Collared

Melissa Cohen

Collared
The Story of a Sir and Her Priest

Melissa Cohen

Alfred Press

Hubbardston, Massachusetts

Alfred Press
12 Simonds Hill Road
Hubbardston, MA 01452

Collared: The Story of a Sir and Her Priest
© 2013 by Melissa Cohen
ISBN 978-0-9828794-7-4

Printed in cooperation with
Lulu Enterprises, Inc.
860 Aviation Parkway, Suite 300
Morrisville, NC 27560

Dedications and Acknowledgements

To my life partner who has never wavered in her love and support of me.

To the many friends and Family of Choice who have been there to lend an ear and shoulder through the best and the worst of it.

To slave sean, who first allowed me to feel what I now recognize as Mastery. Your influence has been invaluable.

To my pup, who I will always own and always love. Words fail to express my gratitude for you being mine.

With special thanks and appreciation to David Stein for unknowingly inspiring me on my Leather Journey years ago, and for graciously allowing me to quote his own book Carried Away: An S/M Romance *within these pages.*

Many thanks to Carpe Noctum Photography for the beautiful cover art which captures 'A Sir and Her Priest' perfectly.

Contents

Introduction

This story began as innocently as any other. What happened next is about as far from innocent as you can get. It's a story that I believe is worth telling but there are aspects of it that may offend the reader's sensibilities, and I am not referring to the smut.

Everything you are about to read is true. Only the names, locations, and identifying details have been altered to give anonymity to those involved.

One of my greatest fetishes may well be for communication, so the majority of what is contained herein are letters, conversations, scene reports, and journal entries written at the time of their occurrence. The rest is just our story, as I see it.

This book has been over two years in the making and my only hope is that it is enjoyable, entertaining, inspiring, and not least of all *hot* to someone besides myself and my boy.

MELISSA COHEN
DECEMBER, 2012

Part I: How It Started

FIRST CONTACT

I am a newbie looking to be properly initiated into submission.

I am smart and sensitive but very shy. I have been submissive all of my life and have gotten more and more into the scene, kind of exploring things on my own, but now I need a mistress to take me to the next level. I know most guys probably say this, but I really mean it: I am not just looking for someone to get me off. I can do that myself. I am totally turned on by the idea of complete surrender to someone else.

I am single, no kids, and somewhat flexible in my schedule. I know that I have a lot to learn, but I am great at serving the needs of others. I am looking for occasional play as a bottom and perhaps more. If you feel like taking a chance on a new guy, just let me know.

I met Joseph online, which is a pretty common way to meet people in this "scene", although not the most promising for long-term prospects. In my eight years of involvement up to this point, I have met only a handful of people online that turned out to be who and what they said they were, and none that were ultimately compatible with me for anything more than a friendship or an occasional play-partner. So what I expected out of this encounter was nothing more than that, and in fact, a whole lot less.

Joseph's profile popped up on my homepage one day, which meant that he was online fairly recently and fit within the criteria I had selected: Male, submissive, under the age of thirty-five, and living within fifty miles of my house. He had posted one nondescript picture of himself, but it told me nothing. It didn't even show his face, but at least I could tell his body was average and on the slim side, which I prefer in a boy.

The content of his profile was mundane, but he did sound sincere. I was at least impressed at the amount he'd written, unlike most who either put nothing at all or a quick cookie-cutter paragraph about how they are seeking a "stern mistress" or "strict domme", of which I am neither. I honestly can't say why I decided to drop him a line. The profile made reference to his inexperience, but even if he had not said so, I would have known. The reek of newness stood out to me from miles away.

Maybe it was the smell of the uninitiated that drew me in—or, as he would tell you, it was something greater than either of our wills that brought us together. Either way, it started one day in early June when I wrote to say hello. I asked him if he'd had any luck and wished him well, but that was about it. Joseph wrote back to me that he had chatted with a couple of women, but nothing more, and thus began our conversations.

After chatting online for two weeks, during which time he didn't start to get on my nerves, annoy me, or piss me off even once (a promising sign!) I suggested that we meet. Joseph was a little hesitant, and explained he had been warned by others that it was a red flag when someone asks to meet so soon. I told him that someone who wouldn't meet so soon was a red flag to me, as I've been strung along by many submissives who claim to want to get to know me but either never commit to a meeting time or just don't show up after we make plans. Still, given his newness, I didn't think it unreasonable to wait a little bit longer.

My expectations were still exceedingly low after years of playing this game: *Meet a man online (the one in twenty that doesn't turn me off from the first conversation). Chat for a couple of weeks. Arrange a time to meet in person. Watch nothing come of it either due to basic incompatibilities or finding out that the man in question wasn't who he represented himself to be. Rinse and repeat.* So went the cycle of my attempts, a veritable "parade of losers", as my friends were known to refer to my quests for a submissive.

So what's a little more time online? I knew it would end the same way it always did. I truly believed that this one, as promising as he seemed from our time conversing, would prove worth nothing more than an hour of my day for a coffee meeting and maybe, if things went really well, giving him a taste of a fantasy here or there as long as he was attractive enough to me (physically and intellectually) to warrant my time.

We continued talking without firm plans to meet up, but much to my surprise, Joseph brought up the topic within a couple of days and declared that he was ready to meet. He had reached the point in his life where he felt as though if he didn't step out into the "real world" now, he just never would. We made plans to meet at a coffee shop near my house and I told him very bluntly (perhaps hoping to calm his nerves) that I expected nothing to come of this meeting. As new as he was, I advised him to explore and meet people but not venture into a relationship until he had a better idea of what he wanted. In fact, I think I told him specifically not to enter into a relationship with anyone, period, during his first six months of exploration. I also told him that there was no way he would be what I wanted or had been looking for. My experience with newly exploring boys has been that they are unreliable and unpredictable. I wonder if I said all of these things to guard myself, and my own emotions, against what may have been a strong intuition of something more with him?

Well, as I now know, the universe (or possibly God) has a way of teaching us lessons that way—throwing us what we need when we least expect it, and proving us wrong at the very moments we are most sure we are right. Despite everything I believed and thought I knew about the way this worked, I was knocked upside the head with a cosmic two-by-four and shown I didn't know much of anything after all.

As it would happen, that coffee meeting was to be the day I met my slave.

◆◆◆◆◆

Let's pause and rewind. Chances are that you don't know me, but what you are reading began as a journal I kept as I realized the relationship between myself and my boy was going to be one of the most truly extraordinary experiences of my life. I was not wrong about that, and I am delighted by my foresight to keep such records of our development. I can only assume that because you have this book in hand, that you are interested in the story we have to tell.

To understand the story, I believe you may need to understand me a bit further. These pages contain many of the most intimate thoughts and details of my existence. I am a dominant, but I am not perfect, not without flaws. I am sometimes too emotional, too moody, to blunt, too self-centered, and many other things. I am exposing all of what I am here for the sake of authenticity, because this story would be nothing without a window into who I am just as surely as it requires the same view of Joseph.

As of the time of this writing, I am twenty-eight years old and have been an active participant in the "BDSM scene" for eight years, though I don't feel as though I have ever been truly a part of this community. I am not a group person. I prefer small circles of friends and intimate gatherings and most definitely have my own philosophies that may not be in agreement with the mainstream SM community (if there can be said to be such an entity).

I go through life as a woman—my body is what science calls female—but I have a greater relation to masculinity and queerness than those in my everyday life would guess. By the look of me you might assume I am a dyke, if anything, but in fact my attraction to females and femininity is quite minimal and I do not identify myself as lesbian or female-centric in my sexuality. In fact, quite the opposite.

Despite my innate orientation, one very important aspect of my life is the relationship with my partner of six years, Heather. Heather and I met in 2006 and found an immediate and strong loving connection, but we were both young and neither of us could have possibly predicted the evolution of our relationship over the course of time. Our ambition was to form a D/s pairing, but despite our efforts it just didn't happen. We settled into a "vanilla" romance and life partnership, but each always seeking some missing piece through other relationships. We are both non-monogamous in our orientations, so this was never a large obstacle.

What makes all of this significant is that at the exact moment in time I was starting to meet Joseph, my relationship with Heather was reaching a critical point. We were both evolving into people we didn't even recognize, as happens when you transition from adolescence into adulthood. We were both becoming the people we desperately wanted to be, but our evolutions were taking us in opposite directions and our partnership became strained.

As I write these words, more than two years later, Heather and I are still in a loving, committed partnership even though it doesn't resemble what it was two, three, or six years ago. As this story is primarily about Joseph and myself, Heather may seem relegated to a background character. However, I am compelled to note the significant and irreplaceable role she has played in my life and in my development. Her well-being is always at the forefront of my mind and our home together is vital to my happiness.

But back to the past. At the age of twenty when I first explored the wide world of SM, I had a hard time finding people that fit with me in the role I knew I wanted. I could always envision the type of submissive I would own, but search as I might, he or she never materialized. Through all of those years, even without a steady boy of my own, I became a skilled top. Inside, I became the person who would be capable of owning and mastering someone once I found him. Throughout this time, I had many encounters with submissive men, some of whom I truly felt could have worked out, but the majority of whom left me disappointed and ultimately jaded.

In my search, I often took two steps forward and one step back. I invested time in the wrong people, I allowed emotions (and sometimes hormones) to overshadow my judgment. I let myself be taken advantage of by selfish bottoms who only wanted to get their kinks fulfilled and who were quickly gone when I demanded anything resembling actual submission.

I was young, and still am by most definitions, but particularly so in this "lifestyle" in which most people don't start dabbling until middle age. But if I am young now, then I was even more so in previous years. I was inexperienced and unready to own someone. That's not to say that I am so much older and wiser now; no, just more humble and more aware of how little I really do know, perhaps.

◆◆◆◆◆

I pulled into the coffee shop parking lot immediately behind the person I was there to meet. I knew him from the yellow polo shirt he said he would be wearing. We parked several spots away from one another and he stepped out of his white Chevy with the Nebraska license plates. *Oh, that's right,* I remembered offhandedly. *He did say he was from somewhere else. One of those flat, square states that all blend together to me ... lots of corn.* Even though I'm from the deep south originally and know other areas of the country are not all stereotypes like you see on TV, I still had little real conception of anywhere beyond the east coast.

It was a warm mid-June day in the suburbs of D.C., and we took our seats outside both to enjoy the weather and for privacy. He introduced himself as John (that was the name he'd been going by online and I had no reason to doubt it was his name) and we began talking comfortably. Even from the beginning I remember feeling at ease with him, and he has told me many times that he always felt the same with me—more so than should have been expected.

We talked for a couple of hours, with me telling him about myself and my experience in BDSM, Leather, and kink (as well as my opinions regarding the distinctions between them) and him telling me how he had always had desires to serve someone, to be submissive, to be used physically. Nothing he told me was much of a surprise, as I've met countless submissive men from the Internet who had never ventured into real life before. One thing we did not talk about, however, was our work. I had mentioned to John that I work in media. In fact, I have quite a "sexy" job in some people's view, and they never tire of asking me questions about what I do and how the industry works. I, on the other hand, frequently tire of talking about what I do for a living, so I had told him the basics of what I did and said I preferred to not discuss it any further. Looking back, he was either just being polite, or he was relieved that the topics of our careers would not be up for much discussion. He had told me he was a graduate student, which came as no surprise since I've encountered a large number of well-educated and intellectual submissive men, so I didn't feel the need to question further.

Our conversation went surprisingly well. It might be because "John" just asked questions and let me talk, but before we both knew it, it was getting later and I knew I should be going. I have a bad habit of telling Heather I'll only be gone for a little while, and then losing track of time and being gone for hours. I also have a bad habit of bringing new boys home to play immediately if my dick is doing the thinking instead of my brain. In this case, there wasn't the initial electric spark that compelled me to swoop John off to my dungeon, but neither was I disinterested in playing with him. John would have liked to go home with me, but I called Heather to see how she felt and she wanted to spend the evening alone, just the two of us.

At this point, I knew I liked the guy, and I looked forward to playing with him. I also fully expected him to disappear after a play session or two, as those who are brand-spanking-new to the scene tend to do. It's a well-documented phenomenon I like to call "boys who go poof!" I've had it happen to me on more occasions than I care to think about but I can generally attribute it to the boy being so new and inexperienced that he doesn't know how to handle all the things happening to him, things that he's only fantasized about for years. Given that, I hesitated to do anything that would lead me to grow attached to John, lest this turn out to be the case with him as with so many others.

So this was my impression of John: the quiet, shy, grad student from the Midwest with a strong drive to serve and submit but without any experience to back him up. Yeah, I'd heard that all before. Not a bad looking guy by any stretch of the imagination either. I wasn't sure why he would ever have any trouble finding a play partner (which he seemed to think he would) except for the shyness. We parted ways and made plans to meet again at my house, four days later.

THE REAL BOY

On the morning of what was to be our first play date, I had an email waiting in my inbox. I assumed it was going to be from John, and that it would be him canceling on me for that night. It had happened so many times before that the pattern was predictable, especially in light of the email he had sent me a couple of days prior.

At our coffee meeting, John had told me that his primary interests were bondage, and some types of impact play like spanking and paddling. Giving him the benefit of being new and wanting to provide an enjoyable experience for his first ever play session, I had agreed that what I would do to him would stay in the realm of the activities we spoke about. Don't get me wrong; bondage and impact are two of my favorite types of play as well, so it wasn't some kind of noble sacrifice on my part. It's just that I was planning to give him way more leniency to direct the specifics of our play than I normally would.

To my extreme surprise and delight, John sent me an email the night after we first met, explaining that he had reconsidered my offer and would prefer that I just do whatever I wanted in terms of playing with him. He specifically explained that he felt it was not his place as a submissive to direct my actions as a dominant. Upon reading this, I laughed to myself because this guy was obviously so new he hadn't run into the "submissives have the real power" crowd who would have clearly told him that it was in fact his place and his responsibility to direct all of our play. I'm not trying to say that I don't take into consideration what a submissive or bottom wants, or that I would ever violate something they explicitly said was not on the table. It's just that the way I play lends itself more to experienced submissives who are comfortable handing over the reins and trusting my judgment. Playing that way was not something I expected to get from John right out of the gate.

Now, the morning of our scheduled play date, another email awaited me, and I realized with a sinking heart that all the good vibes I was getting from our interaction would end the same as ever. He would be sick … his mom would need help moving … his cat would have suddenly come down with cancer. *Oh well, at least I didn't really invest anything in this one,* I thought to myself. I inhaled and opened the email, readying myself for the disappointment.

Thursday, June 17, 2010

Hey Melissa,

I had just a couple of last questions for you. If you get this and can respond, great, if not no big deal and we can work it out tonight.

Eye contact: I know that sometimes subs are required to keep their eyes downcast unless directed to do otherwise as part of their submission. Is this something you desire out of a sub? I have no burning need or desire to do so, but gladly will if it is something you want.

Apologies: I am sure that during my first time, and probably for a while thereafter, I will make my fair share of failures and mistakes. Do you want me to apologize for all of them? I understand that apologies can be a sign of respect and courtesy, but I also understand that it could just get plain annoying. Let me know what you want me to do.

Humbly Yours,
John

Of all the things I thought I might find in this email, I certainly was not expecting this. Here he was, doing it again; defying my expectations and the patterns set by so many other potential boys in my life. My excitement grew and my mood shifted from one of impending disgust, frustration, and disappointment to one of excitement, optimism, and hope. I immediately wrote back.

Thursday, June 17, 2010

John,

To speak to your questions:

Eye contact—I have no preference for limiting or controlling this currently. I believe eye contact is an important aspect of communication and don't want to cut it off. Plus, I actually enjoy looking right at someone, and him looking at me, while I'm hurting him.

Apologies—you're right, excessive apologizing would get annoying. Don't worry too much about making mistakes. As long as you do what I tell you and don't do things unless I tell you, you'll more than likely be fine. If you're not sure about something, ask. If my directions are ever unclear, ask for clarification. I am not holding you to the standards that I would someone who is very experienced or that I've played with frequently. Just remember the basics of how I've told you to behave, how to address me, etc.

I'm looking forward to tonight as well.

See you soon,
Melissa

Evening arrived, and John was at my house for the first time. All of a sudden, I felt my confidence waver as it sometimes does just before I start to engage with a new person. All of my talk and the image I've built up for myself is about to be put to the test. If this person doesn't like the way I play, there's a chance my ego could be bruised. I know that the way I play may not be everyone's style, and someone not enjoying my play doesn't make me bad at it. But still, there's always this moment in my head before I play with someone new for the first time as if I'm about to jump off a cliff and there's no going back.

I brought John downstairs to our dungeon—which, by the way, isn't just a basement with the walls painted black or anything like that. We have an honest-to-goodness dungeon in our basement. Heather is a talented rope top who requires a suspension rig, and on top of that we have a St. Andrew's cross, a bondage table, a cage, a sling, and a spanking bench. The dungeon is divided into two sizable rooms, connected by a hallway where the bathroom is. The large room has two sofas and the small room has a loveseat. This is going to make me sound like a pussy, but I don't care; I enjoy wrapping my bottom in a blanket and letting him sit on the couch after I am done playing with him. Not always on the couch; sometimes curled at my feet or underneath my boots, but one way or the other we are reconnecting in silence as I softly pet his head in stark contrast to the heavy beating I have just inflicted.

I sat down on the couch and instructed John to kneel in front of me while we talked. It was another awkward moment before first play, like two fumbling teenagers who've never done any of this before, but the nerves soon passed as we eased into some conversation. I don't remember what we talked about; I would say it was small talk except that nothing he and I have ever done has felt like "small talk." Every conversation we have is filled with meaning, or at least it seems that way to me. This one was no exception. In fact, this conversation was the first truly important one we would have in our relationship.

As we were discussing our lives, John commented in response to something I described in my relationship with Heather, "I remember counseling couples through something similar." Counseling? Now this was interesting. He hadn't mentioned being a counselor, but he had told me of a prior undergrad and graduate degree before his current studies, so I assumed this must be a career change for him.

"Oh, you are ... or, were, a psychologist? Or a social worker?" I asked, impressed and pausing to truly take mental note of his intelligence and education for the first time.

"Well, no," he replied. "I haven't exactly told you the truth about what I do."

I heard that screeching record sound effect in my head. My brain slammed on the brakes. *Oh boy, here it comes,* I thought. *The part where he tells me he's actually still in high school, on temporary leave from drug rehab, or something equally crazy.* My mind was still going through all the potential things John was about to tell me, but never in a million years would I have guessed the next line that came out. Never.

"I'm a Catholic priest," he said.

I wonder if I laughed. I think that was my first instinctive reaction, but I'm pretty sure I refrained. My head was spinning but I also realized just then that Heather had arrived home, and I excused myself to greet her. She knew I was having my first play date with the boy I'd met a few days prior, and I couldn't contain my excitement and shock at the news. Heather is the daughter of an ex-Minister and has a very unique perspective on clergy members and religion as a whole. She is a long-time atheist, and I thought she would be amused to learn that the new boy that I was about to be doing delicious unspeakable things to, was an honest-to-God (no pun intended) Catholic priest. Obviously, John's career was not something that could be shared far and wide, and eventually only our closest friends learned the truth about what he did. I always used discretion when divulging details on his life, but this first time, this one time, in a state of shock, it was my first reaction to tell Heather immediately.

As I ran upstairs, my mind was racing and I didn't know what to make of it all. My only clear thought was: *Holy Fuck. What am I getting into?*

◆ ◆ ◆ ◆ ◆

John and I played that night like I hadn't played with anyone in years, with the exception of one person. There is one boy, a gay male slave from outside the U.S., who pops in and out of my life with little frequency but great intensity. Our time together is great, but while he is not someone I can truly consider mine, he was the first person with whom I ever felt a true spark of what I can only describe as "ownership". Our interaction turned something on within me that he recognized, and that in turn gave me the confidence to pursue it in myself.

At long last, I felt it again. John and I played ... well there's no other way to describe it except "like I owned him." I had not wanted this at all. I had wanted to give the new boy a good experience, to introduce him to the thrill of a flogging, but that was it. That had to be it, because there was no way he could be ready for anything more. Not to mention the whole other dimension of his career, which would seem to make this (or any) kind of relationship completely off limits. Since he was only in town for graduate school, there simply could be no real future together.

Yet as soon as his clothes and glasses were off and he was kneeling in front of me, looking upwards with the most deep and trusting blue eyes I've ever seen, I felt that all-too-familiar rush of power and possessiveness and lust. All too familiar, that is, because I've felt it numerous times in the past but it's never lasted. Being "mine" is something all boys seem to want for a night or two, or maybe a week, but I played with John to my fullest capabilities and took what

I wanted. I suppose at least a small part of me figured I might as well take while I could, because it wouldn't last at all. The expectation that he would leave and never be heard from again, as so many other new and inexperienced submissive males had done, was still alive and well in my mind.

When we were both exhausted, we crashed on the floor of the smaller dungeon room, and I held him while we talked. I now know that these times after we play are some of the most serene and blissful in his life, as all of his walls are down and he can exist as the object he was meant to be. It was during this time that he admitted to me I still didn't know his real name. It was not John, but in fact Joseph. Of course I understood why he would go by a fake name and I wasn't angry, but I'm sure I did make a point to ask him explicitly if there were any more little details I should know about. I also was relieved that his real name wasn't John. It seems like such a plain and boring name, not at all fitting for as beautiful a creature as himself.

It was two a.m. by then, and I had to be up early the next day for an off-site work meeting. As much as it pained me to send him off, Heather was waiting upstairs, and I'd neglected her all night. I told Joseph we should do it again sometime, still fully doubting I'd ever see him again. I've said the same words to others who have emphatically agreed, and that's been the last I've ever heard of them.

"How about tonight, Sir?" he asked. And we did.

◆◆◆◆◆

By the time Saturday rolled around, Joseph had spent the past two nights being beaten and fucked by me. (This word is used in my vernacular to indicate my anal penetration of a boy with hands, fists, toys, or cock, not penile-vaginal intercourse.) Which looking back now, maybe seems a bit rash, but we both wanted it so damn much. We also spent hours talking about everything from the most mundane to the most important topics. We talked about his life and priesthood, and how he managed to be a thirty-three-year-old virgin, having gone straight from high school to college and then Seminary without as much as a casual girlfriend. "Whoa, no pressure!" I joked with him when I learned the degree of his inexperience.

Thanks to my infinite curiosity, we discussed his current situation as an advanced student of Catholic theology in preparation for continuing his career with the Church upon his return to Nebraska. We talked about his history of wanting a relationship that involved submission and kink, and we talked about how that did or didn't fit into his obligations as a priest. We shied away from discussing how he could reconcile everything (I didn't want to sound like I was accusing him of anything or being judgmental), though that topic came up later in subsequent conversations and I now understand how at least in the beginning there was nothing we did that actually violated his vows.

My mind was blown, to put it lightly, that someone with his background and of his vocation was so down to earth. Growing up Jewish, I had no interaction whatsoever with clergy members of other faiths. I could not, and still to this day cannot sometimes, believe that the small, sexy boy who knelt in front of me, offering himself to me for whatever pleasures I might derive from the use of his body, was ordained to be an instrument of God.

I have to pause here to talk about what my slave being a priest means to me. You should not for one moment think that I am with him because of this, or that it makes me love him any more than I otherwise would. How can I ever say what would have happened if he had been an accountant? Being a priest is part of what makes the boy who he is, and I admire and appreciate him wholly as a person, but I do not have a religious fetish, and in fact I have never found the idea of religious themed play attractive at all.

But I have to admit that the reality of it is so much more intoxicating than a fantasy ever could be. Sure, there are times when I remember how taboo what we're doing is, and it gets my dick hard instantly. But if he is to remain my slave forever, then he will have to give up the priesthood (he tells me that doing both indefinitely is not an option), so I'd better be able to say with confidence that it's not a defining aspect of him in my eyes.

For those of you who are reading this and thinking how terrible, immoral, and sinful I must be for acting as an accomplice to his vice—maybe even for corrupting him after I knew the truth of his life—well, I don't know how to say you are incorrect. I don't believe that what we're doing is wrong or evil. It doesn't feel wrong to us. But there's no doubt in my mind that others will think it is. If it bothers you, please don't read further because this is not a story of us realizing the error of our ways and repenting, or of him deciding to deny his true nature and walk a straight and narrow path.

I suppose the only thing I can say is that ultimately God is the one who will judge us, and that's coming from someone who isn't even sure she believes in God (though I am certainly starting to consider the possibility more than I have since childhood). But one way or another, Joseph was brought into my life and the pieces of the puzzle fit. I don't question things that the universe chooses to give me. I say "Thank you," and accept the gifts graciously.

So after two nights of intense play and conversation, I awoke to find an email from Joseph.

Saturday June 19, 2010

Dear Melissa,

There is something of concern to me that I need to discuss with you. I am going to edit this and try to keep it concise and hopefully not too rambling, so please bear with me.

First, let me say that the time we have spent together has been better than I had ever anticipated. I suppose I was expecting more of what you might describe as simply play experiences: get beat up, enjoy the physicality of it, have a good time and then go home. What I have experienced instead is what I can only call sweet submission. This has been exhilarating but I am now also a bit scared.

Please don't think that I am wanting to back away from you or the scene. Quite the contrary. I feel more like I am addicted to it, as if my mind has truly been altered and I can think about nothing else than the time that we have spent together and when it might happen again. While I find this wonderful to an extent it is also a bit frightening. I was not expecting this to happen, or at least not so fast. As of this moment I truly feel dominated by you, "owned" by you. I know that this is irrational, it is not where our relationship is. We have only met a couple of times, we have not formally established anything more than a casual relationship thus far. But those are my feelings.

These feelings scare me because I know that there are boundaries yet to be maintained in our relationship, but there is a big part of me that would love to just throw them away and be your full-time slave. I am trying to tell myself that this is like an infatuation, a "high-school crush" if you will. It is my first time, and it has gone well so I am overly idealizing or romanticizing it. Do you think this is possible?

Let me say again that I have no desire or intention of pulling back or leaving the scene. It is rather that I do not want to lose control of what is happening here, or at least make sense of what is happening. I welcome any thoughts or advice that you might have. Thank you again for everything. I look forward to hearing from you when you are able.

Humbly yours,
Joseph

I responded at the first chance I had.

Saturday June 19, 2010

Dear Joseph,

Let me first say thank you for sharing this with me. By doing so, you are continuing to impress me with your maturity and self-awareness. It's especially rare, from what I've seen, for someone just exploring a BDSM relationship for the first time, but in general young males are not known for it. Maybe I'm just too accustomed to men under 30, but in my opinion, you have a better grasp than most. Consequently, I think my expectations for you are going to be even higher.

I want to assure you first and foremost that this is completely normal. While I warned you that you might feel a sense of "drop" or let down in the days after first playing, I forgot to mention that the opposite is also possible. It was once described to me as "new sub insanity" or "new sub frenzy", and it's something that I've seen and heard about from others many times. What you've explored the past couple of days is the culmination of who-knows how-many years of anticipation and buildup, and unlike many people's experiences that can never live up to what they've imagined, yours has exceeded it. I'm happy that things have gone this way, and I think that we have an amazing chemistry with each other, which I hope to develop further.

But you're right about the infatuation aspect of it. Of course I don't own you, even though at the moment you feel that way. I am extremely flattered that I've had this effect on you and as I mentioned last night, I've felt the same type of connection—i.e. I am treating you when we are together as though I do own you and it feels like the only possible way to be. But there is much more to ownership than just good play, so don't worry, we're not there yet and I'm confident that in time your rational mind will return.

If, after many months down this road you are still feeling the way you feel now, then we will consider what, if any, options there are. It would be a dream to find someone who still felt this way about me long after the infatuation wore off and even more so, for me to still feel this way about him.

I can only imagine how scary it must be for you, and I appreciate you letting me know immediately. I couldn't ask for a better communicator than what you've been so far. I am a very big believer in transparency in a D/s relationship, so I appreciate that you seem to naturally want to be transparent.
As far as your fear of losing control over what is happening, I have some ideas on how to help that. It would be best to have a conversation to further delve into what these specific fears are. I can only guess you're afraid that you'll sacrifice other parts of your life in favor of time spent serving me or that you may have a lapse in judgment due to this. When we talk about this, I'm sure I can suggest some ways to help you rest assured that you won't find yourself completely out of control.

I look forward to speaking with you later,
Melissa

Joseph and I spoke on the phone later that day as I drove down to the barn where my horse lives. By the end of our conversation, he seemed to be more relaxed and have a better understanding that what he was feeling was to be expected after a couple of such intense experiences. However, there was one thing he said to me during that conversation that still stands out in my mind to this day. One of his fears or concerns about the strong feelings he felt was that he had no freedom or ability to conduct an ongoing "real" relationship as a priest … and yet, "What if this is it?" he asked.

"What do you mean, 'it'? What if this is what?"

"I mean, you know … love. Marriage. What if you're it?"

I remember just laughing or shrugging it off. How silly. Infatuation. Nothing more. And so what if I did turn out to be "it"? He couldn't do anything anyway. He was a priest and not allowed to marry and plus there was no way I was even thinking about marriage with someone I just met a week ago. But years later, that moment still stands out in my mind, and again, I start to wonder about higher powers at work in our lives.

INTEGRATION

As luck would have it, the week I met Joseph was directly before I was scheduled to be out of town for a five-day-long kink event. Heather and I love attending these events, as we only get to be with our Leather Family, which consists of people from all over the country, once or twice a year. Although I love going off to these events, this year's was bittersweet because it meant leaving behind the incredible rush of a new relationship. On top of that, I would feel obligated to play with people I only see at events, even though my heart was somewhere entirely different. I know it wasn't any more fun for poor Joseph, back at home while I was off having the time of my life, or so he thought. Luckily, the place we were visiting had Internet access and I managed time to keep in touch with my new submissive.

Only a week into our Dominant/submissive relationship, we didn't have a clue what the structure would actually be but we were determined to navigate that together. This was the point when I instructed Joseph to call me "Sir," my honorific of choice, rather than my name. I will write more on that in the future, but suffice it to say I am not a "Ma'am" or a "Mistress", or any other female title for that matter. I don't hate my female body and I can't imagine ever pursuing a full gender transition, but I do feel that I should have been born with a physical cock and not just the one inside my head. I do well with what I have, but I do better when people can recognize and accept my masculinity as part of the package. Joseph was never opposed to this, and in fact—to his credit—has never once slipped up and called me any other title than "Sir" the way many others have.

While away at the event, I received an email from Joseph.

Wednesday, June 23, 2010

Dear Sir,

I thought that I would share this with you. I began by simply writing down my thoughts from today, and then decided that you might be interested in knowing this. I have been thinking a lot today about how being a submissive will get integrated into my life as a whole.

It was rather odd getting back into my normal routine today after the wonderful experiences of last week. I kept thinking to myself that I am here among my peers, classmates, fellow priests, and parishioners, but among those titles or identities I now have the added identity of submissive. It is strange to walk around the "normal world" of your life when your life is now monumentally different. How do you relate to people; how do you continue the vanilla activities of life? It is not that I have just found a new hobby, like taking up tennis. I have changed who I am. Before I was someone with certain fantasies; now I am that person. I am a submissive (or at least want to be).

This is certainly not a crisis of conscience or identity or anything. It is the strange experience of looking at the world in a very different way. At least I feel very different, and yet so much of my world has not changed. It is like I am now two different people, a submissive and the person I was before, and am not sure how the two will merge together as one. I know it takes time, and I am not worrying about it. I'm sure it will continue to be an interesting journey.

Humbly Yours,
Joseph

Later, while still away at my event, Joseph emailed me another journal entry that he had written. In the future I would assign him topics to ponder or point him towards online discussions and questions, but this was completely of his own doing and I remember how happy it made me to receive such a thoughtful piece of writing without even asking for it.

Thursday, June 24, 2010

Having experienced my first sweet submission, I am now trying to properly articulate what motivates me for this. What is it about surrendering myself to a dominant that is so appealing and satisfying?

First and perhaps foremost, I am motivated to submit because it is natural to me. It is not just a fun thing to do, a new hobby, but part of my personality, part of me. Submission is truly fulfilling because it allows me to express an intimate and personal aspect of my life that can only be fully expressed by total subjection to another. In virtually every aspect of my vanilla life, in most times and situations, I never feel as if I completely "fit in" or belong to what is happening. There is a constant effort of trying to be "one of the group." Submission comes completely natural, effortless. It is very odd since I have only just begun to experience it and yet it feels like second nature, as if I've done it all my life. This is the ultimate thrill, to be myself completely!

Second, the idea of giving up control over everything is such a delight! I am always very conscious of what I am doing and saying, so as not to do something to look "out of place" or stupid. I am constantly having to monitor myself. In submission I have no worries, no cares, no unnecessary expense of energy. I do not have to think in the least about what I "should" say or think or do. There is only one thing I need do: whatever my dominant desires. In this I am totally free, free to give myself to the moment and enjoy it for everything that it is, even if it is excruciating pain. Is it completely strange that being bound can set one free? But it is wonderful liberation for me.

Third, the idea of being completely transparent is a beautiful thing. In my vanilla life I am rather guarded about what I think, who I am. When you are stripped naked and your dominant looks at you, and her eyes seem to pierce you through, there is nowhere to hide who you are or what you want. You are completely exposed to another. This leads to an intimate connection with another that I never knew could exist. How exquisite!

Fourth, because in submission I have completely ceded control of myself and stand totally exposed to another, I am in a position to be completely accepted. I still do not know why exactly, but with every lash, every stroke of pain on the skin, it is as if my dominant is telling me how much she cares for me. She cares so much that she is willing to do terrible things to me, and I care so much that I am willing to do anything for her. And then, when the pain is almost too much to bear, she comes and comforts me and I just melt into her. I am hers, and I know that I am accepted for everything that I am. I don't have to pretend; she sees everything and accepts me as her submissive and that is glorious.

Finally in this list but certainly not last in terms of importance, there is a thrill I have never known to realize how much my service and subjection and pain can please my dominant. To know that I make her happy, that I bring her pleasure, that I bring her the least smile or the greatest joy is pure bliss. I am willing to subject myself to virtually any torment if only I may hear those wonderful words, "Good boy." I have suffered, I am in pain, I am in distress and she is happy, and that is all that matters. What a new and noble purpose in life.

I don't know if anyone else feels like this, and I don't know if this makes me sound deranged, but I don't care. These are my feelings. I may not have expressed myself the most eloquently or clearly, but the effort is worth it, because the more I bring my motivation into focus, the more my submission will deepen, and the more I will be pleased to be called submissive.

The next missive that came to me was Joseph writing about the idea of being submissive in public, which he addressed as a limit for himself. This wording at first took me by surprise, because we had talked about his actual limits and the only thing he required from me was the promise not to use him "sexually." He defined sex the way his religion had taught him: penile-vaginal intercourse and oral-genital contact. Many other forms of sex, including my favorite type (ass-fucking) were still very much on the table as long as he didn't ejaculate. So this new "limit" of playing or being seen as submissive in public was not something I had expected to read, but after some discussion I realized that Joseph was not trying to limit my use of him in this way, only expressing that he anticipated it being difficult for him to do.

Friday, June 25, 2010

Dear Sir,

In a previous discussion I stated that I have come to the conclusion that in our relationship I have only one hard limit, which is "sex" as we have described it. This is still very true, but it doesn't mean that I don't have limits that need to be explored or pushed. Comments in another of our discussions about mental pain in addition to physical suffering have made me consider one limit, what I think is a particularly big one for me: submission in public.

First, let me describe what I mean when I say "in public." This would refer to acting in a submissive way if we were out in the vanilla world. However, for me, "in public" would also include being submissive toward a dominant in the presence of other people, either other people actively engaged in my submission or simply having them present when I was submitting to a dominant.

As you might glean from my post on "motivation" from my journal, acceptance, identity and emotional security are important issues for me currently. I have found in submitting to you a way to address these issues in a powerful and very personal way. I do not mean to indicate that my submission is in any way self-centered, or that I submit to you only to focus on my own needs. Submission is always about the dominant and meeting her needs, but my own issues remain a major motivating factor in why I choose to do so.

Submitting to one person in private was certainly nerve-wracking at first, but it has led to a wonderful experience of ceding control and enjoying the intimacy of subjection, where everything else is gone but the pleasure of pleasing your dominant. To have other people see me do this, however, scares me immensely. It would mean confronting on a much different level my identity as a submissive. It would mean confronting all of those fears about what other people might think of me, or how ridiculous I might look to them. These are things that normally I would never, ever want to confront—I avoid it out of fear any chance I can get.

On the other hand, however, there is a part of me that loves the idea of being seen by other people as belonging to my dominant. That sort of—for lack of a better word, "objectification"—as a submissive rather than as a person seems exciting. Especially knowing that I would face those fears because my dominant wants it, not because I am comfortable doing it, is also a great source of bliss for me—the real point of submission to meet her desires and not care about my own.

I have no idea if you had or have or will have any plans at any time to interact in what I have described as "public." I am not arguing for or against it. I am writing to help in exploring my own ideas about submission and hopefully better understand my feelings in this regard. I hope that you find this as interesting and informative in reading it as it has been for me in writing it.

Yours gladly,
Joseph

GENDERQUEER

The next day, I received an email from Joseph with the subject line "Genderqueer." I thought that this would be an email addressing my own gender identity and his reaction to it. It only seemed logical. I have called myself genderqueer since I first heard the term, and I felt it really applied to the way I feel about myself. I don't say that I am transgendered, even though I think I would be incredibly happy living as a man full time. But I don't have the drive to go through what it would take to get there, and I am not so entirely unhappy with my typical female body to warrant that. It's really more about what's between the ears than between the legs anyway. My "sex" may be female but my gender isn't nearly as clearly defined.

One of the first things Joseph noticed about my profile online is that I referred to myself as a "Daddy" specifically in relation to Heather. The Daddy/girl element has been part of our relationship since the start, even though it didn't develop into the D/s concept of Daddy and girl that most people envision.

However, as genderqueer as I am, on the trans-masculine side, I am surprisingly binary in my attraction to males. One of the things I very clearly like about Joseph is his boyish look. He is not macho or overly "manly", but he's definitely a boy. He is smooth-skinned and hairless in areas where it's my preference for him to be, but he is equally strong and muscular under his soft skin, with large hands, a scruffy face, and a close cropped haircut reminiscent of the military style. His physical appearance pleases me to no end and I would not want him to change. Particularly, I have no desire for him to become more feminine … so I was surprised to read the following email from him.

Saturday, June 26, 2010

Dear Sir,

I hope you slept well and are enjoying your day today. You asked me at one point what my plans were for the evening, and I told you that I had sat down to begin working on the letter I would send you tomorrow. This was very true but what I did not tell you was that I had put on my bra, panties and heels before sitting down to write. The subject of this letter will no doubt tell you why I did so. I am sorry that I withheld that information from you. I did so in part not to give away the surprise of today's email, but also because it is simply what I do, so often I tell people "what they need to know" and not necessarily "everything else." I do not want to get into that habit with you however.

One of the first questions I asked you was about the way in which you identified your gender. I asked because I was generally interested in how you perceive yourself. I suppose subconsciously I also did so because at times I have had issue with my own identity. For the vast majority of time I am secure that I am male, but there are times—and it happens consistently enough not to ignore it—when being male feels a little odd or wrong to me. So, yes, I have dabbled with some feminization in the past. What comes to mind most clearly is that at times I consider it very strange that I should have genitalia dangling between my legs. I can look at my cock and balls and know that they are a part of my body, but yet feel as if they do not belong to me, as if someone just stuck them on.

This topic has been on my mind throughout the week as I reflect upon one phenomenon in particular. I have been humbled and thrilled that I am able to get your "dick" hard. In our time together my dick has not gotten hard at all, and there is seemingly no desire for it to do so. Yes, it drips all the time, which happens to me any time I get excited or intimate with people. I would like to think that my dick has not gotten hard because perhaps I enjoy being the female to your male. I do so much enjoy calling you "Sir." I originally loved the authority it gave you in my mind, but perhaps I have also been enjoying the gender identity it has assigned to you and to me. I also did enjoy having your, unfortunately plastic, cock up my "pussy" (as it has been called by some of those online Mistresses I mentioned). I told you once that I would gladly give you my penis if I could, and I certainly would. I'm sure that you would use it much better than have I thus far.

So feminization is something that has appealed to me. It is not a large part of my submissive fantasies, but it has its place. Yes, a few months ago I bought matching bra and panties, then I bought some heels and have been slowly getting accustomed to wearing them. As part of that pay site that I have mentioned before, I bought some lipstick and perfume and would have to put them on occasionally. Also, that site would sometimes have me write "slave pussy" across my ass as a sign of my feminization. These things I did gladly. I look ridiculous in women's wear, I know. My body is far from "feminine", most especially my facial hair! However, I think the utter ridiculousness and humiliation of it is part of the pleasure.

We have not yet talked about feminization at all in our relationship. I do not know if it is something that appeals to you. It does appeal to me, again not as a major aspect of what I would like to do but as a piece. Even calling you Sir and submitting to your control and your cock are wonderful experiences of what society has called the "weaker sex", and perhaps that is part of why I am drawn to it. I consider myself weaker, subject to another's authority. Yet I also know that from an early age I have been drawn or at least interested in more "feminine" things rather than the more "masculine" things—for example, in elementary school I was forced into organized sports by peer pressure, although in the end I have come to enjoy them a lot.

As usual, I am not advocating for or against anything in our time together. If you want to explore feminization that is certainly OK; if not, that also is fine. After all, you are in control of what we do together. Mostly I am curious about myself and what new experiences will help me learn about how I view my own gender identity. I hope that this email has been interesting to you and I look forward to seeing you tomorrow (about 32 hours, if you're counting)!

Humbly yours,
Joseph

SCENE REPORTS

When I arrived home from my trip, our reunion was a happy one and we played very well that night. I also implemented the requirement of "scene reports"; journal entries in which Joseph must give his thoughts and impressions of our activities and time together. Over the years I have found these reports to be an invaluable tool in getting to know someone, and I have required them of all previous submissives to one extent or another, but never have they been more valuable than in my relationship with Joseph.

To understand his thoughts, feelings, emotions, reactions, and responses through his own words is a wonderful thing. The act of him composing the report is an exercise in communication and analysis, both of which really turn me on. I never had a submissive in service to me long enough to feel the reports were repetitive or no longer contained new information—until Joseph, that is. Eventually they would fall by the wayside, but for the first portion of our relationship I learned a great deal from his accounts of our interaction. Sometimes I would write journals of my own to reflect upon or process the things we had done, but most of the time we would use his scene reports as a starting point for further conversation.

The first report Joseph ever wrote is below. You will read a lot of these in the telling of this story, though many of them will be abridged to avoid repetition of similar content and sometimes they will be interspersed with my own commentary. It is my hope that through using Joseph's own words as well as my own, you will receive a full picture of how this very shy, introverted, insecure man developed into my boy.

Scene Report: Monday, June 28, 2010

Overall experience: Simply amazing. I cannot believe how much I love submitting to you. It has certainly exceeded any fantasies or expectations I may have had.

Preparation: I was very excited to come once more and experience submission. I was even more excited with the prospect of being able to spend the night. At the same time, I was very scared as I thought about coming over. I was nervous that the "high" of my first experiences would have worn off, which would make it more difficult for me to endure whatever torments lie before me. I was also nervous that you had gone easy on me, that your expectations would be higher, and that you would be pushing me harder than in our first sessions. However, I was very excited that you tied me down so securely. I loved the idea of being completely immobile and at your disposal. I hope to have that feeling a lot more in the future.

Cock-sucking: I am so happy that you remembered your promise to teach me how to suck your cock. I am very grateful to learn, but I must confess that I felt completely strange doing so. Unlike most things we have done together, this did not feel natural. I think this is mostly because I had very little idea what I was doing. I have seen people suck cock before, but never really done it myself. I have no technique or skill at it. But the idea of me kneeling before you taking your cock into my mouth is a wonderful feeling of submission that I want to experience again, perhaps in a better way when I get more used to the activity.

Being fucked: It should come as very little surprise to you that this has become one of my favorite activities to do with you. Not only do I enjoy having things up my ass, but most especially I love having your cock up my ass. This gives me one of the greatest thrills of being completely dominated by you. After all, if someone can stick their cock up your ass they can pretty much do whatever they want to you. And the feeling of you banging into my ass and legs, feeling the power of your thrust, knowing that this is getting you hard, is simply bliss. I could endure that for hours.

Being on the table: Last night was the second opportunity I had to be up on the table and I love being in that position. I love the feeling of being "on display" before you, vulnerable to whatever you would wish to do to me.

Against the door: I was a little startled and very thrilled to be pushed against the door by you. It gave me a wonderful sense of being controlled, and also a small sense of fear to be up against it and at your mercy, especially when you used it as an opportunity to torture my nipples. So far I really do think that this has been the most painful experience—you using the "evil stick" on my nipples. It really hurt, but the best part was being able to look into your eyes as you did it, noticing my extreme discomfort and pain with a wonderful look of mischievous delight. Knowing that my pain brought you such pleasure, and seeing tender caring hidden within that torment (how these two go together is still something of a mystery to me) is a most wonderful image.

Cuddling: Our time cuddling is beyond words to describe. I do feel as if I could stay within your strong embrace forever. Yet, as I said last night, for me the cuddling is good, but it is all of the previous pain and torment endured that bring such depth and tenderness to it. The pain endured is not simply a pretext to getting to what I enjoy, but rather the cuddling is the culmination of all that has happened. I have been beaten and whipped and broken down precisely so that I can be folded up into your strong embrace. And to have you say in the course of our time there that "You are mine!" was unexpected, but completely overwhelming for me. It was like a dream come true, a dream so good you never knew you had it, but now it is real. Our conversation during those times only adds a deeper experience of intimacy and submission. Knowing that I am submitting not just my body but my mind and emotions and everything else is so wonderful. This was truly what I was hoping to find in submission!

The night: I was excited to learn that I would be sleeping in the cage. Of course, sleeping by your bedside would also be a wonderful treat, but I have fantasized about being caged and love the idea of being held secure for someone. The idea you had of me sleeping in a butt plug made me so happy. I am truly the luckiest submissive to have a dominant with such great ideas of how to treat me. Entering the cage was a great thrill, especially as I was once more "on display" for you to tease, like an animal at the zoo as you correctly said. I was surprised by the sudden pang of what I can only describe as sadness when you left. I knew what would happen and yet when it did my emotions rebelled. I wanted to stay with you. I felt somewhat abandoned down in the dungeon while you retreated to your nice bed. Do not get me wrong, I did also love the thrill of being helplessly caged for you, secure in the dungeon until you once more came for me. But I was surprised by the negative emotion that I had never anticipated. Be that as it may, with the butt plug in place and lying comfortably in my cage I had a pleasant sleep.

Today: I cannot say what it felt like to be able to wake up to see you. Here I am lying in my little cage until you come down to rescue me, or rather retrieve me at your pleasure. What a great way to begin the day. You were so kind to let me cuddle with you for so long today, and you were so great to take me outside and whip me. I loved the feeling of being outside, exposed and yet not really, and whipped for your pleasure. I loved having your hand pass over every mark is as if it sealed it as a sign of your care for me. I felt so honored today that you are giving me greater responsibility, testing my ability to massage you (which I plan to read up on and improve my skill for you). Being given the added rule of always being naked in your presence made me so very happy. I had thought about asking you to dispense with my clothes sooner, and it was as if you were reading my mind. It was very hard to leave you today, but what made it more bearable is knowing that I shall see you again so soon.

Even once we were back together in real life, seeing each other every couple of days (or even more often when we were lucky), Joseph would still sometimes just write me emails as time allowed. These emails proved to be wonderful reminders of his affection for me, and in some cases even the impetus for me to start plotting things that would show up much later down the line.

Wednesday, June 30, 2010

Dear Sir,

One of the great things about having the day free is that it allows me more time to think about our activities and discussions. One thing that has been on my mind a lot today was your idea from last night about kidnapping. I mentioned that the idea appeals to me. To be more blunt, the idea is something that I find really hot.

As I thought about this, an episode from Monday night came back to mind. I really love the idea of you being more aggressive in your control of me. The episode that reflects what I mean by this was you holding my hands behind my back, throwing me onto the table and then spanking me. I confess that I was a little shocked when you did so, but I loved it. Normally I would say that I experience you as being very controlling, but also very controlled, in the manner in which you do it. You are normally methodical and disciplined in the way in which you control me—well, this is how I experience you, anyway. I loved seeing a more aggressive side, with more wild and uncontrolled passion in the way you dominate me. To experience that in a more profound way by being kidnapped, having my clothes ripped off, etc. is very exciting to me. It brings in a whole new dimension to the fear and submission I feel toward you, and to the control you have over me.

Of course, this is not in any way meant as a criticism of your style or the activities we have done together. I love being controlled by you in any way. In many ways, I love how methodical and controlled your style is. It means that it is well thought out, well planned, and you are thoroughly in command of what is happening; it is not just a momentary fancy that may or may not work, but a well-organized idea of how to dominate me. This is only meant to express my feelings toward another specific aspect of our play or rather of your control over me. I would welcome any comments or questions you have about what I have said.

I hope you are having a good day.

Humbly yours,
Joseph

Little did Joseph know, from that conversation onward, I was storing the idea of a real honest-to-goodness kidnapping in the back of my head, saving it for the right time to be put into execution. I hoped that I had not given too many of my ideas away, but we had discussed it in enough detail for me to determine that it would not leave him traumatized. Keep in mind, I'd only known him for a couple of weeks, so I wasn't even sure he'd still be around months down the road. There was no way I'd be dumb enough to arrange an elaborate kidnapping for someone I barely knew, so it would have to wait for the right time. Plus, I figured, the further into the future it happened, the less likely he would be to expect it. But the seed had been planted in his mind, and several times over the next few months I would tease him as we were on our way somewhere, "Or, I might just be saying that - and you're really about to get kidnapped." I love doing that type of thing, which acts to actually inoculate the victim against suspecting the threatened scenario at any given time. The more you joke with someone about the terrible thing you're planning, the less of a threat it becomes to them. But then again, there is always a small question in their mind of, "...Really?" And I make a rule of not threatening anything I'm not willing and capable of going through with.

I can realize now that hearing him express enjoyment of my more aggressive side was liberating and empowering. Straying away from the calm and controlled dominant I naturally tend to be is a fantasy of mine, but it was not likely to happen with someone I didn't know well.

As it turns out, a kidnapping is a very nice birthday present...

OVER BEFORE IT'S BEGUN?

In our early days, while I worked a mostly-desk-job and Joseph was still in school, we would chat online while I was at work and he was at his apartment or from his school's computer lab between classes. It was a way we managed to sneak in more time together, getting to know one another, without having to worry about the logistics of meeting up.

This day was no different and we chatted casually while I did my job and he wrote papers. After a bit, Joseph told me he needed to be going in a few minutes. He mentioned he was cooking some soup for himself and his roommate (another priest), and I proceeded to joke with him about this because he'd emphasized to me several times that he was not a good cook and frankly didn't know much about how to cook.

We continued chatting for a few more minutes—perhaps even half an hour—but he didn't indicate during that time period that he was in a rush to go. Then he abruptly ended the conversation by saying he needed to leave right then and there. I jokingly told him to ask me nicely, mostly because the tone he seemed to say it in came across as surprisingly harsh and in direct opposition to his normally submissive and deferent demeanor. But my teasing didn't translate and only added to his frustration and anger. Still, he obediently typed, "Sir, may I please be excused?" So of course I told him yes, said goodbye, and figured we'd speak again later. And boy, did we.

When I got home and logged on to my computer that night, an instant message from Joseph popped up immediately. I was hit with what felt like a tirade from him regarding my disrespect of his time and his outside life. It was like a slap in the face to be spoken to this way by the person who had been so completely passive with me up to this point. I tried to remain calm and talk through what was going on with him without letting my emotions go haywire. It was difficult, but I remember just being quiet for a long time, not typing, letting him blast everything he needed to say out; then responding to tell him how surprised I was at hearing these feelings and how it had not been my intention to convey anything of the sort. I also remember getting the impression that one miscommunication negated all the good faith we'd built up in each other to that point.

I have never told him this, but I was certain at that moment that the relationship was over before it had begun. I feared that this was the point where he'd snapped and would retreat, just like every other submissive who seemed perfect at the outset. Why was I surprised? He would realize that this had been a fun diversion for a couple of weeks, but it was time to get back to real life where he was in control and didn't have to answer to anyone. I started bracing myself to let go and move on. I later learned that Joseph was equally convinced that our relationship was over, but not by his choosing; just by my inevitable rejection of him based on his emotional outburst. Lucky for him, however, a spurt of emotions is nothing I can't handle. I'm a fairly stubborn person and unlike Joseph, I will fight tooth and nail for something I want, and I won't give up until I'm certain there's no hope for redemption.

As we chatted the thought crossed my mind that this whole relationship was nuts, and that Joseph was just a confused, immature boy who couldn't actually know what he wanted … but the stubborn bitch inside me just wouldn't let those thoughts take root. I hadn't felt this way about anyone, ever. I had never connected with a submissive to this extent. No way was this boy going to ruin our good thing before we even had a chance to get it off the ground.

But whatever was going to happen, there was nothing I could do that night. I hate going to bed angry or with anything unresolved, and though there is no way Joseph could have known this, I kept hoping that he would write to me once more before bed to give me some kind of peace or closure to sleep on. I wouldn't be writing to him, since the whole issue revolved around his perception that I was expecting or demanding too much. I sat around refreshing my inbox for a bit, but nothing came. I finally gave up and resigned myself to an uncomfortable night's sleep, but a little voice told me to hit refresh just once more. To my relief, there was a letter waiting, but the relief was short lived because I realized it could just as easily make things worse. Would it be some sort of apology or attempt at reconciliation? Or just another angry rant? I held my breath as I clicked:

Wednesday, June 30, 2010

Dear Sir,

I can only apologize for what I'm sure was a most unpleasant conversation. I did not want to hurt you in any way. On the other hand, I do not apologize for the conversation. You wanted to know me, well now you know what an emotional wreck I am. The difference between you and everyone else in the world is that you now know it. Lucky you, I suppose. But it is good that you know because you should if you want to continue any kind of relationship with me. I have made a few hints or vague references to certain things in our conversations but there is now no hiding the fact that I am emotionally screwed up.

There was more, but it wasn't hostile. Joseph was obviously attempting to apologize even while wallowing in his own miserable opinion of himself. I let out a sigh of relief (or was that my breath I'd been holding the whole time?) and composed my response. Calmly and collectedly, I addressed his outburst:

If this relationship is going to continue, we need to come up with a better way to express unhappiness and dissatisfaction without it feeling like a

tirade to either party. Now, having said that, I'm not really surprised. What we're "playing" with is really intense stuff even for those in the best emotional health.

I don't want you to retreat from me, I don't want to loosen my grip on you, but now I know that there are hot spots that I might step on inadvertently, that would never dawn on me to anticipate, but can set you off into a whole day of suffering. This is not the kind of suffering I enjoy … We also may need to reconsider the sanity of this arrangement. I cannot be party to something that's going to tear you down rather than build you up. And it makes me sad that one day can seemingly undo in your mind all of the positive energy of the past couple weeks.

When I woke up, another response was waiting on me. I was indescribably happy to see we were on our way to moving through this first little hiccup. I was still wary about his intense and sudden emotional reaction, but as I later told him, intense emotions are not something I'm all that unfamiliar with, even in myself. One of my best qualities is probably unwavering, infinite, patience as long as I believe in the worthiness of the cause; and for a burgeoning master, there is no cause more worthy than the building of her potential slave.

Joseph's response was, once again, calm and apologetic:

I did want to say how happy I was, and to an extent surprised, to hear that you "do not want to loosen your grasp on me." I was somewhat expecting to have scared you off, which is not at all what I want. I do think in large part that is why I felt so bad because our relationship makes me so happy and I felt, as crazy as it may be, that was being threatened of being taken away. This is why I do not emotionally invest because it can lead to difficulties like this and because I am emotionally guarded when problems do arise I do not know how to deal with them maturely. And this also makes me feel stupid that I have invested so much emotionally in our relationship so quickly and now there is no way to hide my true self from you as I hide it from virtually everyone else.

In closing, let me say that one day has not undone all the other wonderful experiences that we have had. That is why I do not want to hurt or lose what we have and feel like yesterday may have accomplished that, but it is also why I feel so stupid for what happened yesterday.

Needless to say, we did move on and recover from this. It led to the development of more clearly defined boundaries between what time was mine and what time needed to remain his for the time being so that he could deal with all of his daily obligations (which, between graduate school and helping at the parish where he lived, were not negligible).

As the months went on, Joseph became a much better communicator, and grew comfortable giving me ultimate "say-so" over how he spent his time. I, in turn, respected his prior commitments and did my best not to step on them. This was essential in earning his continued trust and submission, and though it was a slow process, I wouldn't have wanted it to develop any other way.

Within a few days of our first incident, Joseph and I had returned to normal and the relationship was back on track in the direction we both wanted. I had agreed to do whatever I could to assure him I respected his time outside that which he committed to me (which thus became "my" time), while he reasserted that he really did want to be in the relationship, that it was a positive thing in his life, and that he would follow my protocols for voicing concerns and complaints to me.

The July 4th weekend brought us a little extra time together, and in a change of pace from our normal routine, I felt like writing a letter to him in response to our experiences.

Tuesday, July 6, 2010

Dear Joseph,

I have a few minutes before I leave for work so I wanted to write to you. Last night was really wonderful for me and I wanted to give you some feedback to make sure you knew it.

When you arrived and I put you to work cleaning, that was delightful. It was just blissful to know that you were there taking care of things that needed to be done. I was also excited thinking about what I would do to you next.
Now, I am not complaining because you did a very thorough job, but the time was starting to drag on and I was debating whether I should come stop you in the middle and take you away for the next project. I have to admit that I also had a slight fear that after nearly two hours of cleaning and then telling you to handle the rope and trash downstairs, that you would become hurt or resentful and think that I was taking advantage of you by making you do all this work. I know that is kind of irrational, but I believe in sharing with you the same as you have with me.

I need to know that you are happy to serve in whatever way I instruct you, and because this was a new activity that you haven't been assigned before, I had some fear that you would not find it fun, and thus decide you were being treated badly. But I think the rest of the night put my mind at ease about that! The rest of the evening was wonderful for me. I loved having you there, tied up and gagged and plugged, just sitting by me like a room ornament.

I enjoyed watching you breathe and breathe more heavily when I would hit you out of nowhere. I enjoyed imagining what you might be thinking or feeling. I wondered if you felt ignored or dehumanized because I was going about my normal business while you were just … there.

Flogging you was fun, and I could tell that you liked that. The best part, by far, was hitting your inner thighs. I loved the look on your face as I positioned you on the beanbag chair. You just looked so nervous, which I understand was a combination of feeling exposed and vulnerable combined with not knowing what I was about to do. But oh, that look just makes me melt on the inside.
When I started hitting you, I knew I was going to get what I wanted. The inner thighs are a great, sensitive area that many people ignore in play. I didn't know if I'd be able to make you cry and it wasn't in my plans, but when I saw how red your eyes were and then you confirmed you'd been close, well, I could not just let it go then, could I?

Hitting someone to the point of true crying is not something I've gotten to do very often. Most men don't cry easily, if at all. One person I played with in the past year had an extremely low pain tolerance and I'd get some tears and sobs out of him nearly every time we played, but never a full-out cry. It makes me incredibly happy, and it's actually like having a mental orgasm for me when someone does cry. I can't explain it any better than that; it's just the height of emotional pleasure for me to hurt someone to the point of them breaking down, and then I want to grab them and let them cry into my embrace, and remind them how much they enjoy suffering for me because I care so deeply.

I will always do my best to let you know that you are pleasing to me, and quickly inform you when you're not so that you can remedy the situation. I am glad that you told me outright about your dislike of being corrected so that we could have that conversation. To reiterate, you will make mistakes, and you will do things that I don't like simply because you don't know better. It's my job as the dominant to point these things out to you and explain how to do them better, but that doesn't mean that you've failed. Always keep in mind that I wouldn't put the energy into training you the way I like if I didn't think you were worth it. I have had others in the past that I didn't feel so strongly about, and was inclined just to let things slide rather than speak up because it just didn't seem worth the effort to correct them. I feel bad saying that because I was not holding up my end of the bargain, but it's true.

Later that day, I received Joseph's scene report. I enjoy comparing notes and seeing what stands out in his mind compared to mine.

Scene Report: Tuesday, July 6, 2010

My overall assessment of last night was wonderful. I have to admit that for some reason last night was very emotional for me. I don't know if it was just a release of some other frustrations from the day or if our time together is allowing me to open up to all these emotions, but I had several different emotions that I was not expecting. But I could not have asked for anything more out of our time together last night.

I was very content to be able to serve you. If the time was dragging on for you, it was not for me. This is because I like things to be clean, and I am probably too much of a perfectionist in it, so I probably took more time cleaning than you thought I might. Also this was because cleaning for you and helping coil rope makes me happy. I greatly enjoyed being able to serve you in that way and, as I have elsewhere indicated, "give back" for all the wonderful things you give me. In the future you do not need to worry about overburdening me with those kinds of activities. I'm sure that I do have a breaking point, but it would take a lot.

I thoroughly enjoyed the cuffs, as you probably already know, and the new collar was a special treat for me. I was so happy to wear a collar that fit more tightly than the prior chain collar did. I also liked the feel of the heavy chains, even if they were not all that restrictive.

I was initially so glad to be able to wear a blindfold and a gag, I had really wanted that experience. However I must also confess that wearing them made me afraid for some reason. I don't know why. I certainly trust you enough that you are not going to do anything truly harmful to me, but I felt scared; even more so as we went upstairs into what I knew was a strange room. It was in large part because of that fear that I started breathing so hard whenever you touched me or hit me, because that just renewed my sense of fear. I am not discouraging this in the future at all; in some ways I enjoyed the fear, and I'm not sure if I would feel that afraid again next time anyway.

As I lay on the beanbag, I felt very objectified. I felt like your little doll that you left lying there while you went about your other business. It was a new but enjoyable experience to lie there knowing that I was just another object in the room that you would come back to when you wanted; not another person in the room to be acknowledged nor even a submissive in the room to be dominated, but your little man-doll just lying there, because that is where you laid me until you wanted to come back to play with me. It was a great new sense of submission.

I enjoyed both the experiences of the flogging and caning. I like the heavy thud feel of the flogger. It has such a nice impact and can be borne for a while, as it does not immediately hurt like the cane. I do also like the feel of the cane, because it does hurt more quickly. It has a nice sharp sting, which immediately allows me to suffer for you.

Caning my inner thighs was a particularly special experience for me. I am so glad that it brought such pleasure for you; it did the same for me. I was not expecting to cry, but in the midst of the pain that was my natural response in the moment. I remember seeing your great enjoyment at causing me pain and I remember feeling enjoyment at suffering for you. But I also remember how much it truly hurt and that led to my crying which was a thrilling experience of submission! I liked being able to suffer for you and have my body at your disposal. Last night I was also able to feel emotionally submissive to you. You wanted to make me cry and I did; there was nothing I could do as you had control over my body and my emotions. Afterwards, lying there crying and hearing you say "Joseph, you are loved," was one of the most beautiful things I have ever heard. It reaffirmed that every pain I had felt had been a touch of love from you. I truly like being that vulnerable to you.

I was also glad for our conversations. While I have thought about submission for a long time, there are still many of the practical aspects of it that I had not considered and have not yet worked out. I am grateful that you are so patient in answering my questions and allaying my anxieties. Most of all, I just enjoy lying there with you, feeling so completely submissive to you, knowing that you are there in control to keep me safe and I am totally yours. It feels like that is where I have always been meant to be.

Humbly Yours,
Joseph

Later that week, I messaged Joseph to ask him if he would be interested in joining me for a walk that night. I told him about a very private and secluded walking trail near our house that would be perfect. I also warned him that coming on a walk with me might be quite a different experience than what he was used to. "Of course," I ended, "you'd expect nothing less than that."

I wasn't expecting him to say yes. After all, we'd already spent time together on the holiday weekend, but I guess he couldn't resist this chance to see what I had planned. I was a little bit nervous about doing something so public, even though the walking trail was secluded enough. I've been on it a few times and always encountered at least one other person, but late on a hot summer night I figured it was worth the gamble.

We ended up meeting earlier than I had proposed and it was still light out. I told him to wear something grungy, and he came in an old pair of exercise shorts and a beat-up T-shirt. I brought along a leash to attach to his collar, and a riding crop that I managed to hide down my gym shorts whenever we passed by people (which luckily only happened a couple of times). I also tied his arms behind his back. So there he was, walking (or being walked, rather) through the bike trail in a position that would be nearly impossible to conceal if the vanilla public stumbled upon us. I used my riding crop to encourage him along, and he jogged beside me like a good boy. Our walk went on for a while, and it was pitch dark by the time we returned to where our cars were parked. But in my normal fashion, I was not ready to let him go quite yet.

There was a wooden bench near the parking lot where normal people probably enjoyed a relaxing moment before or after a nice walk, jog, or bike. But we are not those people, and that was not what I had in mind. Stopping at the bench, I first pulled out my water bottle and a small bowl from the backpack I'd been carrying. Filling the plastic bowl with water, I instructed my sweaty and thirsty boy to drink from it off the ground.

When he had slurped as much water as he needed, I pulled him up, bent him over the wooden bench, and used my riding crop on his ass and thighs the way I couldn't when we were walking previously. I played with him nicely at first, allowing him to verbalize his agony, and then I became more intense with my strokes and upped the stress on him further by instructing him not to make a sound. It's always harder for him when I require silence and he is forced to fight back whatever reactions he has. It's kind of ironic, being that when we first started playing he was quite the stoic. He still is in some ways, but he is much more expressive now, so it's a challenge for him that takes an emotional toll when I tell him to be completely quiet.

When I realized how late it must be getting and was covered in mosquito bites from the waist down, I decided to call it a night. We got back in our respective cars and went to our own places. I still crave the day when we'll both go home where we belong, together. But for now I have to settle for a part-time pup.

THE GIFT OF BELONGING

I received this letter from Joseph later, and even though it is very short, I feel it's important to include. Ever since we met, he had been telling me how he'd never belonged anywhere or fit in. Coming from a large family (seven siblings and numerous cousins), he had never felt at home and comfortable with them, and even less so at school, college, seminary, and among other priests.

It baffles me how someone could go through life never feeling at ease or having a sense of belonging. In my own life, I certainly have felt like an outsider in many circumstances, but as soon as I was old enough to exert control over my environment, I sought out people and situations that would make me feel included and comfortable. Joseph, on the other hand, continued down the path of what he believed was "right", even though it rarely lead to feelings of happiness or acceptance.

How amazing it is that we discovered each other, and he finally felt he was where he belonged for the first time. In reciprocation, I also have felt as if he belonged with me (not to mention *to* me) very strongly. I nearly immediately felt the same with Heather, so I am not a stranger to these feelings, but they are extremely rare. To me, the feeling of this "rightness" that Joseph experienced from the very start in our relationship was a major indication that this path we were starting down was in fact "right" and it gave me the confidence to continue on that track with him.

Friday, July 9, 2010

Dear Sir,

I wanted to just send along a quick note to let you know that I am thinking of you, but mostly to thank you for giving me a place to belong. As I have mentioned before, in almost all of my life I have always felt out of place (to a larger or smaller degree). As you might imagine this causes lots of anxiety about trying to constantly "fit in" with whatever group or situation I am in.

It is so wonderful now to know that I have a place where I do belong completely; I belong to you. Even when suffering or feeling frustrated I know that I am right where I belong, where I fit. That is a great gift not only for when we are together but perhaps even more for when we are not.

Thank you, Sir, for that gift.

Gratefully yours,
Joseph

The question of "belonging" would become a question of "possessing" very soon afterward. While I was away camping in mid-June, in one of his emails to me, Joseph asked what he was allowed to do with his genitals while alone. He had been hanging weights on his balls, but wanted to know if that was still acceptable. Two weeks after I returned, I finally responded:

Saturday, July 10, 2010

Dear Joseph,

I've been thinking about this since last night when I recalled that I hadn't yet answered the question. I have mixed feelings on the topic; part of me wants to forbid you from doing anything more than the necessary touching in order to keep yourself clean while another part of me wants to allow you the freedom to do as you want with yourself when we're not together.

I think for the time being, given where we're at, I will go with the latter. I do not mind if you "have fun" in whatever way you want by yourself. I care much more about controlling your actions with other people. This is not to say that I will not want to further my control in the future, I just think it's not the right time as of yet.

However, what I do want is for you to keep in the forefront of your mind that your body belongs to me and that I am allowing you to have that control over it for the time being. I want you to remind yourself whenever you do touch yourself pleasurably or use a toy on your ass that these parts of you belong to me and in your mind - or even aloud - thank me for allowing you permission to use them.

It wouldn't be long before I changed my mind on this topic. Within a few weeks from the time of this letter, we had agreed that there would be no touching or playing with himself in any capacity other than to keep his genitals and ass clean and shaven for me.

Everything seemed to happen at an accelerated pace with Joseph but that is because we always knew our time was limited. Looking back, I wonder how different our relationship may or may not have been if our time together were not predetermined on some prior schedule, but that is something we will never know. Despite the accelerated process of ownership, nothing ever really seemed to be happening "too fast" for either of us. As opposed to other relationships in my past where things crashed and burned, or just fizzled out due to us being overzealous in the beginning stages, everything with Joseph has played out as perfectly as I could expect given all the mitigating circumstances of our relationship.

INVADING THE DEEPEST DEPTHS

While at my kinky camping adventure in June, I had learned a new skill. I told my boy that I was interested in trying out urethral play (sounds and catheterization, to be specific) and he expressed interest, even admitting to having stuck "things" inside his urethra before. This took me a bit by surprise, but not nearly as much as it had when he revealed that he had been fisting himself for years. "What kind of things?" I asked him, a bit concerned, and fresh from a very safety-oriented class on the topic.

"Small things—cotton swabs, stuff like that, Sir," he confessed. Not the worst, I suppose, but not even close to sterile. I thus forbade him from doing any more of that, since it can cause urinary tract and bladder infections. I promptly ordered all the supplies necessary for a proper catheterization scene. I already owned some sounds, but had never used them because I didn't believe that boiling in hot water was sufficiently clean. During the class, this topic came up and mention was made to using a pressure cooker as an autoclave to achieve actual sterilization. I mentioned this to Joseph, and to my surprise he promptly volunteered to order the pressure cooker so that I could use sounds on him in the future. For the time being, the medical supplies I ordered online would come in sterile packaging, and I would do the best I could to keep things clean while engaging in this type of play.

Scene Report: Tuesday, July 13, 2010

Overall experience: The evening was far too short but a wonderful and powerful experience of submission.

The catheter became a much more powerful experience of submission than I would have thought. Initially I felt embarrassed by it, not embarrassed as if I had done something wrong, but more from the vantage point of being that exposed and vulnerable in an area that is normally extremely private. How many people do you allow to see you urinate? Feeling the catheter going inside of me was almost like you invading my inner self, in a good way. Whips and canes, in a sense, impose your dominance from the outside, but this was you going inside of me to impose your control. I felt very humbled by that. This feeling was reinforced once the catheter was properly inserted and I lost control of my ability to urinate. A bodily function so private and automatic was now beyond my control. I had to watch my pee flow into the container knowing that there was nothing I could do about it, even though my body's automatic reactions were desperately trying to control it. It was a wonderful feeling of being controlled by you that lasted for a day or so after our session; whenever I would urinate throughout the next day it felt as if I

was only doing so because you allowed me to do it, as if that function was still under your control.

Part II: Becoming Owned

GOING ALL THE WAY

After what seemed like an unbelievably short period of time, Joseph and I had grown to a mutual understanding that what we had together was truly something extraordinary. Rather than just fumble along and see where it took us, I decided that we needed to come to grips with what "this" was and how we were going to proceed.

Feeling what we both felt, we didn't think it possible to go forward as merely play partners, even though that would have been the most logical thing to do. We'd always be holding ourselves back, and never reaching the potential we knew existed for something greater. But knowing he was only in town for a little over a year to complete his graduate degree made it hard to imagine a real future, and nearly ensured heartache if we did indeed become interdependent.

We shot several alternative scenarios back and forth, but ultimately I proposed that we might as well just go all out. If we only have a year to explore this, let's really do it. Slavery. Ownership. These things I had only fantasized about prior to meeting Joseph, but felt the overwhelming conviction that it could happen with him. Even with the extenuating circumstances, there were benefits to our situation that in some way made it more viable to go for a significant D/s relationship. For example, while he was still in school, Joseph's life would be relatively easy to control. Outside of classes, class work, and other random obligations (celebrating a mass here or there, filling in for the pastor he lived with when needed), his time could be used to serve me, and for us to continue to get to know each other. Of course I didn't take his degree lightly, and school would be his number one priority even if it meant our time together suffered as a result, but that went without saying. So we started negotiating a contract to govern the rights, responsibilities, and roles of the relationship.

Looking back on it, I have no idea what made me think it wise to enter the relationship this way. The plain facts of the matter wouldn't lead one to believe this was smart, but I have often been ruled by emotions, passion, and gut instincts rather than logic, and for the most part, I cannot say I have been lead astray. Joseph, on the other hand, is highly logical, rational, and meticulous in everything that he does. Knowing him as well as I do now, I nearly can't believe he went along with the idea, but I can mostly attribute it to the sexual chemicals at work in his brain during the early days of our interaction which made him susceptible and powerless to most of my bright ideas.

I composed the following journal entry to express the state of affairs. Unlike others, this one was not posted for the public to read.

July 14, 2010

In the time since I met Joseph (has it really been just a month now?) I have felt

something I never expected and never have felt before. This time is different for sure, my instincts just tell me.

The one hitch? He's a priest! Let's not ignore this fact. He is a man who has never been with a woman, never dated, never kissed, obviously never had sex, and up until a few weeks ago, never experienced anything physical with another person to any degree. And he's promised himself to God. And what's more, he's only in town for a year to finish graduate school and then he goes back, over a thousand miles away, and we have absolutely no future together. Well, I can't say I've ever been good about following the rules. My life is actually a complete mash-up of things that literally shouldn't have been possible. I tend to just do what seems right and hope for the best. But what do you do when you find your heart telling you This is right! while your head says You are crazy! I am really bad about listening to my feelings and indulging in what may not be the smartest choices when it comes to whom to get involved with. I'll admit it. I've made bad choices on relationships before when my emotions carried me away. But again, something different is happening here. I can't say what, but I just know it beyond anything I've ever known. The certainty with which I know this relationship is right would have me saying God himself told me, if I seriously believed in God enough to make that kind of statement.

Joseph and I have talked about this conundrum. What do we do? We find ourselves inexplicably drawn to each other more than is rational or sane … but we know there is no future. Our time is limited and nothing more can come of it. He's made his decisions in life, his commitments, they cannot just be broken no matter how much he might really enjoy being with me.

So what should we do? Walk away from each other and pretend we never met? Stay buddies but far enough apart that we can't go too deep? Nope. Fuck it all, we say! We've got a year, let's give it all we've got. Go all the way. I don't mean sex … that could come later. I mean slavery. Ownership. The eventual goal being no limits, consensual non-consent, all that comes with that territory. It's a terrifying and exhilarating experiment. I have no idea what is going to happen but I know it's going to be amazing. Hopefully I won't regret this in the future.

It wasn't really true ownership from the beginning - there were lots of limits and stipulations - but in an incredibly short period of time they just naturally fell away. Taking the first step, deciding to do it, to go all the way and just see what happens, that's where we set ourselves up for the biggest joy and the biggest heartache. We both knew it couldn't end well, but we were compelled to do it anyway. We both knew it could only last for a year, but we decided the potential to experience something amazing was worth the risk. What we didn't know or expect was that we would fall in love beyond our wildest dreams and be faced with choices that could change the course of Joseph's life.

We came to this decision to just go for it in late June, and for two weeks we bounced our first contract back and forth via email, making slight changes here and there until we felt it was perfect. This was actually the first time I had engaged in something so formal as to warrant a contract, and the reason why we decided to do that rather than just wing it may have had to do with Joseph's need for very clear boundaries. We also both found the idea of a written contract hot. I asked for Joseph's input in the composition, and in fact he ended up writing the bulk of it.

Our first contract, we decided, would only be in place for two weeks. It was a good trial period to see if we needed to adjust things we just couldn't live with. To be honest, there wasn't a whole lot of negotiation required. We seemed to agree on everything, and besides the deal would be that if at the end of two weeks some of it or all of it wasn't working, we could just walk away without any hard feelings

We signed our first contract on July 14, 2010. It was a beautiful act between us. I told Joseph to get undressed, to kneel in front of me, and to read the contract to me. With a voice shaking with excitement, Joseph read aloud:

AGREEMENT OF SERVICE
Effective July 14, 2010 to July 29, 2010.

Statement of Purpose:
Submission as understood in this contract is an act of power exchange in which the submissive surrenders authority of his life to the dominant, within mutually agreed parameters. Dominance and Submission (henceforth referred to as "D/s") is a conscious and fully informed relationship into which both parties freely enter. It is not an admission of inferiority or statement of superiority, but a mature relationship between equals in which one, the submissive, voluntarily and without coercion agrees to cede control of his life to another, the dominant, according to the subsequent stipulations as a means of providing personal fulfillment and enrichment of life for both parties.

Rights of the Dominant
The role of the dominant is to take control over the submissive within the limits of this agreement so as to provide greater personal fulfillment for both parties. The dominant has the right to receive from the submissive the respect and appreciation appropriate to her position and expects to be treated with courtesy, respect, deference, and gratitude at all times. The dominant has the right to exercise full authority and complete control over the submissive in any and all

ways she so chooses, within the mutually agreed upon parameters.

The dominant has the right to free and total access to the person of the submissive. This includes the submissive's body, emotional state, thoughts, feelings, and opinions.

The dominant has the right to control the submissive's interaction with others within the BDSM/Leather Community—including choosing, approving of, or limiting play partners for him, as well as negotiating the specifics of what he does/has done to him with others.

Duties of the Dominant

The dominant accepts that the owned submissive is a human being equal in dignity who has freely entered into the relationship to provide greater personal fulfillment to both parties, and pledges to uphold the self-esteem and worth of the submissive for as long as he is hers; with the exclusion of clearly denoted "scenes" that would invoke feelings otherwise.

The dominant agrees to induce no permanent harm to the submissive in body, emotion, or intellect, and will take all necessary and prudent precautions to insure that the experiences she subjects him to do not do so.

The dominant agrees to minimize risk of injury, illness, and disease to the furthest extent possible when using the submissive, so as to reduce the chance of accidental permanent harm as well as critical, even if not permanent, damage. Permanent harm and critical damage are defined as an accident, injury, or illness that requires professional medical care and/or impairs the ability of the submissive to function in his daily life. The dominant also agrees not to leave marks more severe than bruises, welts, cuts, and abrasions that will heal on their own if left alone in a matter of weeks.

The dominant agrees not to require more than one hour of the submissive's time daily, unless a date has been scheduled in advance and agreed by the submissive that the time requested is within his capabilities.

The dominant agrees not to infringe upon the "vanilla" life of the submissive, the responsibilities and relationships he holds there, or to engage in activities that would be detrimental to his reputation in his vanilla life causing him personal harm.

The dominant agrees not to infringe upon the submissive's financial stability by requiring him to cover exorbitant expenses in the performance of his submission.

The dominant agrees not to treat the relationship casually, or as such, abandon, dismiss or otherwise terminate her agreement with the submissive without serious efforts to remedy a problem.

Rights of the Submissive

The submissive has the right to receive the basics of care while under the direct control of the dominant. This includes: food, water, shelter/warmth, adequate sleep, adequate free time, and a sense of personal fulfillment. The submissive has the right to inform the dominant if any of the above needs are not being met.

The submissive has the right to expect his core sense of self and human dignity will not be taken from him, with the exception of clearly defined scenes in which this might be the case.

The submissive has the right to freely and openly communicate anything (good or bad) with the dominant at all times, but will do his best to adhere to the protocols given to him for addressing problematic issues.

The submissive has the right to go about his vanilla life without infringement of the D/s relationship. He has the right to inform the dominant if any of her orders are interfering with his vanilla life.

The submissive has the right to not be subjected to sexual contact (defined as genital to genital and/or genital to oral contact) with the dominant or any other person.

The submissive has the right not to be subjected to activities that would permanently damage his physical, intellectual or emotional health or well-being.

The submissive has the right to decline any requests for his time above and beyond one hour per day. However, as scheduling permits, and with agreements in place, he is expected to fully commit himself for the period of time agreed upon, except for the case of extenuating circumstances that require change of plans.

Duties of the Submissive

The submissive agrees that while this contract is valid, he is effectively property of the dominant and his body, time, intellect, and free will are hers to use as she desires without delay or question, within the parameters this agreement sets forth.

The submissive agrees to obey all commands from the dominant and accepts that in the case of his refusal to do so, or in the case of inadequate performance in doing so, he will face correction, disciplinary action, punishment, and eventually dismissal from service.

The submissive does not have the right to "argue his case", though he may be asked to explain himself in certain situations if something has gone wrong. Accordingly, he has no right to excuse himself from the consequences of his actions as judged by the dominant.

The submissive is not to engage in acts of "play" nor in submission or subservience to other people without the express permission of the dominant. Conversely, the submissive is obligated to perform service (of any type except for as defined by his limits) for other parties at the command of the dominant without hesitation and as if the orders came directly from the dominant herself.

The submissive is obligated to inform the dominant immediately if the time spent together or in fulfilling his obligations to her is infringing on his vanilla life and/or if he fears that it might.

The submissive is obligated to inform the dominant immediately if at any time he believes an assigned task, order, or command holds risk of harming him or damaging his vanilla life/reputation/human dignity/etc.

The submissive is required to devote no less than one hour of time daily to the relationship which includes: speaking to, spending time with, or completing tasks assigned by the dominant. If a task only takes part of this time, he is expected to spend the remainder of the designated hour in an activity or meditation relating to the dominant or the D/s relationship such as reading or journaling.

The submissive is required to remain in constant contact with the dominant, consisting of (at minimum) an email or text message to report his status daily if no other communication is possible –with the exception of pre-planned and pre-approved leaves of absence if necessary and true emergencies where contact is not possible.

The submissive has the responsibility to inform the dominant when an activity is causing him serious distress such that if left unattended permanent damage may occur. However, no matter how careful a person may be, accidents do happen. The submissive has no right to seek damages from the dominant for such accidents caused within the scope of activities as outlined in this document.

Terms of Contract

Duration of the Contract: The obligations of this contract, freely assumed by both parties, shall be binding for the duration of 14 days, ending on July 29th, 2010 unless terminated prior to that date.

Reassessment and Alteration of the Contract: As a contract is a binding agreement, it may not be changed or amended without the consent of all parties. A party wishing to change the terms of the contract must receive the express consent of the other party before being freed of previously agreed-upon rights and obligations, or being bound by new ones. Additionally, the dominant and submissive will hold regularly scheduled sessions to check in with one another regarding the efficacy of the contract. This will happen every time the contract is renewed, or no less than once per month if the contracted period is longer than that.

Termination of the Contract: The obligations of this contract shall terminate upon the completion of the above -mentioned period of time. As a binding agreement, no party should lightly seek the premature termination of the contract. However, if there is legitimate need to do so, the contract may be terminated by either party at any time. Reasons for premature termination of the contract may include (but are not limited to): dishonesty or misrepresentation of fundamental truths by either the dominant or submissive; neglect of the submissive's needs on the part of the dominant; disregard for the submissive's limits on the part of the dominant; failure to fulfill the obligations and requirements of the relationship (as outlined above) on the part of either dominant or submissive. Upon termination of the contract, a new contract may be negotiated and put into place or both parties are free to decline entering into further contracts.

I have read, understood, and agreed to the above contract and hereby vow to uphold my obligations as outlined therein to the best of my abilities.

As soon we had both signed the contract, I presented Joseph with his first real collar. Until this point he had been wearing a thin metal chain with a padlock when serving me, and sometimes I would use a thicker, padded leather play collar if I just wanted him to have something around his neck for me to grab onto. But neither of these collars had been chosen and bought specifically for him and neither meant a whole lot to us.

Since he had become my pup, I went to the pet store and found a simple black leather dog collar. To complete the picture, I used one of the do-it-yourself machines to have a blue metal dog-bone-shaped tag engraved. It read:

Pup Joseph
Property of Melissa
If found call (212) 983-4576

Having my phone number on the tag was of course just a cute touch. This is one pup that I can't ever see running away.

Though Joseph is not a "puppy" in the barking, tail wagging sense, his demeanor is very dog-like. Just like my real dog Shadow, Joseph is content to be with me doing anything, or nothing at all, and tries his best to make me happy by following commands. The pup moniker may confuse some people who expect us to be into puppy play, but most people understand that pup is just an affectionate term we use to describe my human property.

Joseph also has more in common with a service dog who attends to his owner and performs very specific functions than any "pet." Those who meet us and see us interact seem to understand. I don't remember exactly when I started referring to Joseph as my pup, but it was early on and it stuck—so much so that the idea of calling anyone else "pup" is entirely unappealing. To me, there can only ever be one pup.

Scene Report: July 14, 2010

Overall experience: Signing the contract and officially becoming your "property" was one of the greatest experiences of my life. I was so happy that I was on the verge of tears for much of the night.

It was very surreal to read the contract aloud. It made it very concrete that I was actually entering into this relationship and making myself your submissive. It was a very good experience, though I had no hesitation at all in signing the contract; I was just so happy to make it official and be yours. Receiving my own collar from you was incredibly special and unexpected. I wish I could wear it all the time. It made me so happy and proud to be your "pup."

Being flogged was a wonderful experience. Almost the entire time, through the use of the various floggers, I was on the verge of tears I was so happy to be yours and to be used as you wanted for your pleasure. I kept thinking how each blow of the flogger was a sign of your care and of your control over me. My approach to the whip was somewhat the same as to the flogging, but the whip does get much more painful much more quickly than does the flogger. It was not long before I was simply enduring the pain, but even here I was somewhat torn. The pain was substantial and I did want it to stop, but at the same time I could feel an endorphin rush coming, and it seemed as if every time it was about to get really intense the flogging or whipping stopped. What is a submissive to do, endure terrible pain in order to get a major rush or forsake the rush to ease the pain? I don't really have that choice, I know, but that was going through my mind and it is a rather beautiful torment in itself, and perhaps all the more ironic since you had no idea you had put me in that position.

I don't need to tell you how much I enjoy you playing with my ass. Being fucked by you on this occasion was especially good, not only for the sensation, but even more for the position it gave me. I remember distinctly looking down one time as I was on my hands and knees in front of you with your cock fucking my ass, seeing my shaved and rather small-looking cock and balls and your powerful legs behind me using me and feeling very submissive, powerless to your control. It was a very good moment. The speculum was a great experience; the feel of it expanding in my ass is wonderful, as is the ability it gives you with its handle to move it around and control me from behind in such a tender area. It was this position of impotence, of not being able to move or go anywhere since you were controlling me with the speculum, which made your strokes with the rubber cane all the more painful. Yes, they hurt a lot on their own, but knowing there was nowhere I could go at the moment with you in control of my ass made the experience all the more humbling.

All of our time together afterward is such a joy to me. All that I go through or rather all that you put me through is worth it as it helps me to be so pliable to you and feel so completely secure in your arms afterward. That time to talk and share is very beautiful for me, and it feels all the more intimate knowing that you have taken away any barriers that I might otherwise want to impose. I wish I could lay in your strong embrace and feel your acceptance of me and your control over me always, but for the moment I enjoy what I can get. And I am just so happy that you are willing to make me yours, that you find me worthy enough to belong to you. That makes me very proud and motivates me to do the absolute best I can in everything so as to not let you down or displease you.

LETTERS TO EACH OTHER

By mid-July I once again had to be out of town for a few days, this time for a non-work and non-kink related commitment. It was not going to be much fun, and I wasn't looking forward to being away from Joseph again so soon. Considering that these brief times apart were becoming more regular, I decided to instruct Joseph on how to keep our relationship dynamic in the forefront of his mind even when we went days without seeing each other. My idea was to implement a daily task, a meditation of sorts (with the assistance of a butt-plug), and this ritual became one that we continued to use whenever we had to be apart.

I was leaving on a Sunday, but I had a friend coming in Friday night, and we planned to go out to dinner and then home to the dungeon afterwards. This would be my last time with Joseph for six days, so there was a "let's make it count" mentality. Actually, I think our entire relationship existed with that kind of undercurrent, considering time always seemed to be against us.

This Friday night, like every night we spent in each others' company, we had experienced some amazing, intense, hot things and the hardest part was always sending Joseph back to his apartment when my allotted time was up. He was certainly my property, but perhaps no one knows better than I do how the outside world can impose limitations on a relationship.

After a night such as this one, I never could just go off to bed, so instead I would sit down at my computer and write a letter to him, trying to capture the happiness I felt before going to sleep as if the memory would be diluted by morning. I have always used writing to help figure out what I'm thinking and feeling, and it has never been a chore to me. Quite the opposite. When emotion and passion are brewing within me so violently that I feel I might explode, to write allows me a catharsis unlike any other.

Friday, July 16, 2010

Dear Joseph,

I am imagining you lying in bed, wearing my collar and with my plug perhaps still in your ass, feeling secure in the knowledge that you are mine. What more is there that I need to be happy?

I could write a book about how much I enjoyed tonight—every part of it, especially getting you to cry. I thoroughly enjoy hearing you describe what's going through your head while I play with you, such as when you said that you knew I would continue hitting you until you did cry, but knew that it was because I cared. Hearing you say "Please, it hurts," is one of the most

hauntingly beautiful memories I have replaying through my head, as is the moment when you started crying fully as I untied you. Wrapping you in my arms, you felt very small and fragile, which in turn makes me feel strong, protective, and powerful. I love these feelings and they touch me at my deepest level.

Assuming we will not see each other until I get back, I want to give you the assignments I have been alluding to.

1. Start thinking of a mantra or meditation, something that you can recite to yourself when we're not together to remind you of your status as owned. Send it to me when you think you've got something close to finished.

2. Once you have completed number 1, use an alarm clock and set it for ten minutes. Make sure you have ten minutes without interruption from a roommate or whomever. Put the jeweled plug inside of you, make sure my collar is on you if it's not already, and kneel down on your knees and elbows with your ass in the air. Then recite your mantra for those 10 minutes.

3. Once you have done this, send me an email or a text to tell me that you have completed your assignment for the day and to thank me for giving you this task.

Lastly, just as a reminder, wear my collar every night when you sleep. For the time we're apart, you are free to wear the metal plug as you like, but I do want to be kept informed of how long and how often you're wearing it.

AN INTENSE NIGHT

Scene Report: Saturday, July 17, 2010

(Note: The assignment at the restaurant Joseph mentions was his task to bring a butt plug with him and go to the restroom to insert it at my command during dinner.)

Overall Experience: The evening was a very powerful and wonderful experience, which far surpassed any expectations I may have had for "going out for dinner."

I very much enjoyed dinner. I was so happy to be able to sit next to you. The anticipation of and fulfillment of your assignment at the restaurant was also a thrill for me. I will not go too much into the nerves/anxiety I felt during dinner, as I think we adequately discussed this issue later in the evening, although I would be happy to expound upon them if you like. I would say this: I need to work on trusting you more and being more open with issues that come up rather than always trying to anticipate what you may want or expect. For example, when ordering an alcoholic drink, I could have just asked you if it was okay rather than just ordering a root beer. It really is not that big of a deal, but I want to be more transparent in the future.

I cannot say how much I enjoyed being tied down so thoroughly by you. I love being in bondage, and I am coming to appreciate rope bondage more and more, as it requires your participation to a much different degree than cuffs. This to me more powerfully symbolizes what I like about bondage—it is an extension of your control over me. The ropes are literally your way of holding me down and keeping me in the position in which you want. That is an amazing feeling for me, and I could just lie there enjoying that feeling forever. Above all, I think I appreciated you binding my cock and balls so nice and securely. It had been a long while since they were tied up and I truly enjoy that feeling—making them feel more objectified, less a true part of myself, and certainly more tender and exposed to whatever you would like to do to them. But just the sensation of being tied down so nicely to the table was a great thrill for me.

I also very much enjoyed the cloth gag you used on me. I like being gagged in general, the helplessness of being unable to speak. I enjoyed the gags used before, but I must confess the cloth was more comfortable than the ball gag and felt more secure. However, what I loved more than the gag was having the cloth blindfold me. There was a wonderful sense of being powerless, not only being tied down securely but not being able to see anything of what is going on. I also enjoy not knowing what you are going to do next, having no sense of anticipating what is coming, and therefore having to completely spontaneously react to what is being done to me.

I was quite surprised by the wax. I knew immediately what it was, having used wax on myself before, and being exposed to wax in other vanilla settings growing up. I was surprised by how much it stung. In the past when I have experienced wax, it was hot but not all that painful. Perhaps it was being tied down which heightened the sensation or perhaps it was someone else applying the wax that added to it, or perhaps the kind of wax being used was different and melted hotter. Whatever it was, I was surprised at how much I enjoyed that experience of suffering. I think I heard some playful laughs from you while applying it which made the experience all the more special knowing the pleasure my displeasure was giving you.

What can I say about the rest of the torment, other than it was pure torment? As I'm sure you know, the "stingy" instruments cause me much more pain much more quickly than the "thuddy" instruments. I was unable to escape, unable to "embrace" the pain. All I could do was endure it as best I could for as long as I could - or rather for as long as you wanted it to last.

In a previous report I mentioned how special it was being made to cry, that not only my body but also my emotions were under your control. I had that experience again on Saturday. The pain had brought me close to crying, but it was not until you started hitting me with your fists and I realized intellectually and emotionally that you would not stop until I really cried, that I was so utterly helpless and under your control, that the tears started flowing. On top of that, I immediately realized that you still would not stop, not because you wanted to punish me or harm me but because you loved me. I cannot adequately put into words what that felt like, to feel so loved, so helpless and in such suffering all at once. All I know is that the only thing I could do in that moment of complete domination was to cry. Maybe the only better feeling than that is to have you comfort me and console me when I do cry, so that I can experience not only your control over me but also your care for me—or at least a different experience of your care for me, as I know everything you do expresses that care. In hindsight, as you mentioned, I do think that the sudden release from bondage added to the second wave of crying. To lose the strong embrace the ropes so quickly left me feeling very alone and completely exposed, and still in a state of complete vulnerability.

I should mention here one other thing. One of the greatest images that I have, which is also one of the great gifts you give me, is to be tied down and be able to look up at you. Your face is always so full of love but expressed in such different ways: concern, merriment, a malicious playfulness, a stern desire to cause pain. I love to look up from my place of submission into your eyes and have a wonderful feeling of intimacy, all the while seeing in your eyes these different expressions and knowing what they will mean for my suffering. I can hardly keep those images out of my mind throughout the following days, and I don't really want to keep them out except for knowing that I have to concentrate on other things.

As always, I love being with you after we play, and especially after such an intense scene. I feel like I just want to curl up completely into your strong embrace, and I wish I really were a puppy so that I could do so more fully. In those moments I feel so completely yours, so open and totally exposed to you, so docile to whatever you would want.

AT HOME

Less than two months since we had first spoken online, I felt confident that my boy was something truly special and rare. This is a feeling I have only encountered a few times in my life, including when I had been with Heather for several months. Even though we still believed Joseph's future was certain and did not include a relationship with me at this point, I was starting to feel equally certain that I could not just let go of him when our time was up.

As such, I wanted him to know that he was part of my chosen family, no matter what the future brought, and I instructed him to start calling my and Heather's house "Home." We have since referred to anywhere he else happens to be living as "his place" but my Home is always Home. Even though at this point he did not fully feel as though my house was his Home, the change in the way we spoke about places began to take root in his brain and instill this feeling over time. Having a place to call Home was a great feeling for Joseph, but even more special to me, knowing that Joseph's history left him never quite feeling at home anywhere—until now.

Scene Report: Sunday, July 25, 2010

Overall Experience: It was a wonderful evening, an emotional evening for me, but wonderful. I greatly enjoyed dinner and the beginning of our evening together. What I most enjoyed about it, apart from simply being with you, was feeling for the first time that I was a part of the house. I have never felt unwelcome, but I have always felt like a guest. Saturday night I felt as if I was not just a guest coming over, but a part of the house. I am using the term "house" because I am not quite sure how else to describe the dynamic between you, Heather and myself. If you prefer, I could say "family" or some other term, but I think you understand what I mean. Anyway, that was a great feeling and it did not come because of some huge event, but simply by my own comfort level and familiarity with the situation and surroundings.

It was nice to be of service when I first came over. As you were still cleaning up, I used my time to tidy up some things in the kitchen and then wash the sink before you asked me to unload the dishwasher. It was also nice not having to be catered to during dinner; you and Heather were busy hanging the curtains and were not obligated to "entertain the guest", which was also a part of me feeling like I fit in. To put it another way, I really felt at home during that whole time, which does not happen to me often in other people's houses.

I am always happy for our time together to talk, and the same was true again Saturday night prior to our playtime. I was also very glad to be able to massage your feet, which helped keep me distracted. It was not at all easy for me to talk about myself so frankly and openly. If I was not able to keep my mind distracted I would have shown my emotions much more, and perhaps I should have anyway. I still cannot believe that I actually confided some of my most painful memories to another person, many of which I never thought I would ever share with anyone else. I am constantly surprised and at the same time so very happy that I can trust you enough to reveal myself to you. I do think, however, that this conversation and the emotions it evoked colored the rest of our evening. As you noted at the end, I did not smile very much even though I did enjoy most of our time together (except for the terrible pain). I was not in a 'playful' mood after talking about myself that way. I do hope that my more serious mood did not hinder your enjoyment of the evening.

I also want to say another word about giving you that foot massage. I know that I am far from an expert in it, but I really enjoy giving you massages. First, it is a wonderful way to serve you and give you pleasure. You give me so much and I am so happy to be able to give back to you (which I know I always do in our time together, but I still like to feel that I am giving back to you more directly). Even more, however, one of the things I enjoy most is hearing your sounds of pleasure as I give you a massage. It is an incredible thrill to hear those sounds coming from you and knowing that you are getting such pleasure out of the experience. I wish I could hear those sounds from you all the time.

I was thrilled to be put into partial suspension. I had been thinking that if asked, the one thing I really wanted to have done to me was to be tied up nice and tight. The time and effort you take in putting me into rope bondage, and also into suspension, is a beautiful sign to me of your care for me. As the rope tightens around me, it is as if you are holding me tight in your embrace to protect me and keep me safe, to keep me exactly where you want me to be. My second time in suspension was another fun experience. It was very interesting to be so limited in my movements yet with enough freedom to squirm around and hang in the air. What a wonderful position to be in to feel your control and enjoy my submission! And to have the thrill of once again feeling your ass-hook in me was a very special treat.

This position was also a very interesting one in which to receive a beating from you. I was of course very exposed to you, and open to the many ways and places you wanted to beat me. I was also free enough to move around to try and evade the pain that was coming. The pain was a very strange experience. The blows started off easy enough, but then it was as if someone suddenly threw a switch and they became very painful. I know that I started begging (a rather sad attempt at begging, I am aware) very early, but it was the immediate reaction I had in the moment to the sharp pain.

The rest of the time was nothing else but pure torture for me. The pain was very intense, and of course I had no way to escape from it. Once or twice I felt on the verge of tears, then my torment would stop just long enough for the tears to subside before a fresh onslaught of pain was given. It was a long time before the pain grew to such a point that my last and only alternative was to cry.

As I began crying, which is a wonderful experience of transparency and openness to you, I felt certain that my tears would not stop your blows, as you had mentioned in the past might be the case. This proved to be true and led to another fit of tears.

The rest of our time together was simply amazing. The opportunity we had to talk—and even more gloriously for me, the ability to simply rest secure in your embrace—was amazing. If I ever have doubts about being submissive, I only need to remember how wonderful it feels to be so vulnerable and weak and yet so safe and protected in your loving arms. It gives me a sense of peace that I can hardly describe except to say that in that moment there is nothing else to worry about or fear. In fact I hardly have any other thoughts at all except the joy and peace of resting safe with you. For me, that is the great reward. It is the reward of being owned by one who loves me. Certainly I get pleasure out of serving you and making you happy through suffering and in other ways. But for me none of that compares to the feeling I have of knowing how naked I am in front of you, and yet how secure I am by you. This feeling of security is a most cherished gift that I only wish I could have always.

DRIVE-IN PLAY

As I may have mentioned, I am not only a human-property-owner but a horse owner (and have been for years). Before you even start thinking it, no, I am decidedly not into "pony play". Yes, there are in fact lots of parallels between owning a horse and owning a human, but none of them include bits, bridles, saddles, or spurs. Not for me at least! But it wasn't long before I introduced Joseph to my other "boy", Thunder, and he began coming with me to the barn on occasion, helping me out with the chores so we'd be done more quickly, and learning how to ride through my instruction. Despite being from Nebraska and coming from a farming family, Joseph had never ridden a horse until he met me.

This particular night, we met at the barn and then went to dinner, after which I was supposed to drop Joseph back at his car so he could get to bed for classes the next morning. But I can't ever resist the chance to have a bit of fun and play with what's mine - and why should I? We were still near the restaurant we'd eaten at and had a little time left before Joseph absolutely had to be back at his car. So With Joseph in my passenger seat, I pulled into the parking lot of a nearby supermarket and told him to go find gloves and lube. "And by the way, you've got five minutes." There was no "or else." There was no threat or promise of consequences, and even though I knew it was unlikely he would make the time limit, this was not just an excuse to punish him as some people create in their play.

I can't say exactly why I gave him a time limit, other than I just like raising the stakes a little; giving him a challenge and some extra motivation to hurry up. As if knowing what I'm going to do with those gloves and lube isn't motivation enough! I also enjoy the idea of him stressing over finding the right items and getting through the checkout in time.

When Joseph returned to the car he knew he had missed the deadline. Impressively, he was only one minute late! I smiled as I imagined him hustling through the unfamiliar grocery store searching for latex gloves and some sort of lube and having no idea what would happen to him if he were late.

Looking back at it, maybe I should have taken the items, thanked him, and driven him back to his car. Now that would have been a good mindfuck. But as usual, my hard dick and lust for this boy won and he got a hot parking lot scene despite being past his time limit on the purchases.

A week later, I arrived back at home on Thursday, after not having seen Joseph since the previous Friday. Even though I was tired from my trip, seeing him always has a way of reinvigorating me. After six days apart we both were due for some well-deserved play time. There isn't a whole lot to say in the way of introduction. It was indeed just another average night for us. But our nights were never "average."

Scene Report: July 22, 2010

Overall Experience: It was a great time, as always, and I wish it could have gone on much longer.

Being tied up was another experience that I wanted to have, and it proved to be as good, if not better, than I had hoped. I simply love the feeling of being bound and helpless and completely at your disposal. I love the feeling of cuffs and ropes on my skin holding me firmly in place. I like the feeling of squirming around and feeling how securely I am held there (these movements are not usually signs of discomfort on my part, but of pleasure).

This new experience was enhanced by being blindfolded and losing that sense as well as finally being able to experience earplugs. I was a bit disappointed in the earplugs in that I could still hear a fair amount, but a lot of sound was blocked and most everything else was muffled, making it very difficult to know what was going on around me. It accomplished its purpose in making me feel cut off from the outside world, deprived of movement, sight and sound. All I had was the interior workings of my mind.

The only difficult part of being bound was the cock in my mouth. As you no doubt noticed, it was working strongly against my gag reflex, making it impossible for me to take the whole thing in. (I would be interested in knowing your intent in this regard, if you remembered my concern mentioned in the past about my gag reflex and being able to suck cock.) I did see this as a training exercise in that regard, and tried my best to take in as much as I could. However, since I could not take it all the way in, my head was left at a sharp angle, making it hard on my neck. I am going to confess that while you stepped out of the room I did lay my head down for a moment to give my neck a rest. I apologize for leaving the position you put me in. I know it was wrong of me and accept whatever consequences arise from my disobedience. I greatly enjoyed just being there, tied up, gagged, blindfolded, and deaf, while you did whatever you wanted/needed to do. Part of me knew that I was not being ignored, I knew that I was not forgotten; I was just not being given any particular attention at the time. From the first, I tried hard to keep reciting my mantra and always remember why I was doing these things: to please Sir in suffering, service and submission. I tried to keep this up throughout the rest of our play time. The feel of your feet on my back, ass, and on your plug only aided in my enjoyment of the experience, reminding me of your presence, your dominance and of being completely owned by you. I would have been happy to remain in that position for hours, if it were physically possible.

The second position in which I was bound was not perhaps as fun for me, but it was equally enjoyable as I knew I was then more vulnerable and exposed to be used by you. As I mentioned last night, I was afraid of what you were going to do for a while. I think the fear comes from the position of extreme helplessness and vulnerability. I was on the floor, bound, blindfolded, and unable to hear. There was very little, if anything, I could do in that moment to escape (not that I ever had any thoughts about escape). I know this is true in other situations as well, but there is something more visceral about this experience than in other settings that makes me feel afraid. It was the same sort of fear as when I was bound, blinded, and gagged upstairs as your "little doll". I should also add that it is a very strange and thrilling experience of being controlled when the cock that was in my mouth gagging me for so long is then thrust up my ass, as if my own saliva is being used as a means of controlling me.

Being flogged this time was a different experience due to the position of lying on the ground. Also, your technique last night was rather playful, lightly running the flogger across my back only to suddenly hit me very hard. Both were great experiences. The position was nice; there's nothing like lying face down on the floor in order to receive a good flogging to make a pup feel his submission.

This was the second time that you flogged me while fucking my ass. This is becoming one of my favorite positions. First, there is the amazing experience of my ass being stimulated so wonderfully and powerfully, and then there is the pain of your flogger so hard across my back. These sensations are wonderful in themselves. What makes this position even better is the fact that I feel so utterly under your control, so much at your mercy. There I am on my knees before you so fully exposed and vulnerable. You have my ass under your control, not allowing me to move or go anywhere unless you direct me. The effect of this is to become your puppet, moved about and manipulated as it pleases you no matter what I may want.

Spending time with you afterwards is amazing. I feel so very close to you then, such an intimacy as you have broken down all my barriers and stripped away all my layers allowing me to be completely naked before you in virtually every way.

MIND CONTROL

It seemed like only moments had passed between the elated signing of our first contract and the night two weeks later when we renewed it for the first time. The second version didn't differ from the first except that the period was now twice as long: thirty days. We signed, reaffirming our commitment to one another as dominant and submissive (the wording of owner and property didn't arise until later), and we marked the night as we did so many others with hours of delicious play.

Unlike other nights, however, there were two exercises I included in our playtime that were designed with a specific result in mind. Normally the scenes I create are first and foremost for my pleasure, secondly for the enjoyment of the submissive, and ultimately to reinforce the relationship dynamic in some way. But rarely ever do I set out with the intention to produce a tangible result—and tonight, I would do so twice.

Since the start of our relationship, Joseph had been brushing up repeatedly against his own issues of whether or not he was pleasing enough, good enough, or worthy enough for me. His self-doubt and insecurities were unshakeable despite my repeated reassurances that he was fully living up to my expectations, and my promise to tell him immediately if he was not. This continued struggle to accept my words at face value frustrated me, because it often lead to negative emotions or mopey moods for no good reason. After all, I hardly ever was disappointed in his performance or behaviors, but he would act as if I were because he felt that way, regardless of my actual approval. On top of simply wanting to relieve him of needless negative emotions, this behavior felt subversive to my authority as his dominant because we agreed that it was my opinion of him or his performance that mattered, and on which judgments would be made, not his own.

This cycle of insecurity and self-doubt had been going on for the duration of our relationship without improvement, so I decided a demonstration was needed to prove to Joseph just how serious I was. To be completely honest, I had never tried using some type of physical or corporal action to change behavior, and I wasn't sure it would actually work. But since talking it out had not succeeded up to this point, I decided to try a different approach.

The exercise went something like this: I tied Joseph down to my spanking bench and paddled him harder than I would "just for fun" and with each stroke he was required to ask me, "Sir, do you find me pleasing?" And I would answer, "Yes!" We did this ten times and since that is far less than any number of hits he would receive if I were just playing with him for fun, you can be certain each one was hard enough to pound the message home.

To my great surprise and pleasure, by the end of the experience, he was transformed. Not to say that all insecurities vanished immediately but from this point forward, if Joseph ever required reassurance, he certainly only needed one affirmation to put his mind at ease and move on. Gone were the constant self-critical pity parties and paralyzing fear of not being good enough.

Let me be clear that I give most of the credit for this and other behavior and thought modifications I have made in the boy to his extreme desire to conform himself to my will, and not some kind of magical power I have over people. Contrary to his opinion of himself, Joseph is an extremely strong person, and this strength has allowed him to adapt to my preferences and internalize my priorities. I don't believe that ability should go unmentioned. It always impresses the hell out of me.

Along the same line, the second exercise of the night also utilized Joseph's mental fortitude. This time the goal was to alter his ability to deal with physical sensations that he would inherently not enjoy. Because he is not a masochist, and sometimes has trouble enduring the degree of pain I like to inflict, I wanted to experiment with a technique for pain processing I'd seen demonstrated in a class. I instructed him to focus on a visualization of light and peace while I was beating him. As Joseph describes below in his scene report, it worked beautifully and allowed me to continue working him over while he experienced an entirely different sensation.

True, I am a sadist, and I don't necessarily just want my "victims" to be ecstatically enjoying their pain, which is why I prefer playing with non-masochists. But my sadism may just be beat out by my desire for control, so that the idea of controlling Joseph's ability to process the sensations I give him is even more exciting than the ability to simply hurt him.

Between these two exercises/experiments, the amount of control I held over Joseph's mind became more evident to us both and gave us the confidence to keep pushing deeper into the territory of internal enslavement.

Scene Report: Saturday, July 31, 2010

Overall Experience: What more can I say than absolutely wonderful! I was very happy to be able to wear earplugs once again. Despite having some initial difficulties inserting them, they worked much better than last time. I was not able to hear any background noises at all. I could not hear you walking around, entering or leaving the room, working on the computer, or anything else. Even your commands to me were muffled and took a moment to sink in. Voices and the vague rumble of the air conditioner were about the only things that I could hear. This was again a wonderful experience in cutting me off from the outside world, leaving me isolated to focus on my thoughts.

I do love the feeling of cuffs on my wrists and ankles, and even now writing this I enjoy the phantom feeling of them strapped tightly around my extremities. The chains add a wonderful sense of weight, in addition to restricting my movements and making me so much at your disposal and under your control.

The butt plug you inserted felt so cold it was so exhilarating. I was thrilled that I could wear it for so long.

The time I spent in the cage was not enjoyable for me. As I told you last night, I find the experience in there to be lonely. You had told me beforehand that you would be putting me in there for a while, and so I was not surprised, but I find it to be isolating. I find that reaction rather strange; I could be tied to the table and left for a long time and feel good because the ropes binding me are so much an extension of you; they hold me in your embrace. I find the time in the cage to be cold in that I don't have that same sense of feeling your presence. I know that I am put in the cage to be kept just where you want me, but the feeling I get (and I obviously know better), is that I am being put in there and abandoned as you go about doing other things. As I lay there, I tried to focus on the words of my mantra as well as the words from your exercise about being your good pup, but they didn't help. They helped remind me of why I was there, what my purpose was, but they didn't help me feel any better about it. Not having any sense of time in there only adds to the loneliness, as I have no idea if I have been left there for ten minutes or one hour. Time goes so slowly in there. I was wondering if my time in the cage was part of my punishment. I knew that I was going to be punished (you later clarified it as reinforcement), and in the past you had made a comment about using the cage as punishment. In either case, the time in the cage makes me appreciate all the more the time that I am not in it and can be with you.

It is still strange for me to walk around the house naked except for my underwear and your cuffs while doing normal activities. It is not exactly embarrassing to be seen by Heather this way, but it is odd. It is one thing for me to be submissive to you and totally exposed to you but being seen that way by others is still a little unnerving. It is not bad; I guess I am still just adjusting to it. At the same time it is exciting to be seen so openly as belonging to you, and to be so free as to not care that someone else would see me that way. I am so self-conscious in daily life, and to be free of that, knowing that at the moment I am doing what you want, what I have been told to do by you, is a liberating experience.

I am always appreciative of the care you take in feeding me. To be honest, while I was in the cage, I was wondering what I would have to eat. It occurred to me that I had bought two potatoes and there would presumably be three of us, you, Heather, and myself. I was wondering perhaps if you didn't have some special "pup food" for me, and was relieved that it turned out as it did. Of course the food was tasty as ever.

The more I think about the experience of being punished for my disobedient thinking, the more I appreciate how you are helping me to grow as a submissive and as a person. I was grateful that you took the time to explain what was happening so thoroughly. I was also appreciative to hear you explain that it was not really "punishment" but reinforcement of how I should think and act in the future. I was already thinking of it in that way, but was glad to know that was how you also intended it. The actual exercise for reinforcement made me so happy. To hear you repeatedly answer me that I do please you really helped me to understand that, and it made me all the more thankful for your goodness to your pup. It was also a bit embarrassing that in the midst of everything I lost count, but you were so gracious about it, as you always are. I know this issue will resurface at some point, but this gives me a beautiful and poignant memory to recall so as to allay any doubts in the future. In that moment my ass was burning from the paddle but my spirit was burning even more as I felt so submissive to you, so docile, and so grateful that you took me for your own.

Believe it or not, I had forgotten about the symbolic action of signing our contract. After receiving such strong paddling during the previous exercise (ten blows being rather painful), I was nervous about how I would get through thirty more. Of course you were so good to me that the paddling was not as severe, but still strong enough to emphasize the purpose of the contract. I can only wonder what it will be like when we sign a longer term contract. How many days are there in six months? It was an incredible experience to have that physical reminder of my submission, along with the verbal pronouncement, to so thoroughly remind me of how I am completely owned by you, and how I willingly submit to you.

I remember well the inflatable gag from a previous scene and I really do enjoy it. I enjoy the experience of being gagged in general, but this gag is particularly fun, especially when it inflates and pushes the limits of what my mouth can handle. To have your gag in my mouth and your paddle on my ass while you were then controlling my breathing was simply wonderful. Something so simple as air, which is so often taken for granted, was being controlled by you. I couldn't make a sound when your paddle hit my ass, because your gag and your fingers had me completely bottled up. I only wish you would have held on a little longer so that I was in greater distress for air, but I realize too how dangerous breath-play can be and understand you not wanting to push it too far.

Getting fucked by you in this way was a new and unbelievably wonderful experience of your cock in my ass. Being asked to relax and lay still while you supplied all of the force made me feel like your little fuck-doll. I was laying there to be used and grasped and manipulated as you wanted in order to fuck my ass. Your cock always feels so amazing inside of me, and even more so last night, as I felt so much an object under your control for your pleasure.

The various ways you can move in and out of me is wonderful. You seem to know how to elicit every bit of pleasure there is to be found. To be hit so hard and fucked at the same time is almost too much sensation to take in at once. It is, as I said last night, as if my body wants to feel pain but cannot, because the other sensation following immediately after feels so good. It is such a conflict, but somehow only makes the experience that much more powerful. I loved the position into which I was bound, sitting there totally exposed before you where I was able to see your expression and everything you wanted to do to me. Then to have you enter my mind in that way to control how I experienced pain was wonderful. It was yet another way in which you asserted your control over me, over the very way my mind interpreted pain. Those kinds of meditations or mind exercises have been challenging for me in the past in other contexts and for a while I was tempted to think I wasn't doing well at it. It was a struggle to keep focus on the light, the heat and peace. But I also recognized that I was enduring your beating much better than I otherwise would have, which meant that I was doing something right, that my mind was bending to your suggestions. I look forward with eager expectation to other scenes where your voice penetrates my mind and reinterprets how I experience our time together.

OWNED VS. NOT

Ever since meeting Joseph, I have had a bit of a one-track mind when it comes to playing. This is a stark contrast from the way I used to be. You might have called me a "play slut" then, and it would have been a pretty accurate term.

Of course I was always looking for that one person I could own and use in all the ways that would make me happy, but since I hadn't found him, I continued to meet and play with new people in new capacities, and I liked it that way to some extent. Once I got involved with Joseph, my desire to do other things with other people pretty much faded away.

But I'm not wired to be strictly monogamous, and there were still people in the world who I wanted to play with. So when the experience arose to play with someone while owning someone else. Joseph asked me how the two types of interaction were different and I tried to explain it to him in a letter.

Sunday, August 1, 2010

Dear Joseph,

I have been thinking about this since you asked yesterday and decided my thoughts would not get organized unless I sat down to write. I hope you are aware there is a huge difference between how I interact with you and play with you vs. anyone else in my life currently. The only person I can compare it to is the last boy I collared, over two years ago. That only lasted three months, and the entire time was a struggle to achieve obedience from him. He was never happy with what I did, and always needed "more" in some way or another. The experience with you has been quite the opposite and I can't tell you how happy it makes me to be able to give so much to you so completely, as you've described.

What I mean is that you are not constantly dissatisfied with the way I play with you, or the extent, or the type of play I do, which was the case with the boy from years ago ... nor are you reluctant to serve in non-play capacities or feel resentful over things I ask you to do.

In the time since him I have played with many people and pursued "potential" D/s relationships with a handful of them. None have worked, though one experience definitely taught me a lot about what I want and need. I need to be able to own someone to the fullest extent possible, it's that simple. With you, your situation makes this both more complicated and more possible. The more complicated part should be obvious, but how I see your situation making it more feasible is that I will never have to worry about you needing the things I cannot provide (i.e. sex, romance, egalitarian relationship, marriage, etc.). If I had a slave who was not in your situation, chances are that eventually he would tire of being with me in this capacity and want to go seek a "real" relationship with someone who would fit more into the traditional life partner box.

So how is play with you different than with others? I think to some degree, only seeing me play with someone else would fully describe it, but I can try. When I played with Brian last night, I felt it was primarily about his interests. I enjoyed our time together, but it was not driven by what I really liked and wanted. It was mutual at best; centered on his fetishes at worst. Not to say it like that's a bad thing because we are friends and I'm glad we could have an enjoyable night together, but though I had a lot of "fun" spending time with him, it didn't do for me what my time with you does. He was not focused on what I wanted or making me happy, because that was not the agreement. He's not my submissive. He is owned by someone else, and it's similar to what I would expect from you if I loaned you out to a friend. I would want you to get a good time out of it, but your purpose and goals wouldn't be to treat the other woman the way you treat me or interact with her the way you do with me. It's more for mutual satisfaction, which ironically doesn't satisfy me all that much.

With you, everything that we do and any time I play with you is an expression of my ownership and your devotion to me. With others now or in the past, play just doesn't hold that kind of meaning.

I've played with very few people in the way as if I owned them. Brian is someone I can play that way with if I want, but it doesn't come naturally to me. I don't feel it and I am not inspired to push him further and further to test his devotion to me. And yes, that is sometimes what I do with you. I believe I told you early on in our interaction, maybe the second night, that I was playing with you as if I owned you, and that only happens on rare occasions. So what does that actually mean to say "I play with you as though I own you"? It means that I am less willing (and sometimes not willing at all) to indulge your fetishes. That's why it's a very good thing that our desires match up a lot of the times because I definitely won't do things to you that I have no interest in, just to appease you.

It also means that I am more concerned with your overall state of fulfillment and well-being, and not so much with your "happiness" at any given moment on a micro-level. I demand more actual service and not just play. I expect all of the things you are well aware of, like emotional transparency. Most of what you know of me are aspects I feel belong in a D/s relationship but not in a "play partners" capacity. I am generally friends with people I play with and enjoy the time we are together, but I don't have that "I could be happy like this forever" feeling. I'm usually ready for the play to be over and for them to go home so I can be back with Heather. And while I do want to make sure everything is back to normal for them the next day, I trust people to be okay on their own and don't expect them to need any sort of follow-up care from me unless they specifically request it. That's not because it would be bad if they did, but mostly because the extent to which I'm reaching them does not call for anything beyond the scene itself. With you, playing is something on many levels, the least of which is probably the physical thing that is happening in the moment. With a person I don't own or intend on owning, the physical elements of play are of more, or even most, importance.

MOVIE NIGHT

I have encountered my fair share of people who are involved in BDSM and claim that no one could possibly live this way "24/7." It would be unrealistic to expect someone to actually be a master or a slave full time, right? The same goes for using terms like owner and property; there are people who believe that it must all be an act because it's too extreme to be done "for real." As such, part of my motivation for sharing this story with the world is to show that some of us do live this way, and the structures of our relationships can and do guide every single interaction. There is no time off from the relationship itself even when we do what we do most of the time, which is just living life.

Thus, I present to you: Movie Night. In which a boy is fed dinner and made to watch a movie. It doesn't get any more "normal" than this, folks!

Scene Report: Sunday, August 1, 2010

As usual this was a wonderful experience for me. At one point you made a comment about hurting me so that I would not feel disappointed. I can honestly say that I was not disappointed by anything from this night at all, except perhaps for it being shorter than I would like, but the necessity for that is completely understood.

I am always happy to be able to help you with chores/tasks around the house. In many ways it gives me an opportunity to experience what I do not often see in my profession—physically doing something and seeing the immediate results. It also allows me to get what I have always needed in my life, which is the approval of someone else. I am happy performing whatever task no matter how small if it helps you or pleases you. The more tasks I perform for you, the more they become a part of the overall fulfillment of our relationship. What began as a desire for mostly playtime is evolving to embrace all the areas of service, and to me that vastly enriches our relationship.

Dinner was very good, as usual, and I am always appreciative of your efforts at cooking. At times I have had to cook for myself, and a few times for others, and I know how difficult that is for me and how much effort it takes. I am always appreciative when someone else makes that effort for me. It was also fun to be able to sit around with you and Heather and watch TV and just enjoy ourselves.

You have the best ways of making watching movies more entertaining. The vibrator feels so wonderful in my ass that at times it makes it hard to focus on anything else. The longer it stays on and the faster it vibrates, the more

I am driven to squirm around and increase the pleasure from it by allowing the sensation to hit different areas. It is simply amazing how good that can feel and for so long. And what is even better is to know that you are at the controls, giving or denying that pleasure however you wish, and immensely enjoying it either way. The clothespins on my nipples also felt unbelievable. In general, I love how you tease and play with my nipples. It gives me not only a great feeling of pleasure, but also a great feeling of submission as you have access to an area of me that no one else ever sees, let alone touches. The sensation of you tugging on the clothespins and then finally taking them off and playing with my nipples is simply incredible. In these, and all of our times together, I cannot help but be amazed at how much control you have over me by being able to give, and deny, me such pleasures.

The movie itself was a lot of fun. It does not rank as one of my all time favorite movies, but it was funny. Most importantly, being able to share that with you, being able to watch it with you right beside me and playing with me the whole time, was wonderful. I was also very happy that for a time I could once again give you such pleasure by massaging your feet. I truly savor every sigh of pleasure you give in response to my actions; it makes me so happy to hear them.

The time we had together once the movie was over was wonderful, as our time together always is. You continued to stimulate my ass so exquisitely. For a time this was accompanied by blows from your crop on my ass, which, rather than adding pain, only seemed to increase the feeling of pleasure. There was also a moment when my cock had grown hard and you pinched it between your fingers. This gave me another firm reminder of who is in control of every part of my body, including my cock, which you don't often touch and/or control for obvious reasons—my limit about ejaculating, and also my cock always being so messy and dripping. There was a brief moment when I felt that you might stroke me (even though I know you respect that limit of mine), and in that moment I couldn't help but wonder how good that might feel. Maybe that limit will change one day? What I did enjoy beyond description was lying next to you, feeling so warm and loved and accepted by you, and then being able to look up and see your face with such a look of complete peace and joy. It made me feel so incredible to see you so happy in that moment and to be able to share in your happiness. In closing, I mentioned earlier that I was not disappointed with anything from this evening, in contrast to the earlier scene in which I had felt disappointed. That is completely true. It may not have been as intense as other times we have played but I think that I am coming to appreciate the variety of ways I can be submissive to you and enjoy your presence.

A GOOD, HARD, BEATING

For the first time, and to my great surprise, Joseph made a request of me to receive "a good hard beating", if I felt like granting it. Though he had endured more than a few intense sessions that left him bruised, welted, and crying for me in the past, he had never requested to be hurt. In fact, I was certain that if I never desired to hurt Joseph again he'd probably not miss it.

Joseph never did ask for much. He would tell me what he needed, as I required, and he would tell me what he preferred when I asked (always leaving the decision to grant it or not up to me) but to flat out ask for something himself has always been a rarity. I decided to indulge him this time, though I warned him that he would probably get more than he had asked for. But what can I say? I'm just a giver like that.

Scene Report: Wednesday August 4, 2010

As always, I was very happy to have your instructions and be of use to you by unloading and loading the dishwasher. I am always grateful that you take the time to cook for me, and the time at the table was nice to be able to visit over dinner.

All day long I had been wanting a good beating or whipping from you and I was so happy to receive it. The desire for such treatment itself surprised me, as I have not considered myself a masochist, but perhaps I am if I am now desiring to be caused such pain by you? Of course I know that the pain is our expression of love and care, or at least one form of it, and I know it was that which I really wanted to feel, a firm reminder of how much you care for me. There is just something so relaxing and rejuvenating by receiving a good beating; in the moment there are no other cares or worries or concerns, there is only the present experience of pain and submission. Of course this is true for submitting to you in general, but a more intense scene makes this focus all the easier.

From almost the moment you began whipping me I began to feel what I will call endorphins. It is a tingling sensation somewhat like when your foot falls asleep but not quite. It is a somewhat strange but pleasurable sensation. It usually begins on the top of my brain and spreads throughout the rest of my body. For a long while my entire upper body felt that way and only later, for a short period, did it spread down my legs. While it lasted, every stroke of the whip brought what I can only call exquisite pain; it was sharp pain but exquisite because it renewed the sensation of the endorphins which felt so good. Perhaps this is what people refer to as "subspace", because I really felt as though I could and wanted to endure much more while this feeling lasted. I was glad to be let down from my bondage and would have been content to have the experience over but even though I had received the whipping I had wanted, you were not done with me yet. The continued whipping and beating on my ass was perhaps the sorest my ass has felt thus far; there were two or three spots that really hurt where you were hitting me over and over. The entire time as I felt such pain I kept thinking to myself how much you love me to give me such torment, and that was (and is) a beautiful thought. Even though the pain was very intense I did not feel close to tears (although I'm sure you could have gotten them if you had wanted to) but I was thinking to myself how long I would hold out until begging.

I could have begged earlier, but I don't want to do so just for the sake of you hearing me beg. I want to beg because I really feel the need to beg from the pain and intensity of the experience. This you finally evoked from me as you kept punishing my ass with your powerful strokes. The thought also went through my head as I began begging that maybe I should not have held out so long before starting, knowing that my begging will not mean you will stop, and I wasn't sure what my reaction would be if you kept going for much longer. I was surprised at myself during the whipping and beating of my ass that I had to fight the urge to curse. I have not felt that impulse before in our time together, and it is very much out of my normal pattern of behavior even under difficult circumstances. I must attribute it to how well you caused me pain during our scene.

The pain in my ass was such that when you first began fucking me with your cock I really did not enjoy the experience. It didn't feel bad, but it didn't really feel good right away either because my ass was still stinging so much. It wasn't until you removed your cock and inserted the butt plug that the sensation began to feel pleasurable. I guess even my ass has its limits when it comes to experiencing pleasure.

It is amazing how something so simple can be so nice, but that is how I felt about crawling behind you into the other room of the dungeon. To have you tugging on my collar leading me, and me on my hands and knees trailing behind was a wonderful experience of really feeling like your pet, of feeling completely submissive to you. I was so happy to be able to crawl back to my clothes at the end of our time together and continue that sublime sensation of submission.

When you played with my ass in the red room it really did feel so good, as by then my ass had a chance to recover after its beautiful beating. You know so well how to toy with my ass and tease it, and then to so quickly withdraw your plug and your fingers, leaving me with a feeling of frustration as I am reminded in one swift motion of your control over my sensations … and then my ass is left there feeling empty and alone and begging for more.

When I got back to my place and was able to inspect your fine work I felt a mixture of shock at how I looked (my ass in particular), a sense of disbelief at what my poor body had endured, and a sense of happiness at having been able to serve you so well. I only wish those marks were more visible so that I could see them more often and thus be reminded more often of how completely you own me and how totally I give myself to you.

D/s WITH AN EXPIRATION DATE

The following is a journal entry that I wrote and posted online, as I often do to process and express my emotions. The kinky social networking site Fetlife.com is a place where I feel safe enough from exposure to the outside world to voice intimate details of my relationship with Joseph (although of course I never have publicized the reality of his job and life). Only a few close friends know, and without those details, the things I have written made little sense to others at the time. Mostly, people couldn't understand why we felt our relationship was so firmly limited in its duration. I usually just said that we both refused to engage in a long distance relationship once he was required to return home after graduating, even though I knew that I would gladly travel any distance necessary to keep him as mine for the long haul.

I found myself in a conundrum. He and I both agreed we wanted him to be my slave in the truest sense: so completely owned that he would never be able to disobey or leave of his own accord. And maybe, though I had no reason to believe I would be successful, I could achieve this. A truly exciting thought for us both! Yet the reality was that his life commitments would force him to leave at the end of his studies unless he made a drastic decision and asked for release from the Church—a course of action that he had told me from the start was not an option.

So given the time constraints imposed by outside factors, I found myself pondering the realities of completely enslaving someone, even knowing it would have to end at some certain date. I thought a lot about this … could it still be real? Was he even capable of being "owned" to the extent we both wanted when we knew he'd have to be released at a set point in the future? If I succeeded in enslaving him, maybe he would come to the conclusion that leaving the priesthood to be with me was in fact an option. But if he just left me on his designated date (still a year away) could I really believe I had ever owned him? These were the questions I mulled over as I wrote and posted it out there to the world, hoping someone would reassure me that ultimately it would all turn out OK.

Thursday, August 5, 2010

We all likely have our own ideas of what "ownership" entails within a D/s relationship, but a key aspect of it for me is that in order to be "real" it cannot just be turned on and off like a light switch.

It is not uncommon for a boy whom I am getting to know to very quickly declare my ownership of him ("Oh Sir, you own me, I am yours, I feel so submissive") but just as quickly walk away from that "ownership" when things

are not convenient for him. It has happened a number of times over the past seven years. Needless to say, I did not own any of them.

If someone is actually meeting my definition of being owned, he or she will not have the ability to just get up and end the relationship. This may sound wrong to some people, and I'm not saying the owned individual couldn't "fall out" of ownership, so to speak, and thus choose to end the relationship. But I think while in a state of actively being owned, it would be unthinkable for that person to even comprehend his or her ability to "break up" with the owner. If at some point the mental status of the owned person shifts, then certainly he or she can (and I'd argue should) ask for the arrangement to end, or at least change to adapt to a different mentality.

So what happens when a D/s relationship must end due to unchangeable life circumstances? For example, if the submissive is in the military and becomes deployed, and if marrying the dominant is not an option, there is no choice but to comply with mandatory separation. If the dynamic of the relationship requires the day-to-day physical presence for both parties and yearlong separations are a deal-breaker for both sides, then the relationship must end. But if it does, and if it can just end, then how can we claim it to have existed in the first place?

To take it a step further, what if the dominant and submissive are aware from the outset that what they are getting into can only be valid for a set length of time? Does knowing this prevent the degree of ownership they would experience if the timeline were left up to chance? And even more confusingly, if not—if it is possible to "own" someone for a contracted period of time to the same degree as you otherwise might with no time restrictions at all—then how do you even begin to "un-own" them on the expiration date?

While no one gave me any real answers, a lot of friends commented with encouragement: "just got for it!" they said. Take it one day at a time. Enjoy what you've got while you've got it. I think I found my answer on my own, in time. It took a while to arrive at but I believe I knew the truth deep down all along. My ownership of Joseph wouldn't end just because we'd hit our "expiration date." We wouldn't be able to turn it off and walk away. By the time it reached that point though, neither of us even wanted to try.

THE PUP LIST

With a couple of months under our belts, during which time Joseph routinely came home and did chores at my direction while I cooked dinner or finished up work from my day job, I had become much more comfortable and accustomed to being served in a literal sense. One may not expect it, but allowing someone to be useful does take some getting used to, particularly for someone as fiercely independent as myself.

I am a proudly self-sufficient person and the idea of someone else doing my laundry or cleaning was at first quite scary and oddly intimate to allow. I also feared that assigning chores would breed resentment in Joseph as it had with some attempted submissives in the past, but Joseph reassured me this was not the case. For the first time in my life, I had met someone who truly "lived to serve."

So it became our normal life routine. Mondays were "our day" because Joseph was done with classes around noon and didn't have any other obligations. At first, Joseph merely arrived home in the early evening when Heather would already be there to let him in and I would still be at work for another couple of hours yet. Eventually, we became comfortable enough to give Joseph a key, and he would come over in the early afternoon to get started on his chores and have the house in close-to-perfect condition by the time I made it home.

Each week Joseph would arrive home on Monday afternoon, undress, put on my collar, leather wrist and ankle cuffs, and whatever else I had left for him (often a butt-plug) and proceed to working on his tasks. On the fridge he would find a note that soon became known as the "pup list"—the chores he was to perform in my absence. And though Joseph enjoyed having a list of things to work through, he was also particularly good at scoping out other tasks that I hadn't specifically left and doing them just because they needed doing.

This was the first time in my life that someone "in service" to me actually performed useful services on a regular basis and I soon learned it meant more to me than just having a clean house. Every time I saw something nicely done, made, put away, organized, or fixed because of Joseph, it would make me smile. What an amazing experience to get home from work each Monday to a clean and organized house and have a boy to help me cook dinner, keep me company, and entertain me through the night. After so long searching, so many false starts and failed attempts, I felt overwhelmingly fortunate and grateful to have found Joseph, which made the doubts about our future all the more painful.

◆ ◆ ◆ ◆ ◆

Soon Joseph's summer semester had come to an end, and he planned to return to Nebraska to spend a few weeks with his family before the fall term started up again. This gave us a perfect opportunity to have him stay at home for a couple of days without any outside obligations. By telling his mother he was still at school and telling his roommate he was leaving for Nebraska, Joseph could free himself of anyone questioning where he was and truly "disappear" into my service. Having two whole days was quite the experience for both of us, even though now it seems like a sad excuse for full-time. But to us, each hour of those two days was precious as gold. Of course, I wanted to know Joseph's reaction to every moment of it. Instead of a normal scene report, I instructed him to write a response to the two days as a whole. Another first is that around this time Joseph decided that he no longer felt it was wrong to ejaculate in my presence or by my hand, if I should want that from him. Because his religious beliefs and the practices allowed by them have always been outside my purview, I always proceeded with caution and in no way exerted pressure on Joseph to change or revoke any limits that were based on his faith. Each time a limit fell away, it was because he explained to me that he no longer felt the activity was wrong, or should be denied from me if I wanted it. This did not always translate into my immediate use of him in that way, though. Each time there was a change in his status I took time to consider the ramifications of using him in such a way before doing so. This case is no different and I did not begin to have Joseph orgasm on a regular basis for some time; but suffice it to say that from this point forward, there will be mention of Joseph coming. This proved not only to be a fun activity for both of us, but also soon eliminated the constant dripping from his up-to-this-point extremely neglected penis.

Scene Report: Monday, August 9 – Tuesday, August 10, 2010

As I mentioned to you, it was a new and somewhat strange experience to be in your house by myself. It was another step toward really feeling like I belong to the home. It was strange because I had never done it before, but it was also very nice for me to have that time there to serve you.

It was such a thrill to be able to put on your cuffs and collar, as if I was physically enslaving myself to you although you were not there. Of course, being able to wear your plug in my ass is always a great thrill for me, and to be able to thank you out loud for my ability to serve you was a wonderful reminder of my status and purpose there.

As I have mentioned before, there is much that I enjoy about cleaning and straightening up and organizing things. I will confess that after about 5:00 pm I did start to get a little tired after so much cleaning, but I think the main reason I was so tired was my disappointment of you not being there. That of course is not to blame you, but simply to say that I had initially expected you to be there, and since you couldn't that was a bit of a disappointment. Also, I hadn't done that much cleaning at once in a long time, if ever. But although I was tired, I kept thinking about my efforts there to serve and please you, and that kept me going right up until the time you sent me for dinner.

I was so happy to be able to help you and Heather get the dungeon put back together. It was also a thrill for me to see the dungeon as it was meant to be, not cluttered due to the painting. The space has a much different character now that it is properly put together. That time was also good for me to see you and Heather interact, and continue to get to know the both of you.

Thank you so much for giving me an enema; it was an amazing experience for me. It is incredible how something that I have done myself many times can make me feel so submissive to you in this new context. It was somewhat odd for me to be teaching you how to do it when in almost every other way you have been teaching me. What I really enjoyed about teaching you, aside from simply helping you to learn a new skill, was knowing that everything I was teaching you about giving an enema would then be used against me. I was teaching you how to make me more submissive, a new way of causing me discomfort and pain. That was a great realization for me.

Receiving an enema from you was a deeply submissive experience. There I was on my knees before you, while you poured liquid into my innards. When taking big enemas in the past I have tended to get bored with the process taking so long, but not with you. With each passing moment as I felt the water continue to seep in, and then as the pressure started and some light cramps came on, I was reminded that all of this was being endured for you. Even further, it was a remarkably wonderful experience to have even the deepest recesses of my insides at your disposal to be manipulated by your control. It made me feel like there is truly no part of me that is not yours.

I was both excited and nervous when you said you wanted me to take four quarts. I was excited because I would dearly love to be able to take as much water as you want me to, to be so at your disposal. I was nervous because I knew that I had never done so before and was not looking forward to the difficulty of the experience. Those difficulties were real. The cramps increased as the water pushed further inside. The difficulty of holding the water in increased the pressure on my anus, and I had forgotten how taking so much water puts pressure on my breathing and stomach; it makes me feel a bit nauseous. But I love the way that water fills me up so much and stretches my abdomen to such an extent. I was grateful that you let me expel the enema when you did, although I'm sure I could have taken a little more. I had warned you that I was beginning to work hard to keep it in, but I'm sure I could have kept doing so for at least a little longer. Be that as it may, I love the feeling afterward when I feel so completely empty, so thoroughly cleaned out on the inside, so hollow after taking so much water for you.

Being beaten by you is still such a conflict for me, but a wonderful one. How is it that I enjoy receiving such pain? "Enjoy" is not really the correct word because I do not actually enjoy it, but it is very fulfilling because being beaten by you is such a physical expression of your love and care. Even though the sensation is at times excruciating, it is desirable, and at times it is even fun. For example, at times when you have two instruments in your hands and are beating me repeatedly, it makes me feel like I am your drum being played for your amusement.

I also never tire of the way you so beautifully play with my ass. The sensation feels so very good and of course mentally knowing that you have the ability to enter into me is a great thrill of being controlled. Having you alternate between playing with my ass and beating me is such extreme sensation that at times it is hard to tell the difference between the pain and the pleasure. That is such a glorious thrill to know that you can elicit that level of reaction from me, control me so thoroughly.

I don't know if it is wrong (in fact I'm sure it is not) but I really like begging for you. By now you know I don't do so just for the sake of begging, but because I feel I need to due to the pain. The fact that you will heed or disregard my pleas is a real turn on. It is such a clear example of my status as your property to be used by you however you like. For me to beg, which again is something I have never done for anyone else, is a powerful experience of my utter helplessness before you, of your complete dominance over me. Of course, begging is also a reaction to something so painful that in the moment I do not enjoy it, but overall, begging is something I am growing to appreciate more and more.

When you finally stopped, my backside was so sore that when you asked about continuing I really did not want any more pain. But then you reminded me that you could if you wanted to, and I felt for a brief moment that I was denying you a fulfilling experience—to continue beating me after I had had more than enough. As I lay there between those two emotions, not wanting any more pain and yet wondering what it would be like to have you continue despite my desire not to, an idea just popped into my head. I had not thought about it before and I don't know where it came from, but it seemed to be the absolute right thing we should do at the moment. So I asked to receive one stroke for every day we would be apart. I am glad I did, and so grateful that you obliged me. Yes, the strokes hurt very much on my already well-worked-over ass, but they were also deeply satisfying. They were like your little reminder that no matter what I do or where I go, I am always yours. And having received those blows, nice and hard, gave me such a feeling of peace. Any frustration that I had been feeling all melted away in those blows. When you finished I was completely at peace and calm, and so very grateful that you are my Sir and treat me so well.

Being able to sleep with you on the bed was an unexpected surprise. I always love to be in your embrace, to be near you and feel your warmth and your love, and what better way is there to wake up than to be lying next to you and see your face first thing in the morning? I am truly a lucky slave. As wonderful as that was, though, it does lose something from being able to sleep at the foot of your bed as I have done in the past, which helps me to feel my status and still allows me to sleep so near to you. I am not saying one is better than the other, but that they are both wonderful for different reasons. Even sleeping in the cage has its advantages, although I do not like it as much.

I had no idea what to expect for Saturday morning and was therefore very pleasantly surprised to have that play time with you first thing. Your playing with my nipples was a special treat of torment. Of course your stick hurts so much as it bores into my nipples, which are so soft and tender, but then to have you bite my nipple was a moment of ecstasy as I was in pain … it was so intimate with your teeth chomping on my nipple.

I was taken aback when you asked about washing me. I called myself a "dirty slave" not because I feel that dirty (naughty) but only because there are areas that I didn't expect you to really want to wash. I cannot adequately explain how wonderful and overwhelming that experience was. I felt so very special that you would take the effort to wash me and take such good care of me. I also felt incredibly submissive to be washed by you like your little pup. It was so sensuous to have your hands running all over, washing me, your fingers constantly probing my ass … and to have your hand working my cock felt amazing. It didn't work me up to an intense orgasm, but it was certainly enough to push me over the edge of ejaculating even though by then your hand was removed and I tried to stop it. As I mentioned to you previously, this was another way in which a barrier of my life was taken away.

As I reflect upon it, I wonder what veils are left for you to pull away; it is as if I am completely exposed before you. There is nothing more that I can say "This is mine," or "This is something only I can do." Not only was I washed, but in the course of it you made me come. Those are no longer "my activities", but have been claimed by you as your own. That feeling of being completely open and exposed before you is beyond words to describe. I cannot think about that scene without feeling very emotional, very attached to you and very much owned by you. To say that it was the best experience I have had with you thus far is probably an overstatement, but to say that I felt it elevate our relationship to a new level of possession and ownership is definitely true. In summary, the time together was far beyond any expectations I could have had. It was the perfect way to spend our last time together for several weeks,

and more or less left me in a trance the rest of the day wishing I could feel that submissive and owned by you all of the time.

BOOK REPORT

After two blissful days together of what felt like stolen time, Joseph finally left for Nebraska. We would be apart for 3 weeks but we would still have daily contact and he would perform the ritual of kneeling and meditating on my ownership while he was away as well as other standards we had established.

Since our time on the phone and computer together would be limited, I assigned Joseph the additional task of reading a book and reporting back to me on his reactions to it. It is one of my favorite books of all time: Carried Away: An S/M Romance by a man named David Stein. It was in reading this book for the first time that I felt something calling me in my heart to have this type of relationship. I don't mean just kink or BDSM, which I had been exploring already for more than a year, but owning someone to his core. This book was also my first exposure to "Leather" as a concept above and beyond the all-encompassing-fetish-community sense of the word.

I read the book for the first time in 2006 after I had already been involved in kink for about eighteen months. I knew I was dominant-identified, but I was still finding my place and trying to surround myself with a community of like-minded people. The female dominants I had encountered really weren't doing it for me. Then I read this book and it was as if some part of me recognized a deep-seated need that I never could have identified on my own but once I saw it staring back at me, it was like looking at my inner self in a mirror.

Ever since then, the book has been a litmus test of sorts for boys I am interested in. If I assign a boy to read it and he "gets it" the way I do, it is a good sign. Unfortunately, this has rarely ever happened. To my extreme delight, Joseph got it. But of course he would!

In addition to reading the book and writing his feedback to me, Joseph and I would exchange numerous emails over the next three weeks while he was in Nebraska. The time apart was, as always, painful. As much as our two days together had been nothing but fantastic, I felt robbed of three entire weeks as every one that passed meant less time with my boy forever. Still, I am grateful for these periods of separation during which we spent more time reflecting on what we had done, what we would do, and what it meant instead of just constantly doing. I believe those times were just as important in our development even if much less fun.

Wednesday, August 11, 2010

Dear Sir,

I hope that your afternoon is going well. I am enjoying time to relax and not have to do anything for a few days. Of course I think about you a lot, especially with no other business to occupy my mind.

I also have been able to read through two more chapters of Carried Away. At this point Matt has just finished his night with Terry in the sleep slack, and they are going to sit down for brunch. All of the activities they have done thus far have been very hot, and it has been a thrill to envision myself in that position, experiencing all of those things with my Sir. What I have found most interesting thus far about the book are all of the thoughts that Matt has in the various scenes. They are so much like what goes through my head at times, and I find that reassuring, knowing that these are normal thoughts of a submissive. For example: when he is licking Terry's boots the position becomes quite uncomfortable, but despite that he has no desire to pull away and enjoys himself immensely. Or when he is trying to anticipate what might come next, and finally gives up all thought and just gives into the experience of the moment. These various thoughts run through my head at times. It is good to have them validated, even if by a fictional character, but it is also good to learn from him of what things I should be thinking or worrying about and what things should just be forgotten and entrusted to the capabilities of Sir.

Aside from kink interests, what I have found interesting intellectually over these chapters are all of the emotions Matt has to deal with concerning his relationship with Terry. Not that I can easily relate to them as I have been able to with other emotions he has gone through, since I have not yet been faced with the possibility of being dumped by my Sir, but it is interesting to see what emotions arise and the advice he gets in dealing with them. In regard to Terry, the two biggest things Matt has to deal with are not jumping to conclusions, and patience (accepting that Terry will or won't tell him what is going on according to his own schedule). Regarding himself, Matt has to do a lot of soul searching about who he really is. Is he really a slave? Some of these ideas relate somewhat to me and my own understanding of myself and a D/s relationship; I am thinking here of my own self-understanding as a submissive or slave, as well as being patient with you, Sir, and accepting things on your terms and schedule and not my own. Not that these are huge issues for me, but it is always helpful to rethink things and be encouraged by the example of others.

Aside from this, there is one thing in particular that I wanted to share with you and get your reaction and opinion on. It is a very interesting description of power exchange in the book. I want to quote a bit of it, as I think it is very beautiful:

Matt: *"Guess we slaves have a lot of power too, Sir! And here I thought it was all about giving up control and becoming open and vulnerable."*

Terry: "It still is. Your power is your ability to surrender, to voluntarily make yourself vulnerable to me - and to your own needs and hidden desires. Keep on giving yourself to me, and you'll find that there's always more to give. There are depths in you that you could never reach except through surrender. My role and my pleasure, is to keep drawing more out of you, as from an inexhaustible well."

Matt: "I don't feel inexhaustible, Sir. You keep pushing me to my limits, and I'm afraid of failing you by not being able to go any further."

Terry: "But you always do, don't you? You keep springing back ready for more. Do you know why?"

Matt: "No, Sir."

Terry: "I think you do: you're drawing on my energy, absorbing the force I pour into you when I beat you or fuck you or piss on you. The energy exchange is never one way - we feed on each other. That's why this works between us. If the circuit broke, if you ever shut down, stopped flowing for me, that would mean I wasn't feeding you, either."

I entered submission thinking much like Matt. I viewed power exchange as me giving power to you. I thought that it was all about my vulnerability, my weakness, and your strength. This passage really spoke to me. In some ways it was as if the light went on about why submission is fulfilling. It is not just about me becoming a weaker person or giving up everything I have or am to another, but it is a path toward becoming a better person, a more powerful person. The power of a submissive is obviously different than that of a dominant and the power of a submissive is always under the authority/control of the dominant, but it is a power. It is a power to please the dominant and it is a power to do more, become more, than you ever thought you could be or do.

When Terry mentioned about reaching new depths inside of myself like an inexhaustible well, that sounded like one of the greatest things I have ever heard. I never considered that I had all that much inside me or all that much to offer. Of course I know that I have done some very good work for many people in my lifetime, I did that and no one else, but that didn't feel like me. It felt like the training I had received, the knowledge I had gained, etc. and I was simply putting that into effect for the benefit of others. But to think that I myself have inexhaustible depths to explore blows me away. I still don't know if I believe that.

So, with that in mind, I was wondering what you think of this notion of power exchange? I hesitate to get too carried away with it (pardon the pun) if you have a different idea of how our relationship is or should work. I also wanted to ask you very matter of fact if you believe that I have that kind of inexhaustible depth within me, and if continuing to explore that is your goal in this and what feeds you?

I will be on sometime later this evening, it might be very late depending how long I spend with my brother at dinner and then afterward. Know that I am always thinking of you and missing you. I hope you had a great afternoon and enjoy your evening.

Your pup,
Joseph

HISTORY

While we were separated during this time, I asked Joseph to spend the time we would normally be spending together in person to tell me more about himself. In the several months we'd known each other it seemed we knew one another impossibly well and deeply, yet nearly nothing at all of the facts of each others' lives. I am an open book and I often talk about myself and tell stories from my past, but Joseph requires much more direct prompting to get him to talk about himself. The following correspondences were among our communication over the weeks Joseph was away.

Tuesday, August 17, 2010

Dear Sir,

Before I address the topic of this email, I want to say something first. I know that I am very fortunate to have the family that I do. My parents loved each other and loved us. They provided for us, always, and cared for us. We never went without what we needed. My siblings all got along well together. I was never subject to any abuse or trauma growing up. I know I was fortunate. I struggle remembering that while also reflecting upon the difficulties I had growing up. I do not want to be one of those people who blame all of their problems on their parents or the way they were raised. So if I come across that way at times it is unintentional. Now, on to the main topic.

One of the things that has been truly amazing and very bizarre for me in our relationship is that I am able to freely pursue my personal desire. I have rarely felt free to do this in my life and it is a wonderful experience to have had these desires for submission for so long and now see them being realized so beautifully with you Sir.

The dynamics of my family were such that what I wanted was rarely ever considered, not because others did not care, but simply because that was the way my family worked. My parents grew up on farms during or just after the Great Depression. They learned to make do with little and save as much as possible, and this was the way we were raised. We got very little of what we wanted. I don't know how often we were told, "Put it on your Christmas list," or "Your birthday is coming," or even "You don't need that." So it was a rare treat for us to get something we just wanted from our parents, and I learned very well not to ask much from them.

They were also raised in an atmosphere where the parents were very much in charge and the kids did whatever the parents wanted, no questions asked. If they wanted us to go pull weeds in the fields, we did it. If they wanted us to go mow the lawn, we did it. If they wanted us to go over and visit relatives, we did it. I don't remember many times growing up when I was asked what I wanted to do, but there were plenty of things I was expected to do: swimming lessons, piano lessons, work on the farm, chores at home, being a member of Cub Scouts, etc. Again, I learned early on to not expect to be able to do what I wanted and just do what I was told or expected to do.

This was also reinforced by my own personality. Looking back, I know that I was a very sensitive child. When my parents argued or fought (which didn't happen very often) I took it personally and it hurt me very much. When I was punished for doing something wrong (which happened on occasion), of course I did not like that very much, so from early on with my parents I learned to not be a burden on them. I did what I was supposed to do and rarely felt the freedom to do what I would want.

This same inability to pursue my own desires was also affected by my older brothers. The way it worked, Samuel and Philip would determine what we would do, the games we would play, etc. If I didn't go along with it I was made fun of. I remember several occasions when I would be playing with my sister and I, or both of us, would get teased mercilessly for it. So, even if I didn't want to, I would feel forced to go and play with my brothers. This was even more challenging because the kids they often played with were a few years older than Samuel, so when they played baseball or football or whatever I was generally too little to be able to compete with them. I would often get very frustrated and upset and stomp away mad. This would also get me made fun of. What then was I supposed to do? If I didn't play with them I was teased; if I did play with them it often didn't end well for me.

I also remember as a younger child I was interested in things which my older brothers or my parents did not approve of. For example, I remember liking certain cartoon shows and my brothers would make fun of me for watching it because it was too girly or not manly enough (you know, not enough fighting). I did also like other things they liked (Star Wars was big with them, sports was big with them, I was very interested in Transformers) but if I deviated from their norm it was not good. This was also an issue with my parents, especially my mother. I remember being interested in certain things that she thought were a bad influence (it was disapproved of to watch the cartoon show Dungeons and Dragons, for instance). My life was about conforming to their standards.

You can imagine the impact of all of this upon my self-image and self-esteem. What I wanted was never "right", and so my life became about never allowing other people to know what I really wanted or thought, as that way I could not be made fun of for it. In middle school and high school I did some things that I liked, but my life really revolved around "fitting in", whether at school or at home. Of course the sad thing is that I never fit in at school and never felt like I fit in at home, but since that was the only way I knew how to survive at the time it was what I continued to do.

My profession is another clear example of doing what I was supposed to do rather than what I wanted to do. I remember, in eighth grade, the panic I felt when the high school guidance counselor told us to be thinking about our future career so that we could get the right high school courses and be able to get into the right college. I had no idea what I wanted to do. I therefore reverted to what I had been raised to do: to pray about things. I started praying that God would show me what he wanted me to do with my life. In time I discerned he wanted me to be a priest, and so until the day of my ordination that is what I did. Don't get me wrong, I still do feel that was what I was supposed to do, and in many ways it is what I wanted to do, but ultimately I feel it was not a choice made because "I really want to do it" but because "it is what I am supposed to do."

In the seven years that I have been a priest you can pretty much imagine what it has been like pursuing my own desires. I have continued to do my best to fit into the present situation, regardless of what I think or feel or want. My true wants or thoughts or desires have always been sufficiently suppressed so as not to be known and ridiculed. Particularly, this interest in BDSM has been felt and explored, but very well hidden. What pushed me over the edge and got me onto the website where you found me, perhaps that is a topic for another email. Suffice it to say, I really feel like this is the first time in my life that I have pursued my own wants and needs with full freedom and abandon (although of course also with prudence). I cannot thank you enough for accepting me and allowing me to live out this fantasy, and I wish I never had to wake up from so wonderful a dream.

You will probably guess that none of this—or very little of it, anyway—has ever been shared with anyone else. I am very nervous about pushing Send and revealing all of these things to you, but at the same time I trust you enough to know all of this. I look forward to any questions you may have about anything that I have written.

Your pup,
Joseph

◆ ◆ ◆ ◆ ◆

Tuesday, August 17, 2010

Dear Joseph,

It was so wonderful to get this email today and to be able to read some things about you that are very personal, intimate, and have obviously shaped your life immensely.

I have to say that the one thought which struck me immediately is how almost ironic it is that the relationship in which you find the most freedom to be yourself and pursue your own desires is one in which you're being controlled. It would seem logical that from the control of your parents you would rebel and want to pursue situations where you are in charge and can do whatever you want whenever you want to, not to place yourself under the strict rules of another person. But on the other hand, maybe growing up like you did imprinted something in you that makes it feel safe to be controlled by someone else. Certainly my control over you is more fun than what you've experienced from other people, though! Reading your description of it, it's just odd because you could just as easily be writing about a D/s relationship. Obedience is very important to me and one thing I like about you is your willingness to do as you're told, without question most of the time.

Should I be concerned that you are not getting what you want and are only doing things because you're told? I don't really think that's the case, but it does make me wonder how is this so different than everything you grew up experiencing?

To respond to some of what you said more in depth: I can imagine the impact of all this on your self-esteem, and this is very sad. I'm sorry to hear that this is what happened to you (and appears to have lasted well into adulthood) but I hope that our relationship will turn out to be healing for you. I don't want you to live your life never letting it be known what you'd prefer. I firmly believe that the only real way to get what you want in life is to ask for it and go after it yourself. I have worked very hard for everything I have accomplished, and I am constantly motivated to "get what I want"; and in turn I often do get what I want because I'm willing to go get it. It's a self-perpetuating cycle. It's hard to imagine living a life so passive; of course you're not going to be happy and fulfilled. Now what I do find really intriguing is that what you find makes you happy and fulfilled is belonging to another person. You are my property in the same way you were your parents' property, are you not? You will, ideally, do what I tell you without question, not always get what you want, and sometimes your opinion won't even matter. Where is the difference, I wonder? I would love to hear more thoughts on this other than the obvious differences.

The issue of your profession is a complicated one for me. Given what you've told me, and that I know you often fantasize about an "easy way out", I find it hard to believe that this is what you really wanted to do. I'm sure you are good at it, and I'm sure that you absolutely believe in what you're doing as a priest, but I am not convinced entirely that if given the knowledge you have now and sent back to do it over again, that you would make the same choice. In my career, though there are aspects I don't love, and though I don't know if I'll stay in it for the rest of my life, I can say beyond a shadow of a doubt that I would not go back and change any part of my education or career path up through this point. I love where I am and the future is wide open for me to continue this path or choose a different one if I want. But I don't get the same impression from you.

What I always want to ask is what would you be if you weren't a priest? What if you knew in eighth grade that you didn't need to worry so much about college or your future yet? That you could have attended any school and spent time finding out who you really were before deciding to pursue one thing or another? I had a similar personal experience with school that I'll tell you about sometime but I took the opposite route as you. I rebelled against it and I went and did some crazy things like leaving a "good" school for an "experimental" one and you know what? I still got into my top choice of college, did great there, and am one of the few people actually working in my field of study. Anyway, this is not to say I don't believe that you truly felt the answer to your prayers was to become a priest because at the time I think it was - it solved the problem for you then - but again, I have this nagging feeling that you want to be a person who is allowed to pursue your desires, to live your life, to accomplish things in the world, to find personal happiness and fulfillment that you haven't gotten from this way of life.

◆◆◆◆◆

Thursday, August 19, 2010

Dear Sir,

I have been thinking about something you wrote recently and want to attempt a response. In your response to one of my recent emails, you asked me about the difference between belonging to you and belonging to my parents.

It is true that I will do whatever you want, within my limits. At times I think I would even break those limits and literally do anything you ask of me, I love you so much and want to please you so completely. It is true that my opinion will sometimes (often?) not matter and I will not get what I want within our relationship. It is also true that growing up I often did not get what I wanted and felt that my opinion did not matter. What then is the difference between our relationship being so fulfilling and my experience growing up being hurtful?

I had not thought of it in those terms before. It is a great question and made me think pretty hard. The big difference for me is that I have freely chosen to be your property while I had no such choice in being obedient to my parents. Let me try and further explain this difference.

I felt, growing up, that my opinion did not matter; that I had to always do as I was told, and that I was not really free to pursue my own desires. I felt all of this as a consequence of people not caring about me. I know this is not true. I remind myself of that a lot now that I am an adult, but it doesn't change the fact that growing up I felt truly invisible. At times I would wonder if I hid myself somewhere how long it would take for someone to miss me? I remember feeling quite often growing up that I was "one of the kids." This was reinforced at Christmas, of all times, when some of my relatives would get a present for my sister and one for "the boys." I remember deciding to run away from home one day in about sixth grade, because I was so tired of living in a house where no one cared about me. I got a block away before my reason kicked in and I realized that I would have no place to live, no food to eat, etc. so I returned home without incident.

In a more general sense, I seldom if ever remember my parents taking time to talk with me - not just with "us kids" - but with me personally about how I am, what I was doing, etc. I never had "the sex talk" with either of my parents at any point. I don't remember spending much time individually with either of my parents ever. They were both busy with many different things and several kids at home. I actually don't remember them spending much time individually with any of my siblings. either. This is the cause of so much emotional pain in my past.

Belonging to you is almost completely different. I have chosen to give myself to you not because I just like being abused but because I know that you do care for me. Even when my wants or opinions are not met or even considered, I know that underneath it all everything you do is out of care and love for me. This has been one thing I have enjoyed about our time together at the barn; I see how much care you show Thunder when you control him and even when you have to correct him, and I am reassured that the same amount (if not more) of care and love are given to me while I am being controlled by you. The pain of your whip, your paddle, even the sharpest pain of your evil stick are all felt as extensions of your love. Even being driven to tears I experienced as a sign of your care for me.

There is another difference, as well. When I was growing up and feeling as if my ideas and desires were not considered, it caused me to put up defenses against my family; to emotionally shut down with them. Why share what I think or what I want if that is only going to cause me pain or embarrassment? That is what I did very well, and what I continue to do with them. This is completely different than our relationship, where my surrender to you, and your ability to consider or ignore my wants and desires, leads to the breaking down of any defenses or emotional barriers. I feel like ever since I met you, you've been peeling away layer after layer of who I am until one day I will be there totally exposed, me without any barriers or defenses, completely transparent in every way to you. That is such a beautiful thought to me. I have spent so much energy over the years in maintaining those kinds of barriers with people as the only way I knew how to relate to people and cope with relationships. Why it is that your ability to reject what I want has a completely opposite reaction to the way I experienced it with my family growing up? I think it all goes back to the care and attention and love I know that underlies everything you do, even when my wants are not considered, or are considered but not indulged.

Why do I need to experience care in the form of submission? I think a lot has to do with my personality and especially the way it was formed over the years. Having been told often that my ideas were wrong, and having seen efforts of my own fail, I have come to hate making decisions, especially difficult ones. I know by personality I am not a leader and never have been. I know that I work best when I am given a task and then given the space/time to complete it. I know that I am constantly worrying about myself and my actions, and love the freedom of not having to worry because someone else has taken that burden upon her shoulders, and all I have to do is say "Yes Sir." I know that from a very young age I have been a people-pleaser, and so pleasing you in so powerful a way comes naturally to me. I know that for many years I have fantasized about bondage, whereas fantasies about "normal" romance or marriage have been almost non-existent. In short, as I have said before, being a slave seems like what I was born to do.

I will also admit, as I have told you before, that I have viewed part of our relationship as therapeutic. Not that I am just using you or our relationship to meet my needs. Nor that I expect you to be able to solve all of my problems. But I have felt stunted, as you aptly put it, and I was seriously looking for a Christian-based counselor early this spring to address emotional issues which mostly revolve around what I have been talking with you about: self-esteem, desire for love, inability to form intimate relationships, etc. Counseling didn't work out and so I decided to try a different route. Rather than talk with a counselor about my desire for BDSM and other things, why not try a relationship, and through real-life experience of love and control overcome some of these other issues? I hope that doesn't sound weird or misplaced.

That is about as much of an answer as I think I can offer to this question. I welcome any further comments or discussion on what I have written. Again, I cannot believe how easily I tell you some of my most painful and intimate memories, which I never thought I would ever share with another person, but it feels right that I do it and I want to do it. One of the many reasons I treasure our relationship, and one of the many reasons I can truly say I love you, Sir.

Your pup,
Joseph

◆◆◆◆◆

Thursday, August 19, 2010

Dear Pup,

It was painfully obvious to me that your relationship with your parents and siblings had owner/property traits, for lack of a better word. Now I think all parental relationships do to some extent, but some much more so than others due to differences in parenting styles. So of course my first concern (which has already been resolved, don't worry) was that you were seeking out a D/s relationship for unhealthy reasons in some way to emulate your past experiences even without knowing it. We can never say for sure why you have the desire to be owned, controlled, and used as my property; it may have to do with your upbringing, who knows … but I am convinced for now that you've wanted these things for long enough and clearly enough that deciding to be a submissive or slave is not a passing whim or something you are doing because it's the only way you know how to function. You did mention this once recently in conversation; you were wondering if becoming a slave would be, like the priesthood, an easy way out. I don't think either path could really be termed an "easy way out", but we can talk more about this another time.

Your family culture seems to come from an old-fashioned "farming" mentality (I'm sorry if I'm stereotyping or making untrue generalizations, but this is the way I see it) that the good of all comes before the good of one. It's vital for survival in large families, especially where labor like farm work is needed to survive. It's something I read about in college when studying cultures and societies. The idea that children are unique, individual "people" is relatively modern and urban in nature. So while you may have compared yourself to peers or families you saw on TV, your parents were still raising the kids in a more old-fashioned way.

My parents lived in the suburbs and had professional jobs (lawyer and nurse), and I was an only child, so we grew up in opposite situations. I was given lots of personal attention, encouraged to explore my unique interests and talents, and told that I was special, one of a kind, and all of that. Even when I didn't get the attention I wanted from my parents or we didn't do the things I would have preferred to be doing, I didn't ever feel unloved or not cherished by my parents, and I think that has shaped a lot of the way I am as a dominant. As I've told you before, I am a Daddy. I may not be your Daddy, but I can't eliminate that force from my personality entirely.

I've heard of people being slaves from the perspective of childhood programming, and I've also heard quite the opposite. The "I'm a perfectly capable human being who could be dominant if I wanted to be but I just choose to be submissive" kind of thing. I don't personally hold one to be better, more real, or truer than another. I have always intellectually preferred the slaves who come at it from a place of their own empowerment, who are not lacking in self esteem but just get something so much more out of being under another person … but emotionally, I think I tend to be drawn towards the damaged, weaker types because I have a lot of strength that I enjoy sharing, and I especially like to see the results of my efforts on other people. I don't know why I enjoy taking on responsibility so much, but I guess it does thrill me to have ultimate control that comes along with it.

For the record, normal romance has no appeal to me either. As a kid and teenager, during my sexual awakening, I couldn't find any interest in normal romantic stuff. I found bondage porn very early on, so I knew what turned me on … but in the more mainstream areas, I'm very attracted to the darker things like vampire stories, which often have extreme D/s undertones of ownership and torture. Stuff that should be seen as traditionally romantic leaves me dry … or "soft", I should say.

In my opinion, there is nothing wrong with viewing our relationship as therapeutic. I have personally been in and out of counseling throughout my life. While it hasn't always been helpful, I don't think I'd understand myself and other people so well without it. But above all of that, my experience in relationships has been what has healed me from many of the wounds of childhood and adolescence. We all have them. I think that the biggest part for you is that you haven't had the relationships, or even friendships, to help you grow up and move beyond what being a kid was like. These things are still much fresher in your mind than in those of other people our age who have replaced memories of not being loved with new ones to the opposite effect.

One role of a partner in any relationship is often just to allow us to work through issues. I still have many issues, but Heather is wonderful for me, and I think you have potential to help me through some things as well. So no, therapeutic is not a bad thing. The only "bad" thing, in my mind, is if someone gets into any relationship expecting the other person to just "fix" them or heal them. It's quite different than the inherent healing that happens over time through the acts of loving and being loved by someone.

To me, being in a relationship requires both giving and receiving acceptance as well as love, and both of those things can be quite healing to give and get. I look forward to talking to you later.

With love,
Melissa

♦♦♦♦♦

Monday, August 23, 2010

Dear Sir,

I think it's time now to talk about your questions about my career, and how slavery might seem like an easy way out, just like the priesthood. Let me explain what I meant by this.

 Most people would think, like you do, that the priesthood is not an easy way out. That is true in many ways, of course. The priesthood is demanding and requires certain sacrifices, but in another way, it can be seen as an escape from personal responsibility. I am not saying that is why I entered the priesthood, as I firmly believe it is and was a calling for me. Sometimes I looked for some reason to leave seminary and do something "easier", but I could never convince myself that these doubts or considerations were valid enough to allow me to abandon the conviction that this is what God wanted me to do.

That being said, the priesthood is still an escape from personal responsibility in many ways. You don't have to worry about going to job interviews or about job security. You affiliate with a diocese, and then they take care of you for life: paycheck, retirement, healthcare, etc. You don't have to worry about where you will live, as that is assigned to you. You don't have to worry about certain small decisions, like what to wear every day to work. All of this was appealing to me when I was going through seminary, as at the time I was insecure enough that I couldn't imagine going out into the world and doing all of that for myself.

In a similar fashion, I wonder at times if my desire for being a slave isn't the same sort of escape from personal responsibility. As a slave there are many things you do not have to worry about because your Sir will be making those decisions for you. Again to be clear, I am not saying that the reason why I want to be a slave is just to escape personal responsibility. I just wonder at times how much of a factor that is in my desire for slavery, if that fine distinction makes sense to you. I know that to an extent there is nothing wrong with that desire, as many slaves very much enjoy that aspect of slavery. I just want to make sure that my desire for this lifestyle isn't an unhealthy desire for escape. I would welcome your thoughts on this topic and perhaps exploring this more with you in the future.

Again, I am sorry that I missed you this morning, but most likely you are busy with work or other things. I will try to be on again this afternoon and hopefully talk with you then. I miss you, but the time is growing short before I get to see you again. 77 hours.

Your loving pup,
Joseph

♦♦♦♦♦

Monday, August 23, 2010

Dear Pup,

Just a brief thought on the this before I have to run... when you described the way of life you live as a priest, to me it sounds very much like being a slave. I am coming at things from a different perspective than you are, of course, but my first thoughts are almost the opposite of yours. I am wondering if you really were cut out to live the "slave life"—i.e. under constant control and protection of someone else, limited decision making, among other things— but as you didn't realize this was an actual possibility, you were drawn towards something very similar. This is not surprising to me at all, as I have encountered loads of submissives who have gone into the military looking for structure, protection, and that type of life where you're taken care of as long as you follow orders. Without taking away from the sanctity of what you do as a priest, it's a similar way of life.

So in my view, the same elements that attract you to slavery are what attracted you to the priesthood (again, not dismissing the actual calling part but just saying these were attractive elements) - as opposed to your view of "escaping" the real world in the same way through both vocations. To me, you are not only the perfect slave because we get along so well in so many ways, but on top of that you have already proven your inclination for living this type of highly controlled life before we even met. I know this may not make sense to you, but the more I'm with you, the more I realize that your "newness" to the world of D/s relationships doesn't really matter, because you have more years of experience living a structured lifestyle, under the authority and control of another entity, than anyone else I've pursued a relationship with.

This fact solves one of the largest issues I have encountered with submissive men in the past: that they have no conception of what living as a slave actually means, and they retreat when the reality of the situation does not stay true to their fantasy version of it. I feel I am a very lucky master to have found you, to reap the benefits of your past experience, and for so many other reasons.

Love,
Melissa

BEGGING (BADLY)

The night before Joseph would return home to me, I decided to play with him on the phone. It had been quite some time since I had allowed him an orgasm, and I figured that he would be very enthusiastic to get the chance. Showing emotion isn't generally Joseph's strong suit, but I thought for sure that if I got him aroused enough and instructed him to beg me to come, that I would get some sincere pleading. It turned out to be more difficult for him and more awkward than I had imagined.

Previously, Joseph had only begged within the context of our play when he felt he couldn't handle any more pain. Begging usually preceded crying and you'd better believe that type of begging sounded real! I suppose the difference is that while Joseph is very invested in avoiding pain where possible, he is quite a bit less invested in his own pleasure. Ultimately, I still allowed him to come even though he had utterly failed at begging for it. I know he did try and that it was not easy for him.

After we hung up the phone, I received this letter, much to my surprise and delight. I am always proud of Joseph's attempts to live up to his promise of "transparency" with me even when it's an uncomfortable topic.

Wednesday, August 25, 2010

Dear Sir,

I beg your pardon for my very pathetic attempt at begging this evening. I know it is not a big deal, if a "deal" at all, but I do want you to know how it felt to me.

First, I have never begged anyone for anything for as long as I can remember. Maybe when I was a child I begged my parents for something, but I don't remember doing so, and I am not counting any of our activities as begging. I get nervous and very uncomfortable doing new things, especially when I don't know exactly what I am supposed to do. Therefore, not knowing what you like to hear or want to hear from begging, I was nervous and uncomfortable.

Begging would also require extra energy for me to move out of myself and express in an over the top kind of way something I would really want; as you well know I do not readily express a lot about myself, and never in the overtly, overly enthusiastic way of begging. I didn't feel that energy, and you not being there in person didn't help me to find that energy. Lastly, when the moment came for me to beg I felt rather stupid and silly having to do something as humble (or humiliating?) as begging. It is an expression of humility, of my status as a slave, which I accept intellectually but have a hard time always embracing emotionally.

I should add one more thing. I also felt bad that I could not properly beg for you, even though I know it didn't really bother you at all. Again, I do not see this as a big issue, but I do want you to be aware of how I experienced it especially in case you want me to beg in future. I am so excited to see you tomorrow, only 17 short hours from now! I miss you and love you so much.

Yours,
Joseph

Mine Once More

After three weeks apart, and more emails, phone calls, and online chats than we had exchanged since first meeting, Joseph returned from Nebraska. We used the same method as before to steal a little time away together during which he was mine completely with no outside obligations.

The two days he spent with me ended with a Saturday night party at a friend's house, since Joseph had to return to his place Saturday night for Sunday obligations. Heather and I stayed at the party a little longer, but as soon as we were home I couldn't stop myself from writing to Joseph. The words poured out effortlessly as I was still high from the thrill of reuniting with my boy.

Saturday, August 28, 2010

Dear Joseph,

We just got home and I'm exhausted but also a little wired. I wanted to write something to capture my feelings right away so I don't lose any of them. This weekend (I'm sure I don't have to tell you) was purely incredible for me. Having you for 2 whole days was beyond words can describe and now I miss your presence even more. You are such a force of positive in my life - you don't even realize what you give me. Someone who doesn't talk back, argue, or complain. Someone who endures what I want to put him through—happily— accepting more or even asking for it. Someone who follows directions very well and goes out of his way to make things easier for me. It's so different from what I get in all my other relationships, friendships, and partnerships. I wish I could fully show you how much the role you occupy in my life means, but I suppose you really do understand, even if from your own vantage point, the uniqueness of it.

Tonight was absolutely amazing and you did very well. Putting you in the "electric chair" was such a thrill for me, and I look forward to doing more of that in the future. I am not kidding about the look of anguish on your face. It's so beautiful. I'll have to have Heather take pictures sometime. I love watching you suffer at my hand and for my enjoyment. I know some things you enjoy for their own sake but the vast majority of what I do to you and what you are starting to crave is very difficult and not outright "enjoyable" for you. The fact that you go through so much for me means something I cannot accurately describe in words.

Whipping you was equally incredible, and I felt you could and would have gone on forever. Not because it didn't hurt but because you wanted it so badly, because you want to do whatever I will do to you and go as far as I could want you to. I'm glad you were with me when Sally and Bill played and she used a safeword. It's good for you to see scenes like that; scenes that "normal" people do. If I had been Bill and you had been her, it's doubtful I would have stopped that soon; but then again, you wouldn't have told me to. It's just not the way you are.

I also really enjoyed having you on my lap for the next little while (I wish it could have been longer of course). I don't know what you think about, if anything, when you're like that after we play. I imagine you just being happily zoned out, enjoying an overall warmth that spreads across your body after a good beating, and enjoying melting into me with no will left to do anything but be there and be mine.

He wrote back to me, thanking me and telling me how happy it made him to know that he had made me proud. Then, hesitantly, he brought up our most sensitive subject, yet again.

I did want to mention here one thing I was struggling with, last night in particular. It was the stress of knowing that our time was coming to a close, and that I would have to reintegrate back into my normal life. There were a couple of times where I thought "What in the world am I doing? I am a priest and a 'normal' person; why am I doing this?" The thought came and went quickly and I didn't pay much attention to it at the time, but looking back I can see where it came from. Serving you so completely for two days was such a change from what my life is otherwise like, and was so enjoyable, that the idea of having to go back to my other life and still be your slave was a little daunting. I think the time we shared was another stepping stone moment for me. I had gotten used to fantasizing about these things, and then exploring it online, and then the idea of meeting someone, and then the idea of serving you occasionally while still living more or less my normal life. But now this was another step toward intensifying our relationship, and the idea of trying to integrate that into my life as a whole was a challenge. After this morning, however, back into normal vanilla activities where the world hasn't stopped and life is fine, I am feeling better about it. I hope you realize I am not saying I want to back off from our relationship or spend less time together or anything of the sort. I only want you to be aware of what I was experiencing yesterday. I will leave it at that for now, but I did want to communicate that experience to you. I am looking forward to seeing you again very soon. I hope your day has gone and continues to go well. Thank you again for being my good Sir, and always taking such good care of your pup.

Yours,
Joseph

Two Days In The Life

Scene Report: Monday, August 30, 2010

Dear Sir,

Perhaps what I learned most over these two days is not how much I enjoy suffering for you, which I have done in the past, or how much I enjoy talking with you, which I have done before, but how much I enjoy being under your care. Having you select what I would eat, what I would wear, what I would do, what I should say (if I should say anything) was an amazing experience for me.

Honestly, over all of that time I never felt as if I wanted to rebel against something you decided, or that I didn't agree with or like what you had decided for me. I may not have always preferred the way you played with me (the electricity, the amount of pain, etc.), but I never felt like rebelling against it or not wanting your control. Your presence is steadying, calming and reassuring, and I appreciate that very much. Your care and love for me come through so often in the way you treat me that I cannot help but want to serve you better, to please you more.

Looking back over the weekend, I realize that what we experienced was not "real life" slavery. If I was your live-in slave full time, I know things would be different. I know we would normally not play that often, nor have that much time together for various reasons. I know that if I was your live-in slave I would need to have more time to myself, as I am an introvert and need time to be alone in order to recharge; I cannot change that, but I wanted to get as much time with you as I could out of those days, and I am glad I did so. In spite of all of that, the idea of being with you more permanently was only strengthened by this experience, which in some ways I think added to some of the difficulties I experienced.

One of those was adjusting to the pace of longer-term service. It isn't just gearing up emotionally for one scene, but living out a daily life together. The other difficulty was having to readjust to my vanilla life. The longer I spent with you, the more that lifestyle became appealing, even if parts of it seem very foreign or even contrary to my current way of life; and the more appealing it became, the harder it seemed to leave it behind and try to readjust to my vanilla life. Also, I think ever since seeing Father Jim outside of the barber shop, I was nervous about the collision of my vanilla life with my service to you. Even though in the past I have talked as if I wanted it to happen in order to force a decision, I know that was mostly fantasy, and meeting him was a firm reminder of what could possibly happen. Only after coming back into my vanilla life for a while and seeing how nothing bad has happened has that nervousness gone away.

In summary, the time I had with you was a wonderful experience of what it could be like being your live-in slave. The fact that things didn't always go as planned, that it wasn't just one long scene—this helped me to understand how wonderful full-time service to you could be, even if what I experienced still wasn't quite reality. I only hope that I may have the opportunity to one day experience the reality of life as your full-time slave. Until then I will have to content myself with what time we have.

But now onto the weekend! When I finally got there and saw you it felt absolutely incredible to fall into your arms; it felt like I truly came home where I belong. That feeling of warmth, belonging, and love is truly beyond words, but I could have reveled in it forever. To see you once more and immediately fall into service felt like the perfect gift. I was so content to once more be naked, at your disposal physically, and being able to serve you. I felt as if I was doing what I was supposed to do—cleaning up for you, serving you, helping to make your life easier and better.

I was very excited when you were able to "milk" me for the first time. It was an interesting sensation to feel the large metal wand inside of me, stimulating my prostate. It felt good, but not really pleasurable like when my cock was being stimulated. Of course, the wand in my ass did feel pleasurable, as you might well imagine. The feeling of being milked—to know that you were inside of me manipulating my body as you wanted, making it do what you wanted when those things are not even under my control, was amazing. To feel you emptying my juices from inside was a fabulous thing.

I still cannot believe how wonderful you are for taking the time to bathe your slave. It is an incredibly sensual experience, as well as a very submissive experience. It is sensual because it obviously feels so good: the warm water flowing over me, the pleasant fragrance from the soap, your strong hands rubbing soap across me. It is a wonderfully submissive experience because it makes me feel very much like your property, your pet, that you would wash as one washes their dog or their car. That I am not even allowed to wash myself; you have taken control of that aspect of my life as I kneel before you in the shower.

As I drove back to you, one of the fantasies that kept running through my mind was of the measurements you had taken, and the anticipation of receiving a permanent collar from you. I was incredibly thrilled to have that longing fulfilled by receiving your ankle cuff. It feels so good, so natural, around my leg constantly reminding me that I am no longer my own man but I belong to my Sir. Of course I don't need a collar to know that and to be happy belonging to you, but the physical symbol of my status is a truly beautiful thing, and I am so proud to wear it for you.

One thing that we had discussed and that I was elated to experience was you exercising more control over me. Not only did you order food for me, but then to have you dish out what I was going to eat was an incredible thrill. It felt exactly right. You give Thunder what food he should have, and the same with Shadow; and why not the same for your slave? It helps, of course, that you are very considerate in ordering what I might like, and also that I like most things, but I welcome the times when you give me something I don't like or give me very little to eat; whatever you decide your slave should have. That reminder that my ownership extends to all aspects of life is truly rewarding and fulfilling for me.

I was a little nervous at first when we started dinner, walking in naked in front of Heather's friend Ashley. I have gotten used to doing so with you, of course, and with Heather, but to do so in front of a total stranger made me a little nervous. But that quickly subsided when she seemed to take no notice of it. I kept telling myself that I was only doing what my Sir wanted, and that made it all okay. I was also very glad for your instructions that I did not have to worry about making conversation. I like the idea that I am there to be seen and not heard, sort of like the dog who comes to eat while everyone else is having dinner - people know the dog is there eating, but pay him very little attention. I like that idea of being "the slave eating his dinner" who people can see but not notice, like part of the furnishings of the house.

It felt so good to once more be under your whip and flogger. As much as I do not really enjoy the pain, my body had been aching to feel the effects of your control. That is what I really love about being flogged or paddled or caned or whipped by you. Every stroke is a reminder to me of my status—that I am your property to be used by you however you wish, and also that you are using me because you care for me and love me. These were the thoughts in my mind as I felt each blow become harder and more painful. I kept thinking, "I am a good boy for Sir. I am doing this because she owns me and can use me however she wants. Sir always uses her property with great care and affection." I like it being hard serving you, suffering for you, because the more I have to work, the more it shows you how happy I am to belong to you.

I was equally thrilled at being able to get into the sling, even though the sling was a little rough after having my backside beat up so well. It felt exhilarating as it always does to be bound and rendered completely vulnerable to you. This was made all the more exciting by the fact that my eyes were blindfolded so well, and my mouth was gagged so effectively that I was unable to see or speak.

Unfortunately, though, the blindfold and gag also caused some unpleasant feelings. The pain you were giving was so exquisite that I felt myself growing nearer and nearer to needing a release. I was in no position to beg, so crying was the only option available, but when I tried to cry I found that it was almost impossible The bandage that blindfolded me kept my eyes closed, not allowing many tears to form, and the gag impeded any sobs from escaping. That made me feel frustrated and confused; I needed a release and could not find an outlet, so I shut down emotionally.

As always, though, you take such good care of your boy. I am continually amazed that you can read me so well to know when something is wrong with me, although in this case I am sure it was very obvious. You removed the gag and blindfold immediately, and when you asked if I wanted you to make me cry, I could hardly believe my ears. I quickly said yes. The thought came to me, "How messed up are you that you want someone to hurt you bad enough to make you cry?" but I knew it was what I needed. Your care of me at that time was utterly amazing, so stern ("…I am going to keep beating you until you actually cry; fake crying or almost crying won't cut it!") and yet so loving. You know exactly what I need, and you take me to places that I would never be able to push myself in order to attain it.

When I sobbed that I wasn't able to cry—I really felt like I had no tears at that moment—you wouldn't accept it and continued pushing me. You said, "I will beat you all night until you cry," which of course initially struck me as almost cruel, but I knew it was anything but cruel. When you did make me cry; to know that you were able to make me do what I could not make myself do was a fabulous feeling. I cannot say how grateful it makes me feel to know that I have such a good Sir to look after me, and how lucky I am to belong to you. I am a very lucky pup.

I don't think I can adequately describe how wonderful my time was on the bondage table the next day. I absolutely love the feeling of your cuffs on me, binding me, immobilizing me, controlling me. It is the very extension of your control wrapping around me, holding me in place. I could lay in that loving embrace of immobilization for hours, and I was even more thrilled when you began binding your cock and balls. It feels so wonderful to have them snugly tied up, especially knowing that you are doing it as an exercise of your ownership over every part of me.

Then you started the experiment of trying to make me ejaculate, and it was wonderful beyond words. Not only does it feel very pleasurable, of course, but what I truly love is feeling you use your cock as your toy. At that moment it is no longer a part of me, my cock bringing me closer to orgasm, but it feels truly like your plaything to be manipulated and stimulated however you want. You came back repeatedly and used me again and again, and it was almost more than I could bear—the feel of your strong hand stroking your cock, of the vibrator stimulating my ass, balls and cock, the movement of the wand over my prostate. I know what the Catholic Church teaches about such things, but in the moment (and ever since looking back on what happened), I can see nothing wrong; it was simply an owner making use of her property however she wanted; not out of some illicit desire for pleasure, but out of her right of possession.

I do so love being tied up by you. I also enjoy the feeling of suspension, even partial suspension, as it leaves me so vulnerable to whatever you want to do to me. Initially, however, I was nearly regretting such vulnerability because you were really laying into me—kneeing me, punching me, etc. There was a power, an emotion—an anger?—in it that I hadn't felt from you before. It really did make me scared, seeing a new dimension to your personality; I felt it most powerfully when you slapped me in the face. One of those slaps was so hard it almost felt as if something would come loose. I know it is never your intention to damage me, but I would also like to say how much I enjoy feeling afraid in front of you. It is one thing to receive blows knowing that it will all be held within a certain safe limit, but to see you in that way, not knowing what you are capable of in the moment, knowing that I am helpless to stop you— that is a truly fabulous feeling of powerlessness and submission.

I was so happy that you allowed me to come up on the bed with you afterwards. Seeing your face so close to mine, that look of happiness and authority at seeing your boy next to you, is a great joy. Feeling your hands go wherever they like on your slave's body is thoroughly exciting to me—and then to feel your kisses is more than words can express. I was actually hoping that you would do next what you did - kissing me and penetrating my mouth with your tongue. I must confess it was a somewhat strange experience to feel another person's tongue in my mouth for the first time. I was comforted, thinking back to our conversation that all I needed to do was lay there and allow you to kiss me (and that "we" were not kissing, I was being kissed and penetrated). You have now exercised your authority over every orifice of my body, this time penetrating my mouth. I cannot think of any area of my body that you have not now laid claim to.

As I continued to lie there, I was overjoyed that you would once more reach down to play with your cock. I could hardly believe that after all of its use it was still responding so well to your manipulation, and even gave out a bit more cum. I did not like the idea (or the taste!) of having to lick my cum off of your hand, but it made me feel very humble and obedient to you. It was also a good way to serve you by cleaning off your hand so that it would not be filthy with my juice. As I slipped quietly from your bed, careful not to wake you, I was in such a state of contentment that I easily drifted off into a pleasant sleep on the floor, knowing that my good Sir was so close by my side.

I was very happy to be able to drive you to the party the next day. I know you appreciate being able to relax going somewhere and let someone else drive, and I am very happy to be able to chauffeur you around. I was excited to arrive at the party, but also nervous. Even though I have played in public before (both at the Club and in Baltimore), to me this was a different kind of atmosphere, a more intimate party among friends. That made me feel more nervous; it meant that everything we did would be seen and noted by those attending. When we first went in, my nervous feeling was confirmed even further; you knew most of the people there and it was a very tight space— but at the same time, I found myself fitting into a scene that is so very new and incredibly different.

This tension between feeling totally out of place versus feeling like I completely belonged continued throughout dinner. I looked around the room and saw a variety of different kind of people (gender, age, race, etc.), none of whom I knew, which is itself enough to make me uncomfortable. Some of the discussions were rather vanilla, and some were discussions that I wouldn't normally ever hear (for example, the talk about the "dick on a stick"), which added to me feeling out of place. This was compounded by the fact that the others knew one another, or were at least more adept at mingling and getting to know one another, a skill I really do not have. All of that being said, I knew I was where I was supposed to be—right next to you. That realization would come back to me over and over, making me feel like a perfect part of the scene. While I was sitting on the floor next to you, I really felt my submission; it also stated loud and clear to everyone else that I am submissive only to you. In that respect, it alleviated a lot of my nervousness, because I didn't have to worry about being another person mingling in the crowd. Instead, I was free to be who I am—your slave, responsive to your will. This feeling of freedom and submission was reinforced by the way you chose what I was going to eat and the times I was able to perform services for you. My time at your feet was also challenging due to the hardness of the floor; I thought about mentioning this to you but in the end decided against saying anything about my discomfort because I don't want to come across as a needy slave all the time (and certainly not as whiny), and I didn't want to have to join everyone else on the furniture and lose my rightful place at your feet. Ultimately it wasn't that bad anyway. If I cannot endure some discomfort as the price of carrying out my duties, then what kind of slave am I?

My first thought on entering the dungeon was that they had some nice things but it certainly wasn't as good as your own. It made me realize again how lucky a slave I am that my Sir has such good equipment and facilities to use on me. The "electric chair" made me uneasy just looking at it, mostly because I thought (like many people) that the entire chair would be electrified, and I wasn't sure if I could take that, or how much of that I could take. Needless to say, I wasn't overly thrilled about being the first person to be in the chair, but I did love how freely you volunteered to strap me in and try it out. As I have said several times before, there is a great liberation in serving you and doing things out of obedience to you that I would never do on my own initiative. This is one of the great thrills I get out of following your desires so implicitly, and it was certainly true in this case.

The chill of the dungeon combined with the cold metal of the chair, however, did not help me to relax at all. I did greatly enjoy the positioning of the chair, particularly having my legs spread so wide apart. Of course, I could not help but be aware of the presence of others watching the entire time. Being put on display in front of strangers made me a little uncomfortable (especially when I am self conscious about the way I look) but it also made me feel very proud to be seen serving you and surrendering to you.

When I learned exactly how the chair was going to work, I must admit I was slightly disappointed. True, I was nervous about having the whole chair electrified, but I also thought it would be a tremendous rush to feel electricity jolt all across my body. The initial jolts I did feel were a mixture; some were barely felt, some were more like tickles, and only a few were painful (especially on my nipples, as you quickly learned). What made me happy, though, was to see how much you were enjoying this new-found torture: the looks on my face, the ease with which you could torture me, the various ways and places of shocking me, even kissing me or touching me yourself.

My confidence increased when our next activity was something very familiar to me. Having seen the St. Andrew's cross used already that night, I felt as if it was our turn to show others what could actually be done on it, which is another way of saying I felt a deep sense of pride to suffer long and well for you. I was so happy when you went back to your bag and brought out your ass hook, as it is a wonderful way to have my ass played with, and also to be bound more fully by you.

The whipping I received from you felt so good, and yet in some ways more painful than ever. I do believe that I was "tenderized" enough from the previous night that the strokes I was now receiving felt more painful than perhaps they otherwise would have. I also believe that everything I had been experiencing at the party added to my emotional state, and my reaction to your whip. Be that as it may, I loved the idea of being bound and exposed while receiving your lashes. My only thought was to make you proud by what I was willing to suffer, and my good, strong reaction to the pain you wanted to inflict.

Sometimes I felt on the edge of completely breaking down into tears, but I struggled against that; I did not want to appear to be a weak slave in front of other people. But your words during the moments of rest were a great source of new strength for me to carry on, even when it felt as if I might not be able to endure much more. I do wonder what I really mean by not being able to endure it? Certainly there will be a point of tears, or pleading with you, or both, but does that mean I wouldn't endure any more? Again, I find myself amazed at how you are able to pull new strength and energy out of me which I would never have thought I possessed. I did end the scene feeling very proud not only in what I could suffer for you, but most importantly that I could suffer it for you. There were no more thoughts of being self-conscious about how I looked naked in front of other people. I was your slave and being with you, however you wanted me to look, was the only thing that mattered.

STRENGTH IN SERVICE

All the talk about "service" is good and well, but having a slave means nothing, even if he is willing to do the dishes and clean the house, if when you really need someone he isn't there. On September 1st, 2010, I experienced the most truly traumatic event of my lifetime. I can't think of a personal experience that even comes close, and I hope to God I never will again. On this day, my workplace was invaded by a domestic terrorist who took several hostages, and threatened to pull the trigger on the homemade explosives strapped to his body. The employees were herded around the building and eventually evacuated as hostage negotiators did their work; luckily, no one (except the terrorist himself) was physically harmed.

In the rush of the event, we had been instructed to leave everything behind and move to safety, so I found myself out on the street with no money or identification, without keys to my car, or the ability to go back to retrieve my items. Thankfully, I had been clinging to my cell phone since fleeing my desk several hours earlier. Joseph was the very first person I called when I was in the relative safety of a locked office with my coworkers. I have never been a religious person, or one to believe in the power of prayer ... but in a situation like this, it seemed like the right thing to do.

"Hey. It's me. I don't want you to panic, I'm sure I'll be fine, but I need to tell you there's a gunman in my building and we're not sure what's going on. Please ... pray for me. I love you."

"Yes, Sir, I will," he said. "Be safe, and if there's anything I can do for you, call me. I love you." His calm presence helped center me as it has so many times in much less serious situations. I found the strength to call Heather and my parents so they wouldn't panic when they heard what was going on, as it was all over the news channels by this point. But hours later, on the street, I felt a sense of powerlessness like I'd rarely experienced before. Fiercely independent and self-reliant, I hated being in a position of complete helplessness. No money, no car, no ID, no credit cards, and a quickly dying cell phone. Most of my coworkers could take the metro home, or had friends and family close enough to call for a ride. I had neither, and my house is not possible to reach via public transportation, but the local streets within a half-mile radius of our building had been cordoned off for safety and there was no indication of when we'd be allowed back into the building to access our cars. All I wanted was to go home.

In a situation like this, most people would just think to call a friend. I'm sure I could have thought of one person who would be able to get me home if I hadn't had a slave. Even Heather, who worked far away and would have spent two hours getting to me, would have done so if I had asked her. But there was something inexplicable about the state I was in and the absolute vulnerability I felt that wouldn't allow me to take help from anyone who offered it. The only thing that felt safe—the only person I felt safe enough to see me this way—would be my boy.

Fortunately, Joseph was at school and had been camped out in the library after classes to work on his thesis. I was able borrow a few dollars from a coworker and catch a train to his campus, where his parked car awaited us. Riding home, I was still in shock. I felt detached from my emotions and I calmly recounted the events of the day to Joseph, who listened while he drove. But once we were home, our shoes and jackets kicked off and my exhausted body resting on the sofa with my head in my boy's lap, I finally lost my composure.

So many times in the past, I had made Joseph cry from things I'd done to him, and I had been the one to comfort him and relieve the pain I had inflicted. So many times in the past he had been naked and vulnerable in front of me, unable and not permitted to hide his emotions. Now, for the first time, I allowed him to really see my suffering, to be emotionally naked in front of him, and to give him the joy of serving me with his strength in my time of weakness.

To my surprise and pleasure, a few days later an unprompted journal entry appeared on Joseph's Fetlife account. While he glossed over the actual seriousness of the day's events, I was able to see how being there for me in a time of true need had strengthened the sense of reality surrounding his identity as "mine."

Thursday, September 1, 2010

Still being relatively new to the scene and to life as a submissive/slave, there are times when I am still trying to wrap my head around the idea of living as a submissive. Sometimes it can almost seem like a game that I am playing, or a fun diversion to do in my spare time. Some people probably play in that way, and I am not speaking badly about them in any way. I am simply trying to understand my own life in submission as something more for me.

Recently something happened that reinforced why submission is not just a game or a diversion for me. My Sir went through something very difficult and was in need of assistance, and fortunately I was available to serve her in her need. There was nothing of play or fun about this, but only my dominant needing the services of her boy. Of course it was terrible for her to have to go through what she did, but I felt a personal level of fulfillment, and even happiness, at being available to serve in that way.

It was a strong and clear reminder of the relationship that we have built and are continuing to build. Being able to serve in a difficult moment helped me to see once more how service is not something that I do just for kicks or for the thrill, but because it is truly and deeply a part of who I am.

My one great desire is to make sure that Sir is happy and her life is as positive as it can be. I long to serve in whatever way I can to help achieve that for her, as her betterment is my fulfillment. While I hope she never has to go through anything close to that terrible again, I do look forward to serving her in any capacity I can in the future, and continuing to live as the submissive that I am.

A PERMANENT MARK

It has always been my fantasy to own a slave that I feel so certain about my future with that I would mark him properly with a piercing or tattoo. Despite being with Joseph for just a couple of months, and with our future nowhere near resolved, it seemed like the time to do such a thing might be closer than I'd imagined. I guess fantasy is one thing and reality is another!

By mid-September we were newly into our third contract period, spanning August 28th through November 28th, 2011. In this version, the previous wording, "...The dominant also agrees not to leave marks more severe than bruises, welts, cuts, and abrasions that will heal on their own if left alone in a matter of weeks" had undergone a revision to include the phrasing "with the exception of intentional markings such as tattoos, piercings, cuttings, and brandings which are to be planned in advance and executed in an appropriate, safe, and sanitary manner." This contract version also specifically stated that "...the dominant has the right, and sole discretion, to mark (pierce, tattoo, brand, cut, scar) the submissive in whatever way she chooses and in a location of her choosing, as long as the process is performed in a safe and sanitary manner and all marks are concealable under everyday clothing."

Needless to say, these revisions were not made unilaterally, and Joseph had been in absolute agreement that as the owner of his body, I had the right to make alterations in the future if I chose to. No firm plans had been made, though; we were only speaking hypothetically of a nipple piercing or a tattoo at some point in the future.

Then I realized quite suddenly that the person I would want to perform the piercing would be in town from the West Coast for just a few days for a kinky camping event. While I normally wouldn't have ventured to mark my property quite so soon, something just told me that it was right and that we'd not regret doing it. It was also important to me that this specific piercer be the one to do it, and given the geography, it could be another year before we ran into her again.

I first mentioned the idea concretely to Joseph about two weeks before it would have to happen. "So, pup...I was thinking. I've always wanted to pierce my slave's nipple when I knew he was going to be mine for good."

"Yes, Sir." He replied. His standard, non-telling response to just about anything I ever said or suggested.

"Well, how do you feel about that?"

"It's a good idea, Sir. I never would have gotten my nipple pierced myself, but if it's what you want ... I think it's hot."

"I'm glad you think so. Of course it is hot. The thing is, I'd really like Suzanna to be the one to do it. She's pierced me before and she's really good. She'll be in town for camp in a couple of weeks, so let's see if you can come up just for the day to have it done."

"Yes, Sir."

And that's the way most of our conversations went from the start, whenever I came up with new ideas. Even when my brilliant ideas meant something painful for him, he never balked or gave me reason to think he wanted anything less than to please and obey me one hundred per cent. I honestly don't think I've seriously suggested anything to him that he hasn't initially—or very soon afterward—considered a good idea. I don't know if we are just that perfect of a match, or his will so easily aligns with mine, or he is so open to suggestion … but I'm not complaining! It's wonderful. And even in the rare instance that he doesn't immediately find something a good idea, it never takes long for him to realize on his own that it is, in fact a very good one.

The entire experience of planning out and executing the piercing was very special and meaningful to me. I contacted the piercer and made sure she was available—and yes, she was. We set up a time, and Joseph arranged to come up to the camp that day. I hadn't even really explained to the piercer the depth of meaning in what she would be doing for us, but somehow she inherently knew, and the impromptu ceremony she created was just beautiful.

Before the piercing, Joseph and I talked in depth about its meaning to us. We knew instinctively that we had each found something extremely rare in the other one. Regardless of what the future would hold, we had begun to tell each other that he would always be mine. I knew that this was true, even if it didn't play out the way it did in my dreams where he left the priesthood and pledged himself to me for life. Even if he remained a priest, we had come to the agreement that he would never seek another dominant and even less so, another woman for a vanilla relationship.

So this piercing was the first mark of my permanent ownership, though it wouldn't be the last. I liked the idea of only piercing one nipple, and Joseph—no fan of pain and needles—had no objection to not having both done at the same time. I decided on the right nipple, since left and right-sided adornments have traditionally "flagged" top (dominant) and bottom (submissive) respectively.

The day of his appointment with Suzanne, Joseph arrived at the campgrounds just before lunch. I gave him the tour, and showed him around the places where I had made so many fond memories over the past few years. Finally, we were called inside Suzanne's cabin by her boy and assistant, Chris. There was a little bit of prep work, and as the ethical practitioner she is, Suzanne made sure Joseph was good to go ahead with the act. When it came time for the actual piercing, we positioned him face up on the bed. I knelt by his head and held his hands. Other than my grip, he wasn't restrained in any way. The boy doesn't "enjoy" pain and he particularly dislikes needles, but he does have a deep love of ritual, meaning, and symbolic acts (go figure!) so I knew this whole experience was significant to him.

Without any prompting or preparation from me, Suzanne began to speak on the meaning of what she was about to do. She said that she was just being a conduit and acting on my behalf, and that it was actually me piercing Joseph and claiming ownership of him through this act. Even if I had told her what to say, I couldn't have done a better job.

The actual piercing was quick and easy. Joseph winced and gritted his teeth as the needle slipped through but it was less pain than I've given to him on many occasions. With his eyes closed, Joseph didn't know what stage the piercing was at and didn't know that the needle was already through his nipple, so Suzanne—God bless her sadist heart—decided to have some fun with him.

"OK, are you ready for the crazy part?" she asked.

The poor boy, thinking that first sting had been only preliminary, gulped and said "Yes," bravely and firmly. It made my heart skip to think about how much pain he must have thought was coming, yet he never hesitated in his commitment to the act. Suzanne just smiled and said, "The crazy part is that's it, you're done!"

I don't even remember my pup's response at the time, I was so proud of him.

Part III: Life As Property

GOOD THINGS FOR GOOD BOYS

Scene Report: Tuesday, September 21, 2010

I am always so happy to be able to spend time at home, especially knowing that I am helping to make it a more comfortable, pleasant place for you and Heather by cleaning up, organizing, etc. That is why I am always reluctant to leave, even when I know I need to get back to my place. Even while wearing your collar and piercing as tokens of your ownership, they cannot convey the same sense of peace that I get from being with you. I have almost never experienced that kind of peace before in life, and certainly not as regularly as I have with you.

Giving you a massage is always a rewarding experience. I think the more techniques I learn, the more competent I feel at it and the more I enjoy doing it. The fact that you were sore and in serious need of a massage made my service all the more fulfilling. You know how much I love hearing your sounds of pleasure as I work your muscles in various ways, but what was even better for me was the fact that you fell asleep. On one hand, it was disappointing, as I could no longer hear those harmonious sounds. On the other hand, it was a truly wonderful feeling that you could fall asleep and get the rest you needed. It was also very affirming to hear you afterward say that I was just as effective as a professional. For my own self-image, I need to know that I am competent at these things.

Back home, in the dungeon … I was indeed in for a huge treat with your new toy, the thigh strap-on harness. I never would have guessed what it was, but it felt so great. As I lowered myself down onto your leg your new cock filled my ass up very nicely, and then when you grabbed my cock I felt as if I was in total bliss. The feeling I had was that of being completely possessed and used by you, your cock playing with my ass and your hand playing with my cock. When you gave me directions to ask if I could please come, I was thrilled not only knowing that I would (or at least might) be allowed to come, but knowing that it would only happen when you wanted, and that I would be denied many times first. I quickly discerned that you wanted me to either come during or after your orgasm, which made the experience even more exciting. I felt perfectly at ease begging for release in that context, and I found myself getting more and more into the spirit of it. I was disappointed that I came so early, not only because I knew it was sooner than you had wanted, but also because it prematurely deprived me of the joy of the activity. In my mind, when you use me that way, my cock feels less a part of "me" and more like an object, a toy that you are playing with. When I came, it was less like "I came" and more like you made your toy come. I enjoy that sense of detachment and objectification of your cock.

I was very happy to have you beat my ass. It had been a while since my ass had received much attention in that way from you, and it felt so good. I especially enjoy it when you spank me, or beat me with your fists, as it is a very personal and intimate experience every time your hand strikes me; but even the sharp pain of the cane felt good. The remainder of our time together was simply wonderful—totally relaxed, completely at ease and in peace lying down with you. I lay there as you read to me, and your voice sounded so beautiful it was almost hypnotic. I love to listen to you read.

For four months, Joseph had been accompanying me to the barn where my horse was boarded, helping me with barn chores, and watching while I enjoyed riding my horse Thunder. He had never expressed an interest in riding, and I was surprised to learn that despite growing up on a farm in a very rural area, he had never so much as sat on a pony. I quickly decided that this had to change. I also quickly learned that Joseph had no desire to try out horseback riding, and he was in fact quite averse to doing anything new that he might not be good at. Knowing this only made me more eager to push him, a pattern that has continued throughout our relationship whenever he is hesitant to try something new.

Even though he willingly agreed to get on Thunder's back from the first time I commanded it, Joseph definitely didn't like what he was getting into. Fortunately my horse is very well behaved and particularly calm with beginners, so I trusted that my pup would not be in harm's way. As it turned out, having Joseph ride was a great experience for both of us in terms of bolstering his self-esteem. To his surprise, he was actually kind of good at it, and seeing Thunder respond and follow his commands gave him a confidence he'd never experienced. Sure, he wasn't ready for the Olympics or the Kentucky Derby yet, but it made me incredible content to see my boy trust me enough to try something he was hesitant about and even afraid of outside the context of an SM scene, and to be successful.

Giving Joseph his first riding lesson was pushing beyond a barrier. It was ordering him to do something that he really would have preferred not to do, but that was not the least bit sexy. Later that night, we pushed past a different type of barrier. After four months together, I allowed my boy to see my entire body without clothes for the first time, realizing that this would not only be a first for me and him together, but the first time in his life he had seen all of a woman. The idea of being yet another "first and only" for him thrilled me.

Scene Report: Saturday, September 25, 2010

At the barn, the first thing that I noticed (after how happy I always am to see

you) was how comfortable I felt being there. I was now used to the people and the horses and the setting, so it felt good to be there and not feel nervous or self-conscious all the time.

I was nervous for my first ride, but when I first got on Thunder it felt very natural. I was very glad that he is such a good horse and quickly adapted to me as the rider. It was a great experience for me to be able to try something so new and feel comfortable with it, so much so that I would like to try it again. Usually I try something new and it doesn't really "work", because I'm not experienced at it and don't really know what I'm doing, so I don't want to do it anymore. But riding Thunder was a lot of fun, especially following you on the trail. It was a great time.

You made a comment about whether I truly get anything out of helping you so much, and the answer is resoundingly yes. First, I have told you before the satisfaction I get out of seeing a job well done. Mostly, however, the opportunity to help someone else has always been fulfilling for me. It is even more fulfilling to be able to help my Sir and making her life better than it is to help some random person. Not to mention it is time together to share a common experience. Standing around toward the end waiting for the guy to trim Thunder's hooves did get boring, but I understand those things happen sometimes, and that you were doing your best to get us home.

When we stopped for dinner, it occurred to me that I am very happy that you are so conscientious about ordering food I like, but there is also part of me that would love it for you to push me a little more and order other things that I haven't specifically said I liked. Of course both are good; the first option shows your care for your property, and the second would give me a powerful reminder of your control. In any case, having you order my food and serve it up to me is a wonderful experience of my submission. I liken it to the way you feed Thunder or Shadow; they don't choose what to eat but you give them what you want them to have. I love that experience of your dominance.

◆◆◆◆◆

"You Know I Find You Sexy, Right?" I messaged my boy some time later.

We had been discussing how his academic career turned me on, and he observed it was interesting to know what got me going. Which in turn compelled me to tell him that *he* got me going quite well on his own.

"Yes Sir, I do," he replied. "I am often amazed by that, but I know it's true and am very honored and grateful for it. But I do appreciate hearing it."

Then, after a brief pause: "I don't suppose I have ever actually told you how sexy I find you, have I Sir?"

"I don't suppose you have," I mused.

"Well, I do. How strong you are, and yet how gentle you are. How intelligent and competent you are. How commanding and controlling you are. How sensitive and communicative you are. All of that I find sexy."

My dick was instantly hard and I wished I had my boy in front of me to relieve the aching. *That's what I get for talking to him at work…*

REACHING DEEPER, TAKING HOLD

This scene report came after a week that had been difficult for Joseph, but had ultimately been a big milestone in his development as a person and as my property. One of my requirements has always been his transparency, and he has told me many, many times over how opposite this rule is to everything he has experienced in life till now.

Before me, Joseph's self-criticism, and perceived and real criticism from others, kept him in such fear of judgment and ridicule that he found it better to keep all personal thoughts hidden from the world. This has never been acceptable in our relationship, even when sharing something with me has the potential to upset me. During this week we experienced a communication hiccup that was really no big deal, but the actual "big deal" was that Joseph did what he was supposed to do—expressing his uncomfortable and unpleasant emotions to me so that we could work them out.

I was so proud of him for doing it, even though it never comes easily. But even more than pride, I feel that each time I witness Joseph setting aside his natural inclination and former habit of just keeping everything to himself, and opting instead for obedience to my rules about honesty and intimacy, I am conquering new depths and owning him more deeply than before.

At the same time, this week witnessed another milestone in the depths of my ownership and control. Prior to this point, Joseph felt uncomfortable touching my genitals, which I refer to as my "dick" or "cock" instead of the more traditional female terms—which are not to be confused with my-cock-the-strap-on-dildo or "my cock" that resides on Joseph's body! Over time, his discomfort fell away and he only craved to be used in any capacity I wanted. So for the first time, I allowed him to touch me and help me with an orgasm.

Scene Report: Sunday, October 3, 2010

I was once more elated to be "fucking useful", not so much by the few things I helped to move but just by being able to be there with you and help relieve the stress of the morning. I hope you will never hesitate about asking for my assistance whenever you need it; I cannot always promise I will be able to be there, but I will always want to help and will do so if I can. Being able to be of service to you in important events in life makes me truly fulfilled as your slave.

I was so happy to have time to relax with you before dinner. Even though it was a painful conversation for me, I was happy to have it. I know that I have a lot of emotional baggage that I need to overcome, and I know that I can't do it on my own. I need someone else to push me to get rid of it, but unfortunately until now I have not been able to find that person. I know that I can tell you anything, and you will be considerate and supportive ... and that means the world to me. A relationship where I can be this open and this transparent has been a fervent prayer of mine for years. I firmly believe that you are the answer to that prayer; you are certainly everything I could have asked for.

Our conversation yesterday was particularly difficult, as I divulged what I would call the deep secret of my life: how truly empty my life has always felt, so much so that I have often wished not to live. To be able to share that with someone and not be judged for it, but instead be understood and supported, was truly wonderful. I know that I have not yet overcome that feeling, but being able to talk about it is a great beginning. I am so thankful that you want so much to make me a better person, and that you feel confident that it will happen, given time.

The time we had after dinner to play was truly special. I love the feeling of being pinned underneath you, and the rush I get from that experience of your control. To have you on top of me, hitting and beating me, biting me, manipulating my limbs and body as you wished, gave me a deep feeling of submission.

When you put my hand on your "cock" to please you, I felt an intimate connection between us. It was a deeper, more intimate feeling of connection than I have had with you before, for all of the feelings I've had for you. As my fingers rubbed across you and I could hear how much pleasure you were getting, I felt wonderful that I could be such a good sex toy, which is how I felt in that moment—that I was your toy. As your pleasure reached climax it felt as if I experienced some of that pleasure myself, I felt that connected to you. As you correctly said, the fact that you were getting so much pleasure while I was being denied it myself only added to my enjoyment of my predicament ... and as you saw afterward, I was fulfilled and at peace from the experience of being used. The only thing better than getting pleasure myself is being denied it so as to better please you. It is experiences like last night, the culmination of the entire evening, that so much confirm why I want to belong to you.

You are truly the greatest thing to happen in my life and I cannot tell you how much I appreciate all you give me and do for me.

COLUMBUS DAY PLAY

Heather and I spent the Columbus Day weekend out of town with our Leather Family. As much as I enjoyed the time away and the company we had, my experiences never felt quite as complete without Joseph. His obligations with school and helping out at the parish prevented him from going most places with us, but if I couldn't enjoy using him directly, at least I still had the luxury of using his service from afar. My dog was being held at the vet for the weekend and we would arrive home on Monday, so I arranged for Joseph to pick up Shadow and be waiting at home for me when we arrived.

Scene Report: Monday, October 11, 2010

Being able to pick up Shadow from the vet gave me not only another way to be useful but also a greater feeling of truly belonging to the home. I really felt as if I was not just going to pick up your dog, but my fellow pup. That goes along with the increasing feeling I have every time I go home, that it is truly "mine"—not in the sense that it belongs to me, but in the sense that I really belong there. Having my own key now helps me to feel that I really am a part of the home rather than just someone who comes over.

During the day I had the extra incentive to really make things nice for you when you got home. It had been stressful for you before leaving; I wanted to make your return as comfortable as possible. To that extent, I even did a few things I hadn't tried before (like making the bed and cleaning up a few things in the bedroom), all with the intent that you could come home and not have to worry about working as soon as you got back. I do so enjoy making your home a nice and relaxing place for you, which is why I was also pleased to be able to go pick up dinner for us. It was one less thing for you or Heather to worry about.

It was very nice to hear about your time away over dinner and just to be with you again after a few days. I was very happy that you wanted to shower with me, as you know how much I enjoy that experience. Having you give me an enema in the shower was amazing. The feeling of you pumping water inside of me is truly a feeling of domination; to have your hands working my cock and ass at once felt wonderful, and yet slightly frustrating. It felt so good to be allowed to come, but I could not give myself as thoroughly to the orgasm, since I was concerned about holding in the enema.

Once again I so much enjoyed giving you a massage. It is such a wonderful way to serve you and to feel connected with you. Heather joined in, and where I once had some struggles with that, this time I simply focused on the added attention and pleasure you were getting from it and that made me all the happier. When you told me to massage your dick as well, I initially felt hesitant, because it was a new experience ... but I soon learned what you expected from that kind of massage, and it felt very natural and very good. I enjoyed being able to see the physical reaction of your body to the pleasure, which was all the motivation I needed to keep doing everything I could to make you feel that way.

Kneeling upon the table I very much felt like your slave, objectified, presented there before you. Ninety-six strokes, even though I made it through them last time, still seems like a lot, and my heart sank as you told me you were going to give me twice that. I really did not know how I was going to make it through that many - I knew I would take them, but didn't know what kind of shape I would be in after doing so.

As you started, my mind focused on only a very few things: properly counting the strokes, doing my best to take each one, and remembering that I was doing so because it was your right to use me however you want (and sometimes you like to use me hard not as punishment, but as another way of showing your dominance and your care). Some of the strokes really hurt, which made me wonder all the more about getting through a hundred and ninety-two of them. I don't know whether coming before it started increased the sensation of pain, but I do know it hurt quite a lot. Through it all, I kept coming back to those three things: counting properly, taking each stroke as it came, remembering why I was doing so.

I felt as if I was on the verge of tears for a long time as you were beating me. I wanted so much to let go and really cry, but knew I had to keep the count until I was finished. When one hundred and ninety-two finally came, I could hardly believe it. I would not say it wasn't as bad as I feared, because my legs were sorer than I can remember in a long time; but I felt a great sense of accomplishment at having done all of that for you, at being used by you so well.

However, the greatest joy I received the entire night was in my apology to you for my disobedience in touching my (your) cock without permission, and your acceptance of me. I knew I needed to tell you I had made a mistake and was sorry, but it still took a lot of effort to find the right moment and the right way to tell you. I really did not know how you were going to respond. Part of me thought you might be really angry and want to punish me somehow; I was prepared to accept that. Part of me wanted to imagine you finding my apologizing hot and not being upset at all. Mostly I was hoping you would handle it the way you did: you were upset by what I had done (and rightly so), but not furious at me.

When I looked into your eyes, I felt truly ashamed at what I had done, and I could feel the hurt it had caused. In that moment, despite everything else in our relationship, that nagging fear came back about being rejected. To hear you say that you accepted my apology and that I was still your good boy were the most beautiful words. I cannot tell you how much that meant and means to me. Not that I ever want to hurt you or disobey you in the future, but it was almost worth having done so to hear those words.

I have said it before, but it bears being repeated. I am truly the luckiest slave to have such a good master who loves me so much and who I can love so much.

As time went on, Joseph's and my time together became more and more mundane. Not in the sense that we played less or did less exciting things; only that these things were our normal routine now, and every little occurrence didn't seem quite as remarkable as it once had. Rather than being disappointed that our life was becoming so routine, I found myself thrilled and marveling at just how different my life now was from before I had met Joseph. His scene reports continued, even when all he had to report was a quiet night at home.

Scene Report: Thursday, October 21, 2010

My experience tonight felt like a quiet, normal, enjoyable evening at home. It was great! There is something amazing about the feeling that we didn't do anything special, no extra effort, just what we always do in the evening: everyone gets home, we eat dinner, I get flogged. What a wonderful life. Doing laundry, cleaning up the kitchen, being pestered by Shadow: it all felt as if I was right where I belonged. I love the feeling of fitting in so well, of being perfectly at ease and at home doing what a slave is supposed to do— being useful. What was even more enjoyable was being useful when you got home.

I loved the position you put me in for the flogging. I was spread out nicely, making movement difficult, but it was a very comfortable position I could hold easily for a long time. Your blindfold is wonderful as it takes away my sight. The earplugs fit well enough to limit what I could hear; I enjoy not being able to hear you walk around, because I don't know if you are behind me, in front of me, or even in the room. It is a great feeling of total submission and dependency that I don't even know from what direction you might be coming at me.

I wondered at first what you were planning when you removed my collar, and then was thrilled when you put on the posture collar. I had seen it before and had wondered what it would feel like to wear it, and I was not disappointed. It felt great as it encased my neck and limited my mobility. You applied it fairly tightly, making breathing more difficult; that concerned me slightly, but mostly made me remember how you control everything about me, even my breathing. Your gag completed the effect beautifully so that I could not hear, see or speak. I felt like I was in a cocoon, shut off from the world and even distant from my body.

That feeling of "separation" or distance made the flogging an interesting experience. I could feel each stroke, but in some ways it felt disconnected, as if I was experiencing what was happening to someone else's body. It also made the flogging a bit more impersonal, as if the blows were coming out of the darkness, and not from you. Of course I knew they were coming from you, but there was still something of a distance-effect created by my sensory deprivation.

The blows themselves felt very painful right from the start, but as much as I don't really get off on pain, I did enjoy being unable to cry out or do anything about it. The most I could do was squirm around a little in a vain attempt to soften or elude the blows, and that feeling of helplessness was wonderful. I quickly realized there was nothing I could do but endure, and that was a great thought.

The moments when you put your arms around me were both reassuring and controlling, as if you were telling me by those actions to deepen my submission and surrender within the moment. That was especially true when you held my nose and cut off my breathing, reminding me not so subtly that my very life-breath depends upon you.

I heard the sound from your single-tail moments before I felt its first strike. I relish that sound, as it always make me think "Oh no, here it comes!" just before the pain starts. It was the searing pain from your whip that immediately pushed me harder in my endurance and submission.

As much as I was glad to have the scene end, there was also part of me that wished I could have had more. Being "pulled down" by you afterward was one final act reminding me that I am your property to be used and moved about at your will. I feel so used, so tired, so molded to your will by the experience. And to feel all that while being cradled in your lap is a most amazing feeling.

DINNER AT THE RECTORY

To say that Joseph's "other life" is a bit of a mystery to me would be an understatement. I know where he lives; I have dropped him at the front door several times when giving him a ride home from the Metro (mainly as an excuse to see him a little longer), but I have only been inside once for a quick tour as I dropped him off one night.

The rectory is a very large house that used to be the parish's convent many years ago, so it has more rooms than would make sense to house just one or two priests. The first floor holds the Church Office, kitchen, living room, and dining room. On the second floor is a long hallway of small bedrooms, dormitory style, with each two rooms sharing an adjoined bathroom. Joseph has two rooms of his own—one with his bed, dresser, and TV; the other with his desk, bookshelf, and a small sofa. In between the two rooms is his very own bathroom. So all in all, it's pretty nice (though not fancy) and it's more private than I had imagined, given that I knew he lived in a rectory with another priest.

Through my time with Joseph, I always heard stories about the other priest he lived with. Father Patrick was an interesting man, from what I could tell. Joseph once told me that some people accused him of being too "worldly" because he enjoyed a lot of material things—going out to nice restaurants and the theatre, cooking gourmet food, decorating the rectory, and that sort of thing. I asked Joseph if he was gay, because from the description it sort of sounded that way. Joseph denied knowing anything about it, which might be true, but I do still have the impression this might be the case. Joseph also told me that there was a bit of an unwritten "don't ask, don't tell" rule about what priests in large urban centers do with their free time. Either way, it matters little to me. I only find the idea of a gay priest and a kinky priest living alongside one another, but each in their own respective closets, to be amusing.

Regardless of my far-fetched speculations, I had wanted to meet Fr. Patrick for quite some time. I was excited to finally be invited over to dinner, but a little disappointed that Joseph would be doing the cooking, not his roommate, considering how much I'd heard about Patrick's cooking skills. Then again, this would be a treat since Joseph never cooked at home. The evening went well, and beyond just eating dinner and getting to know Patrick a little bit, some other things happened. Things I cannot believe we actually did in the rectory! Even though I didn't grow up knowing anything about Catholicism and didn't even know what a "rectory" was until meeting Joseph, something about it still felt taboo enough to make it hot.

Scene Report: Saturday, October 30, 2010

I was excited and nervous to have you come over to my place for dinner.

I wanted you to meet Patrick and see more of what my place is like, and I wanted to cook for you, but I was nervous about how the food would come out. In the past my attempts have not always been as successful as Saturday night. I was also nervous about you meeting Patrick; I wasn't sure how the two of you would get along, and of course the possibility of something slipping out about the true nature of our relationship was always there. In the end, though, I was thrilled at how well you got along.

Alone together, it was like my slave-life came crashing into my vanilla life, which I know is not true because I am always yours, but it was a powerful reminder. Of course, the idea of being with you and doing our activities in the rectory with my roommate down the hall added a touch of scandal or excitement for me.

What I enjoyed most about our time together was simple being together. Having you play with my cock as you did (not being able to see I'm not entirely sure what you did with it) felt amazing. It did not feel erotic in the sense of lovers having sex or making love. It felt sexual in the sense of you doing to me whatever you wanted, not only to make me feel good, but because every part of my body is yours to use however you want. In return, I was so glad that you allowed me to again touch your dick and make you come. It is always an honor for me to be able to give you that kind of pleasure and serve you in that way. I was even more happy that in the course of doing it, I was able to find your G-spot and make you feel another kind of pleasure. When you finally had to leave, I could hardly believe that it was after one in the morning. Apparently, I lose all track of time as I am enjoying so much the time I have to spend with you.

ANGER COMES OUT TO PLAY

Halloween: one of my favorite holidays, and not just because of the candy! Joseph and I had planned to go to a midnight showing of *The Rocky Horror Picture Show* but I didn't want to give up the chance to play, so I had warned Joseph to expect some of that as well.

But the more I thought about it, the more I wanted to play with him differently than I had ever before. Normally I'm very careful to warm him up and ease him into the activity we're doing, but sometimes I just want to play rough. This night was one of those times, and it led to a side of Joseph I'd never seen before. Even though once in a while he would become angry during play, it was nothing like this. All throughout our playtime he was screaming at the top of his lungs, thrashing, pounding on the cross, and cursing. We were going places we hadn't been before, for better or worse … and going through experiences that grow our relationship is second to none in terms of my enjoyment, so canceling our plans to see a movie was a no-brainer. He wrote about the scene later:

As soon as you hit me hard the first time, I got very angry. I can only guess that the anger came from being tired, and perhaps some resentment about it being unfair because I wasn't in the mood. I think part of it may have also been from being a little worn down emotionally by not having had much time to myself over the previous several days.

With that first stroke, when my anger came out, I initially thought that maybe I shouldn't be reacting that way. But then I remembered how you always tell me that you want me to do what is natural, and anger at the moment was coming naturally. Since you did not say anything to me about my behavior, I assumed you were all right with my behavior until I was told otherwise. At times I surprised myself at my reaction to things and even scared myself a little at behaving that way. I never would have pictured myself being that angry and wanting to lash out; I felt like hitting someone or breaking something. Since you were the only one around, those thoughts were somewhat directed at you, or at the cross. But even in the midst of that anger I did not want to be disrespectful toward you, and I was careful to answer you when you spoke to me. At times I also decided defiantly that I wasn't going to make a sound or show any kind of response. I felt in many ways like a little boy throwing a tantrum and pouting.

When you were finished and took me down, I still felt angry and wanted to pout. Somehow, however, that energy was still not directed at you. I was not mad at you. Even with that anger, there was still part of me that wanted to be with you and cuddle with you. In the midst of that I was so touched by your understanding of my emotions and your support of me and what I was, or may have been, going through.

Later, when I was tied down, I was thrilled that you indeed intended not only to suck my (your) cock, but also allow me my first experience of sucking your flesh cock. It felt so good just to have you place a condom on my cock (I think I have tried that once before just to see what it feels like but it certainly is not a common experience for me). To then have you take my cock into your mouth felt so amazing. I was truly disappointed about coming so quickly not only because it denied me of that pleasure but also because it deprived you of doing what you wanted. I was also surprised at how quickly I came; at times I feel like I have more control than others and apparently Sunday I had very little control. Being able to suck your flesh cock was wonderful, too. It was my first time and I did not know what to expect, but I quickly got into the spirit of it. I did not feel overly adventurous about what I could or should do, but I could tell from your reactions that my actions were very pleasing to you. It was indeed an honor and a pleasure to be able to serve you that way.

Thus, an evening that began with a lot of anger ended with a lot of pleasure. But what I most enjoyed, what was most fulfilling, was the support and encouragement I felt from you through everything. It was that support which made it a truly special night.

BUMPING UP AGAINST THE FUTURE

You may have noticed that by this point many of Joseph's limits regarding sexual contact had fallen by the wayside. We were engaging in oral sex reciprocally, both achieving orgasms (and excellent ones at that!), and "deep kissing" (originally an act Joseph had written off as too sexual) had become a normal way for me to penetrate my boy. Other than the using strictest definition of penile-vaginal intercourse, there was no remaining way in which Joseph could claim to be a virgin.

I have said it before, but it bears repeating: I did not ever urge or force any of these limits to be dropped. Each time Joseph fell deeper into being owned, he told me that it felt more and more unnatural to deny me the use of his body in any way I could desire. There was also the undeniable fact that he was starting to doubt his future as a priest.

In the beginning, our relationship seemed like an amazing dream that could never possibly be Joseph's reality, but as time went on and the feelings only increased instead of lessening, the idea that he might actually have a *choice* about his future became a new and ever-present thought. Joseph also maintained the philosophy (as did I) that as long as we were doing this whole Owner/property thing full force for the time we had, he might as well experience it fully. Since that was so, within the confines of whatever time we were to be together as owner and owned, it became unthinkable to Joseph to limit my use of my property.

I completely understand if hearing this in light of his obligations as a priest might make people question our morals. I cannot explain his actions other than him just not feeling that our relationship was wrong. He knows what the Church teaches about the activities we engaged in, but he personally never expressed feelings of guilt over our relationship. Not being Catholic, or even religious in any way myself, my own morality has more to do with what I believe to be right or wrong. I try not to do harm to other creatures, and I never viewed allowing Joseph to shed his limits as harmful. Even with the clarity of hindsight, as I write this now, I can say with a clear conscience that I never felt bad about anything we did together, and I have no regrets.

Still, even as we fell deeper into my ownership and possession of his body, mind, and heart, we couldn't avoid encountering reality once in a while. We would speak as though the future were certain; that he *would* be mine permanently someday, and for the most part we would act as if that were the case. But I knew that Joseph still had a lot of internal conflict to work through before a decision was made one way or the other.

Because of these conflicts, it was his idea to enter weekly counseling with a therapist and spiritual direction with a priest at this point, to gain two outside professional perspectives on his life and his newfound dilemma. I supported his decision, but the weekly sessions left me with a more emotionally raw boy than I was used to, and that sometimes brought issues to the surface for us as well. As someone who had spent his entire life keeping feelings to himself, and hardly even acknowledging them *to himself,* Joseph was now being held accountable for his honest emotions by not only me, but two additional people now. I don't take lightly how difficult this must have been for him. After one particularly intense day at counseling, followed by an intense night together, we conversed over instant messenger rather than having him write a scene report. I told him, "I can admit that I have been treating you as though you will be mine forever. It's the only way I can do this. I can't keep it in the forefront of my mind that this will all be over in six months."

He assured me that while he felt a great deal of pressure to stay, he knew that I was not intentionally laying it on him. "We have both spoken about what it will be like one day," he said, "and it is a great thought, and I have indulged in it a lot. But the reality is I have not made that decision. At times it seems very likely that I will be yours, and at other times it is not so easy to say."

"You've also said flat out that you want me to make that decision for you, to forbid you to leave," I pointed out. "I don't fully believe that I have that much power, but I'm not convinced I don't either, if that makes sense. I have a lot of belief in us and in our future. That's all I can say. I *know* nothing is certain, but nothing ever is. When you make your decision, whichever way it goes, I want it to be based on the reality of what it means either way, and not on some fantasy image of it. I'm glad that we've hit this point now, for you to see if being a slave still has the same appeal after the glossy newness is long gone. So, for what it's worth, consider the pressure off. I don't have expectations either way, just hopes. I maintain that the decision is yours, but if I am successful at mastering you, there won't be much room for a decision. Not to say that you won't still have to choose, but the choice will be so simple and clear if I've actually enslaved you to the extent I know we both want." Then I added, "But even if this only lasts till August, it still will have been the most amazing experience of my life."

◆◆◆◆◆

Not long after my first experience at the rectory, we had the opportunity for me to spend a night ... which of course meant a lot more than just sleeping. Father Patrick was out of town and it was exciting for both of us getting to explore our relationship in a new environment. Of course, the excitement was at least in part because we knew it was "wrong", but it was also the fact that for both Joseph and I, expanding my presence with him (and thus control over him) in a new *physical* realm also created new heights within the relationship.

Just like when I crossed other boundaries and Joseph realized that things he once considered his own were mine to take, my presence and use of him in the rectory gave him the feeling that the space was no longer "his." To give a more concrete element to this feeling, I brought over a small rolled up sleeping mat that Joseph would use as his bed not only when sleeping on the floor beside me, but from then on, permanently

This occasion was also the first time I had played with Joseph while he wore his clerical garb, and used it deliberately as a factor in our mutual excitement. Until this point (and still, for the most part), I tried to keep our play very separate from his profession. This separation is more due to oversensitivity on my part regarding fetishizing something very important to him than any discomfort he's ever expressed about such things, but I cannot deny that seeing him—or even imagining him—in his black suit with an entirely different type of collar has always just been *hot*.

Religious fetishes are not uncommon, but I never had one. I never gave a bit of thought to actual clergy, and seeing people dressed as priests or nuns in SM clubs would have gone right under my radar, meaning nothing to me at all. Why then am I so instantly hard at the sight of Joseph in his clerics? And why am I even more aroused when I see him in the vestments he wears for celebrating Mass?

The obvious answer, that I have developed a fetish for Catholic priests, is actually not the entire truth. Seeing Joseph acting as my slave turns me on immensely, because I see an authentic part of him that is beautiful and pure. It didn't take me long to realize that seeing him as a priest also showed me a part of his core self that comes from a place of truth, beauty, and love. I wish that the world allowed a man who has so much of these attributes to inhabit them fully in both ways … but this is a heavier discussion for another time. Joseph's scene report documents how thrilling and exciting it was for him to be under my control "at his place."

Scene Report: Thursday, November 18, 2010

I was very excited the whole day knowing that you would be coming to spend the night at my place. Your assignment for me to pick out five items from the dungeon to take back to the rectory was both exciting and a little nerve-wracking. It was exciting that I could pick out items for you to use on me, but it made me a little nervous in that I wanted to pick out items that you would approve of or find fun.

When we got to my place, my excitement continued to grow. It was simply amazing to think that you were there, not so much as a "guest" as when you came for dinner, but completely as my owner. To walk into the guest room in my clerics ready to be used by you, to have you take off my clothes … it was thrilling. As you were taking off my shirt, the thought went through my mind that it would be very hot for you to just rip it off, sending buttons flying and all. But to have you physically strip me was a beautiful experience of your control and ownership.

Seeing myself in the mirror across the room, gagged and in only my undershirt, was made even better by seeing my master. I truly enjoyed being thrown down on the bed by you. The only difficulty in this instance was the gag at times actually making me gag, which I didn't indicate not only because talking was out of the question, but because going through something difficult for you is also part of the fulfillment and excitement for me.

It was a huge rush for me to hear your surprise and delight that I had brought that particular cane. When I was selecting items, I was thinking not only about what I wanted, but what you would enjoy. I knew you would enjoy using the cane and the small quirt on me, and your enjoyment is what I enjoy. When you asked if I wanted you to beat my ass so raw that I would be unable to sit the next day, I could not respond at first. I was just stunned—part of me very excited at such a hot idea, and the other part of me frightened at having to endure that much pain in order to get my ass that raw. Indeed, the pain from some of your blows was so intense that once or twice I felt I had to restrain myself from biting through the gag. In spite of that, in some ways I was disappointed when the beating was over.

Also, the plug—whenever you inserted it, I forget when because you did so many wonderful things to me—felt great in my ass; it was so pleasurable and filled me up nicely. Having you tie me up so that the plug would stay in place was a wonderful treat. I particularly love having my cock and balls tied up, but having your ropes decorate me anywhere is great.

I was very excited when you gave me the assignment to make you come. Telling me that the amount of time it took me to make you come would be the amount of time you would do something to me was a really hot idea. Of course I had no idea if it would be something pleasurable or painful, and I don't know if you knew at the time either. But I quickly set any thought of that aside and simply focused on giving you pleasure. It was especially wonderful for me given my position where I could not only hear, but really see how much you were enjoying what I was doing.

It was so peaceful lying there together afterward and both of us drifting off to sleep. I remember waking up and seeing your face, so peaceful and beautiful. As much as I didn't want to disturb you, I knew you needed to get into a better position to sleep in my small bed, and so I tried my best to gently wake you. I was excited to spend the night sleeping on the floor, but also very happy that I could spend time with you in bed until you fell asleep. It was the one last service of the night I could do for you, to lie there with you and help you fall asleep. What a feeling of contentment when you finally did go to sleep, and I could slip from the bed to take my place on the mat! I went to sleep knowing that I had served you well, and now could rest so close to my owner.

Waking up early was another little thrill for me. It made me think of myself as the slave waking up early to make sure everything was taken care of for my master when she awoke. Of course I knew I wasn't doing that, but that I was waking up early for another reason: to celebrate Mass. Still, that was the feeling I got from it, and it made me excited the whole time I was away, thinking about my master being at my place waiting for me when I finished with my morning duties. What a rush to come back and be able to see you off for the day.

What I think was so special for me about you spending the night at my place and playing with me here was that it gave me a renewed sense of my submission to you. It is no longer that I go home to play and serve you but that even here now I am truly yours. Of course I know all along I have been yours wherever I have been, but having you here really helped me feel and experience that in a new and deeper way. In a certain sense, it was a new experience of the boundary between my two worlds being taken away. My vanilla life here and my slave life with you are really and truly one and the same. That was, and is, a most beautiful feeling for me.

RESPONSE TO "ESTABLISHING PROTOCOL"

Dear Sir,

I just finished reading one of the posts on that online forum you had asked me to read—the journal entry about how to establish a protocol. As you asked, I will offer my thoughts after reading this post.

In general, the post made me excited as the basic idea of a protocol is a hot idea to me. I love the thought of knowing exactly what you want me to do and how you want me to do it, so that I am most pleasing and helpful to you. I thought it was an interesting idea that a protocol should reflect what you want out of the relationship. I suppose it is a very simple and basic idea, but one that had not really occurred to me. I just assumed that you entered a D/s relationship and protocol was a natural part of it. However, it makes sense that the protocol will reflect what exactly you want out of the relationship: strictly a service relationship, play experiences, slavery, etc.

There were many good thoughts about developing a protocol for yourself. Of course the protocol has to be your own. Borrowing ideas from others can be helpful, as other people think of things you do not, or they might have helpful suggestions about how to make protocol practical for day to day life—but ultimately it has to be about what you want. Here, of course, I really mean "what the master wants". Yes, it should be somewhat reflective of the submissive as well, which is why feedback from both is necessary. If the submissive is required to do too much by the protocol, or has to constantly do things he does not enjoy, it might become too burdensome and make him want to leave; ultimately, though, I do think the protocol is more reflective of what the owner wants out of her property. It is simply important to make sure that the slave is capable of living up to it.

For that reason, the idea of starting small and allowing the protocol to grow "organically", so that the slave is not overburdened with trying to learn huge numbers of protocol all at once, was a great idea. Also, the idea that protocol will need to adapt and change over time is another concept that I would not have considered, but it makes a lot of sense. As the relationship develops, so does the protocol. Something that once was very meaningful may cease to be so, and thus the protocol should change to reflect what is meaningful to the relationship at that time. With that being said, I would think there are some basic elements that would never change, or you would end up changing the whole dynamic of the relationship (calling you Sir, for example).

I was also very relieved when the article mentioned options for release from protocol during down time. As much as I enjoy following your orders and living up to your expectations I can see in myself that there is time needed to escape from that. I don't mean escaping from the relationship and its basic dynamic, but just escaping from all the formalities, having time to relax, not thinking or worrying about doing things exactly one way.

Those would be general comments, theoretical comments. I would say in regard to our relationship specifically, it has always been exciting and relatively easy to follow your protocol. I have not felt the need for release from your protocol, as I get that a lot in my vanilla life. If anything, I think I would enjoy being given more protocols, or at least being held to it more often when we are together. However, the most challenging thing for me thus far in terms of protocols is that sometimes it is not clear how strictly I need to follow protocols! For example, quite often it seems like we have time to relax and be together where strictly following protocol is not that important (e.g. keeping my hands behind my back, or walking behind you on the left). At other times, it will seem to me like suddenly you expect me to be doing so. This is not offered as a complaint, but as an observation. It may be that the fault is mine, and if so I would be happy to know it and correct my behavior. It may be that your expectations have not always been as clear as they need to be. Just offering that for your thought.

Of course, I do think that following a protocol will be much easier when (if ever) I am with you full time. Yes, I can follow protocol during the times we are together, but it will be much easier when I can get into the habit of doing things day in and day out as you want them to be done, rather than trying to remember "I am with Sir now and need to do X."

SAFEWORDS

I'm just going to come out and say it. I don't "do" safewords. Every so often (i.e. daily), people get into online discussions about the merits, or lack thereof, of having a safeword. I have long believed that they don't really keep anyone safe, and on the contrary, can lead to dangerous situations by providing a top with a false sense of security ("…The bottom is fine, he/she hasn't safeworded!") When I play with anyone that I don't own, all they have to say is, "That was too hard," or "I want you to stop," or "My hand is falling asleep," and depending on the arrangement we have, I will stop or adjust accordingly. If they are actually my submissive and not just a bottom, I will work with them to once again find motivation to keep enduring. I've heard this referred to as "coercing consent", though the word "coerce" has some negative connotations that I am not trying to imply in this use. It's more like helping them find the motivation to continue consenting even when it's very difficult. But, of course, if the person no longer wants to play, I stop.

It's entirely different when someone is not just bottoming to me, but as in the case of Joseph, is owned. Clear communication in plain English without code words is always my preference, but with Joseph it goes one step further. He cannot expect that I will stop just because he says something hurts or is unpleasant. In fact, that moment is likely just the starting point for my enjoyment.

It's difficult to write this in a way that doesn't come across as insane … but at the most basic level, it's all about consent. Joseph has consented to be my property, with no right to refuse orders or stop me from doing what I want; but I have in turn agreed and vowed to him that my intention is not to harm him, and I will take it seriously if he ever informs me that something is harming him, or that he sees the potential for it to do so.

Playing without safewords is something I recommend to everyone. Learn to speak up about your needs, negotiate well before you play, and give feedback before, during, and after the play. None of that requires anything other than the English language (or your shared fluent language of choice).

On the other hand, *living* without the ability to revoke consent is not something I recommend to anyone. I'd probably advise most people against it! It just so happens that it's the only way I can feel authentic in my position as an owner, and I believe that for those who are called to live this way, they neither need my encouragement to find it, nor would my discouragement dissuade them from doing so if they truly wanted to.

Living in a structured relationship without the ability to revoke consent means that Joseph can say any word as long and as loud as he wants, but I'm not going to stop unless or until I believe there is a problem. It puts all of the responsibility for what transpires in my hands, ultimately, which is where I want it. But on the flipside, it requires him to give me very good information about what's going on with him and it requires me to both *listen* and *trust* that information. This dynamic would not work with a submissive who didn't sincerely want both to please me and push himself in the process. However, just because he doesn't have a magical word that stops the action doesn't mean I ever ignore the information he gives me. Again, therein lies my trust that he does not say things frivolously, or with the motivation of trying to control the outcome.

Due to my own personal biases, the quickest way for any person to get me to stop whatever I'm doing is to indicate they are about to puke. Other ways would be displaying any sign of distressed breathing, out-of-control heart rate, dizziness that could result in falling and hurting oneself, signs of shock, panic attacks, nerve damage, and so on. Because I know the onus is on me, I am probably hyper-vigilant when it comes to picking up on these signs. This has been demonstrated by the rare instance when there has actually been an issue, and I have noticed it and asked Joseph what's wrong before he even thought to tell me.

That isn't because I'm a mind reader or Super-Dom. I just pay attention and make sure I know what's going on at all times. I trust my boy to tell me when anything out of the ordinary is going on, because he has no fear of gaining control, stopping the scene, or ruining my fun. He has long since internalized my desire for complete transparency, and accepted the ramifications of my making decisions based on what he informs me; he knows that he is not responsible (for better or worse) for the results of those decisions. I also give Joseph all the credit in the world for sincerely wanting to endure as much as he possibly can for my enjoyment, and never attempting to get me to stop just because he is uncomfortable. The boy has begged and cried and screamed and had outbursts of anger, but when push comes to shove, if I ask him bluntly, "Do you want me to stop?" he will reply that he does not. Ending my enjoyment for anything other than the fear of actual *harm* would feel like cheating to him. (Oh, how I love my boy.)

This has been our relationship from the start. I'm sure I told Joseph my view on safewords as we were getting to know one another, and he, being new enough to not even have an opinion of his own, simply accepted mine without objection. It had never been an issue between us, but like many topics within our relationship about which Joseph had defaulted to a position of complete agreement with me, I still remained curious to hear his views, after enough time had passed for him to develop them

Out of curiosity, I posted a discussion on safewords to an online Master/ slave forum. I pointed Joseph towards the discussion and instructed him to respond to it, mostly out of a desire to learn how he had come to see the topic

Dear Sir,

In your post you had asked three questions, but since you already know the answer to two (no, we don't use safewords, and no, I don't know others who do) I will respond to your other question. "Does having a safeword negate someone's status as M/s in your opinion?"

My basic response to this question is yes. Initially I had thought that it didn't, but as I started thinking through my reasons why, it occurred to me that it has to affect your status. It does not remove you from the realm of D/s or M/s but it does change your status.

A safeword is basically meant to protect the submissive so that no harm comes to him: physical, mental or emotional harm. In this sense, the safeword keeps one in the realm of D/s, in that the dominant still has ultimate control of the submissive, but respects their needs in that moment so as not to cause him harm, and thus stops the activity when the safeword is used. The submissive will still remain submissive in the relationship. He only needs the dominant to cease this activity in the moment for the sake of his well-being and their long-term relationship.

However, even that bit of control alters the status of the relationship. How can I say that I am your slave and that you are ultimately in control no matter what, if I have the ability to make you stop some activity at some time? Even if it is for the sake of not causing me harm? As you and so many others point out, it is through good communication that the slave can indicate a perceived need to stop, and the owner can assess whether or not this perceived need is correct and respond accordingly. Of course, if the slave is truly at risk for harm, the owner will want to stop or at least slow up in order to protect her property. If it is only a perceived need, the owner can continue to push the slave to do more than he thinks he can in the moment without any real risk of harm, and with ultimately greater satisfaction for both as limits are pushed. The slave's trust in his owner is thus increased by this experience.

I do see the need for the slave to be able to ask for assistance in the midst of play, and I also see the need for the owner to respect those requests and take them seriously. However, if this must be followed either as a safeword or some equivalent, then he is not really a slave. He may be a submissive or a bottom, but he has not surrendered ultimately control and authority to his owner as a slave must. In my opinion, anyway.

Your pup,
Joseph

LOVE

While out of town, spending time with my biological family, I received the following email from Joseph a few days before my return. As I have mentioned before, I am frequently the more emotive partner in my relationships, and never before more so than with Joseph. It was easy enough for me to tell him I loved him once I realized that I did … but though he returned the sentiment right away, he still seemed to have trouble saying the words without prompting. Joseph was always the "I love you too" type, and I sometimes wondered why it was so difficult for him to just *say it*, particularly because each and every one of his actions *showed it*. Then, one day, out of nowhere, he told me.

I have been thinking quite a bit recently about this whole topic of love. I am happy to say that I love you and mean it, although there are times when I wonder if I even know what "love" means. And because of that I sometimes feel bad that I cannot feel as enthusiastic about telling you how much I love you as you are about sharing your love with me.

My mind goes back to my first year in seminary when my spiritual director more or less said that I didn't know what love is, and that I had never really been loved by anyone. That caused me incredible sadness and made me very angry with him. I cried harder that night than I can ever remember crying before. Unfortunately, my mentor on staff was not really able to understand what I was going through and help me, and I was not in a position personally to go back to my spiritual director and really discuss this. But what hurt so much was that he was right, I knew he was right, and it made me feel so awful and alone.

It seems like such a simple thing that everyone knows. From our earliest days, aren't we taught what love means through example and experience? I can give you book definitions and ideas about what love is, and I have even spoken about this topic many times in church, but at times I feel as if I really have no idea what it means to say that I am in love, or love someone else. This makes me wonder what it says about me as a person.

This is not the cheery letter I wish I could write to you, but it is something that has been on my mind again as of late. I wanted you to know what is going on with me, not only because you want to know everything that is going on with me, but also because I want to make sure you know how much I care about you … even if at times saying those words may be somewhat awkward for me.

Your pup,
Joseph

BIRTHDAY KIDNAPPING

The idea to "kidnap" Joseph had been brewing for a long time. I knew from much earlier conversations that he found the fantasy hot (as did I, obviously!) and I didn't feel like it would be too extreme of an experience. But could I actually pull this off? I don't believe in doing things halfway, so I knew that if I was going to go through with it, it had to be well thought out, realistic, and scary as hell. Luckily, I have some friends who are equally intense as I am, and whom I knew would be willing to help out.

When I proposed the idea to Heather, she immediately suggested a restaurant with a huge, desolate parking lot where we could snatch Joseph. The plan started coming together, including the decoy of a birthday dinner out with just myself and Heather, and the real surprise of an actual party back at home after the abduction. For the friends that were not interested in helping conduct the kidnapping itself, there would be a party at our house with plenty of food, and the "guest of honor" arriving a little bit later in order to be tortured by all who wanted.

Joseph's retelling of the event (drawn from his scene report) is below, but I have filled in the story from my perspective to complement his and paint a fuller picture, including many details that he couldn't possibly have known.

Friday, December 3, 2010

I was really looking forward to coming over for my birthday. I knew you had something special planned from the few instructions you'd given me, but I was expecting some ass play and maybe getting my limits pushed physically and didn't have any clear idea what you might have in mind. The thought of kidnapping had idly popped into my mind, though. It occurred to me as I pulled up in the driveway at home, but then the idea completely went out of my mind. Standing in the parking lot at the restaurant, I had no idea at all. When I first heard the leaves rustling, I was expecting some animal to come out of the trees; even when I first saw Jack, I still had no idea what this guy was doing.

Pup's birthday landed on a Friday, which was perfect. I had spent several weeks ahead of time planning and orchestrating this kidnapping-slash-surprise-party; now it was time to implement it. I left work a little early and arrived at home about 6:00 to find Heather and Joseph waiting for me. I told Joseph to go get in the car, and I'd be right there. I texted our friend Jack who was to be the head kidnapper, while Heather gathered up the necessary rope, put it into her purse, and joined me in the car where Joseph was waiting obediently.

As we drove the eight minutes to our destination (yes, I had timed it!), I chatted idly about how good it would be to try a new place we'd never been before together, how Heather had told me it was good, and I hoped Joseph liked it. Throughout the drive, at each red light, I was checking my Blackberry to make sure Jack was waiting in his spot.

As we arrived at the restaurant, the parking lot was as empty as I could have hoped. Still, I drove to the far end of it where the pavement bordered nothing but woods, muttering about how I didn't want to risk a single scratch to my brand new car and it was worth the long walk to the restaurant, despite being a chilly night. If Joseph thought this was strange, he didn't mention it. Since I had just bought a new car two weeks earlier, it was the perfect excuse to park absurdly far from the entrance, up against the curb and bushes that separated the parking lot from the woods.

We got out of the car, but I hadn't gotten a text back from Jack yet and I didn't have a good reason for us all to hang out by the car. To buy time, I started messing with my blackberry and cursing at "work" for sending me emails that needed to be responded to immediately on a Friday night. Fortunately, this was completely normal for my job at the time, and both Heather and Joseph were used to us being out to dinner while I was interrupted by an email that needed immediate attention. As always, Joseph stood patiently by the car waiting to take his spot to my left when I began walking to the restaurant. I never did get a response from Jack, and I was growing more anxious about having to stall our entry to the restaurant, when out of nowhere his ninja-like figure sprang from the bushes and grabbed Joseph from behind. Jack quickly threw a hood over Joseph's head and whispered into his ear, "We can do this the easy way or the hard way. I, myself, prefer the hard way."

Faster than even I knew what was happening, Jack and Heather had my boy hogtied, and I was turning the car around so they could easily hoist him into the back. Between Jack's size and strength and Heather's rope skills, they made quick work of it. Jack is six and a half feet tall, built like a football player, and a former marine, so he was chosen for this position in part because his size gave him a great advantage over my five-foot-nine, hundred-and-sixty-pound priest. Not that I suspected Joseph would fight back at all, but the use of someone so massive would ensure he couldn't do any harm even if he tried.

As for the trunk of the car, I had specifically planned this part with my new hatchback in mind, since with the seats folded down the trunk is one with the backseat. There was no chance of suffocation, but without being able to see, Joseph surely thought he'd been tossed into an actual trunk.

When he first grabbed me, it dawned on me what was happening and I was excited. When he put me on the ground with his foot on me, however, the fear started welling up inside of me. The reality of being kidnapped was sinking in, as was the reality of not knowing what was going to happen. (Where would I be taken? Who would be playing with me? What would they do?) Being tied up and blindfolded only increased these fears, as I was put more and more at

the mercy of some stranger. Rationally, I always knew you were behind it and in control of it, but that rational thought was put very far out of my mind due to the strong emotions I was feeling.

Being lifted off the ground was another rush of fear—I could so easily be manipulated and moved around and I could do absolutely nothing about it. I was sure I was being put into some other vehicle, as I knew where your car had been, and I was carried somewhere else. Once inside, I thought perhaps it might be your car, but could have no idea for sure. Your brief words to me before driving away really helped me. I knew that whatever happened, you would be there, in control.

As we drove around, I cycled through moments of fear and moments of relative calm. At times I was fairly certain I was in your car, and at other times it seemed I had to be in somebody else's vehicle (the strange music, for one thing, confused me). I spent much of my time just trying to stay in place and not slide all around the vehicle. I knew that we might be just driving around to throw me off before going home, but I also knew by now we could be any number of places. Essentially, I had no idea where we could be.

The car ride with Joseph in the back was one of the tensest parts of the whole experience for me. Rationally, I knew he was relatively safe. I was driving at no more than thirty miles per hour around the vicinity of the restaurant and back to our neighborhood. He wasn't in danger of suffocation; he was just inches behind me in the back seat with the seats folded down flat. The probability of any kind of accident was small, and I knew I had side airbags that would deploy even if the rear sides were hit. I felt reasonably safe in my new car with nothing like a broken taillight or expired tag to draw attention, but still, my biggest fear was being pulled over by the cops. I was sure that no one had been around when we abducted him, but I couldn't know for sure if there were cameras in the parking lot, or if someone had noticed the "getaway" out of the corner of their eyes. I needed to drive around for a while to disorient Joseph so he wouldn't just assume we'd ended back at home … but damn, I wanted to get home quickly.

I played a Spanish music channel very loudly to disorient Joseph further, but I did at one point speak to him so that he'd be sure it was me in the driver's seat both literally and figuratively. I wish I could have kept silent until he was home, but I decided giving him that small comfort was not going to ruin the entire experience.

When the car finally stopped I was relatively calm until once again I felt myself lifted out of the vehicle. The reality of being "there" set in, not knowing where we were or what was going to happen next. I knew we were walking through the grass, but while I hoped we were home, I still had no real idea of where we were. The feeling of being carried around, feeling at one time as if I might fall to the ground, ignited my fear once more. Being thrown down so quickly and in such a manner seemed to bring those fears to a head.

I was glad to have the ties undone, and also glad to have you there with me, but not knowing where I was or what was going to happen made me unable to calm down. Being stripped only made me feel more exposed, and in this case more vulnerable to what might happen. It also made me cold, which was part of why I was shaking, but my continued fear didn't help either. Even with you there trying to calm me down, I just couldn't. I still cannot explain why my emotions were so strong, as part of me knew all the time that you were there and that nothing harmful was going to happen to me, but that thought could do nothing to lessen how scared I felt. For a few minutes I was able to calm my mind, but then as I heard voices and then all the footsteps coming down the stairs I was almost sure we were somewhere else. And whatever calm I had achieved vanished instantly as I had no idea who these other people were or what they may be about to do to me.

When I pulled into our driveway, Jack once again slung Joseph over his shoulder and carried him around the back yard and through the back entrance to our dungeon. Joseph had never come in that way before, so I was confident he wouldn't recognize the sounds of that gate and those doors. Once we got him inside, I took off all of his clothes, but of course left the hood over his head. He was shaking from cold and fear, and I decided to give him some alone time to mellow out while I went upstairs and worried about the mundane party details (baking instant pizzas and showing people where the cups were). After a few minutes, people started milling downstairs to observe our prisoner. Knowing Joseph's shy and introverted nature, I was excited to see how he would react to a group of people whom he couldn't identify observing, and even being part of, his torment.

You had tied me up, and that did help me some to feel secure, but whatever effect that had was countered by the presence of others watching. I was not only afraid of these other people and what they might do, but also embarrassed to be so exposed and scared in front of all them. Even you fucking me with your cock was difficult, as in the moment I experienced it as just one more way of being exposed and used in front of these people. The casual talk of the people in the background made me feel all the more embarrassed. It was both powerful and scary to be taken so casually by them, and sometimes they would make a joke or laugh, which really got to me. I feared they were laughing at me, making fun of me and my situation. I know you have said differently, but I am telling you my experience in the moment. I know there were many little things that happened, but it is all confused right now. One thing I do remember is you leaving for a moment and telling someone to "keep an eye" on me. She came over and started digging her nails into my flesh, and that about sent me over the edge. Yes it hurt, but it was more the idea of someone I didn't know doing something to me. She could obviously tell how scared I was and that amused her. I also clearly remember you asking me at one point if I wished that I had been given a safeword. I struggled with trying to answer the question, because I was so scared and overwhelmed by the experience. Part of me thought the idea of a safe word might be good, but then it occurred to me that a safe word really would not have changed a thing. I had the same ability to tell you that I needed it all to stop, but I didn't want to. A safeword would not have changed anything, and most importantly, it would not have changed the way I trust you to play with me.

As opposed to how it felt to Joseph, the party was not actually comprised of very many people. I believe it was less than ten, including him and myself, and specifically only my trusted friends—most of whom had spent significant time with Joseph and me in the past—were invited. There were perhaps seven or eight other people sitting on the sofas in our dungeon while Joseph was naked on the floor and I played with him in whatever way I wanted, including fucking his ass.

At first people casually socialized, made small talk, and laughed at my pleasure and Joseph's suffering, but as time drew on my friends became more interested in the kidnap-and-torture activities. I left the room briefly to check on the food upstairs and put Miss N in charge of him. She is a dominant and sadist who I have known for several years, and I trusted she would not do anything while I was gone. It seems silly to even need to say this. All of my friends know that Joseph is my property, and none would ever overstep their bounds as friends if tasked with watching him. Luckily, there was an understanding that some fingernails and teasing were well within the rights of a friend.

It seemed only appropriate to offer up my captive for birthday spankings to anyone who wanted to give them. Since no one knew how old Joseph was, they were allowed to guess, and give him as many as they believed him to be. Lucky for him, the boy looks much younger than the 34 years he was turning that night. Only Heather, who went last, knew his real age. I was looking forward to these birthday spankings, because up to this point no one else had ever played with or hurt my boy, with the exception of letting him try out some canes by a woman at a "Dungeon 101" night once.

I enjoy playing with my own property, of course, but it's a different experience to watch someone else have fun with what's mine. To watch him being used from an outside perspective allows me the ability to just relax and enjoy the show, rather than having to *be* the show.

I was not looking forward to "birthday spankings", though I was not really afraid of the pain of the blows. I was scared and embarrassed simply by being used by these unknown people. In some ways the spankings felt good; at least they gave my mind something else to think about other than fear. When you finally asked if I wanted the blindfold taken off, I was torn. I really wanted it off, as it would take away the last piece that was keeping the scene going and keeping me in such fear. Once that was removed, I would know where I was and who was there, but I really did not want to face the people. I felt embarrassed at how exposed and vulnerable I had been in front of them, at how scared I had been in front of them, and at how they had laughed at my predicament. So I told you that I did not want it taken off. What I really wanted was to somehow just escape the situation and go somewhere where I could feel safe again.

As if you read my mind, you took me into the red room to be by ourselves. Finally, I could let out all of my emotions and fully cry. So often during the scene I had felt so close to really crying, but restrained myself from that, as I did not want to cry that way in front of these unknown people. I needed to maintain some sense of dignity in the scene. It felt so good to finally let it all out, but mostly to just feel safe and loved again in your arms.

As for the rest of the night, there is not a lot to say. I was emotionally drained from the experience, and still somewhat embarrassed by what had happened. I was content to just be with you and feel protected by you, and so glad to be able to sleep with you in bed that night. Being able to sleep with you, feeling you next to me to keep me safe, was very needed and deeply satisfying.

The party had gone on for quite some time. I knew it was getting later, and I knew Joseph would need a good bit of recovery time. Plus, there was still birthday cake to be served to the guests and poor Joseph hadn't gotten any dinner this whole time. Worried that his body might soon crash due to the adrenaline, fear, pain, and lack of food, I asked him if he would like the blindfold removed. The unspoken words, we both knew, was that this would end the kidnapping.

I was expecting Joseph to say yes, and to be able to "give him what he wanted" in a kind gesture at the end of what had been a rather unkind night. But for his own reasons, he didn't exactly want the blindfold off right then, and he surprised me with his "No, Sir."

"Well, you should remember it doesn't much matter what you want, pup." I stated matter-of-factly as I removed the blindfold anyway. I quickly led him to the smaller room of the dungeon where we could be alone, and at this point he overflowed with all the emotions of the evening. It was a beautiful thing to have him so completely raw and naked, more so than I had ever experienced before, but it was also the scariest part of the experience for me. In all the months we had been together, I had experienced a wide range of emotions from Joseph, but I had never seen him like *this*. He was completely limp, but clinging to me with all the strength he could muster. He was crying, hard. Shaking. Sobbing. Burying himself so deep in my arms that he'd have disappeared if it were possible.

For a few brief moments, I wondered what I had done and if I had taken it too far. I had never done anything like this before to anyone; not even close. My greatest fear was that I had misjudged Joseph's ability to cope, and done something that would change our relationship forever. Perhaps even ruin it.

In fact, it did change our relationship, but only for the better. I don't want to minimize the risk it took to pull off this endeavor. It really could have gone wrong, and I was prepared to abort the entire mission at any point if it went off the rails and needed stopping. I am still somewhat amazed that I did manage to find the right balance between authentically scary and ultimately safe enough.

I don't want to imply that Joseph walked away without any lasting "scars", either. Like most of the physical marks I leave on him, the emotional marks took a couple of weeks to fully fade, but as I told him later that night, it wouldn't be long before he was looking back on the experience as the hottest, most intense, most incredible scene and fantasizing about it happening again. And I was correct. Once he got past the short period during which every date I made with him was another potential abduction and every parking lot harbored boogiemen just waiting to jump him, he was looking back on his birthday with fond memories.

TELL ME ALL YOUR THOUGHTS OF GOD...

With the holidays approaching, school was out for Joseph and we managed to once again steal some time for him to stay at home with me. Five days of blissful, uninterrupted service ... but the price to pay would be two weeks apart for Christmas and New Year.

Because he was one of the few priests in the area fluent in Spanish, Joseph was obligated to celebrate Mass for the Hispanic community every other week for a nearby parish. He could get out of all his other daily obligations because of his school break, but he could not shirk this one responsibility: nor would I have wanted him to. It was only one evening of all the days we had completely to ourselves, after all. And besides, I had never before had the opportunity to witness Joseph *be* a priest.

Sure, I knew he was one, and I had even seen him in his clerical garb a number of times, but it was a whole different experience to see him going through the rituals and ceremonies of celebrating a Mass. I had never been to a Catholic Mass before. (Hell, I haven't attended synagogue since I was thirteen years old). What I found amazing, though, was that despite the ceremony being in another language (and it not even being my religion), the service was beautiful. It is a memory that will stay with me forever.

When the hour-long service was finished, I waited for Joseph in his car while he greeted parishioners and closed up the church. It was an odd feeling of pride and reverence, sitting in the parking lot in the space "reserved for clergy" and awaiting my boy (now stripped of his vestments and simply wearing the black suit and Roman collar known as "clerics" that I've seen him in countless times) walking back to me. Once again, I felt a surge of pride as his owner, the same as I had felt when I watched him celebrate Mass. Yes, he is a priest doing the work of God, something that is more important to many people than anything else in this world ... and yet he is always *mine*. I definitely saw my boy through different eyes that night, and for the first time, the significance of who he is really hit me.

On the ride home, I teared up as Joseph asked me how I had enjoyed the Mass. For the first time, I paused to wonder if it was right for us to even *think* about him leaving his commitment to God behind to be with me. I am not a religious person at all. In fact, throughout the time I have owned Joseph, I have thought, written, and talked more about God and religion than in my entire life up to this point. Even growing up as a relatively "practicing" Jew, I didn't give much thought to matters of God. But as I have said before, I am guided by a strong sense of intuition and some sort of moral compass, for lack of a better term. I do have feelings about what is right and wrong, and I am usually told such things by what I can only describe as "The Universe" communicating to me. I ask a question—What am I to do? What is the right course of action?—

and I allow the answer to present itself to me. When it's the right answer, I just know. There is no doubt left in my mind; no wavering or uncertainty. That is my "religion", so to speak. But can I say I believe in God? I don't really know for sure. I would say it is an evolving belief and Joseph has definitely played a role in how it is evolving.

◆◆◆◆◆

The day Joseph left for Nebraska, we scheduled an online chat to check in that evening when he stopped at his halfway point hotel. After some pleasantries and catching up, we moved on to a heavy topic.

"I woke up this morning with songs from the Spanish mass in my head," I told him. "The whole thing was very beautiful to me in some strange way—strange to me because I never found Jewish services like that. I was driving into work today thinking about whether or not I believe in God, and what the real meaning of 'belief' is. What I mean is, some people seem one hundred per cent sure that God exists—or to be specific, that their God exists. I don't feel that way. I feel very much on the 'Who knows?' side. To me it's equally likely either way, yes or no. But I started wondering, whether some people choose to believe because they want to, even if they are not fully convinced. Because today a feeling just came over me that I can best describe as 'I may not be certain about anything, but I can believe it if I want to, and it's OK not to know for sure.'"

"First, I am glad that you found the Mass beautiful," he answered me. "I wasn't sure what you would think of it, and I'm pleased that it was a good experience for you. Second, I am impressed that you have those songs in your head; I cannot honestly remember what they were myself!"

He went on, "Third, because they are convinced, but what you mean by 'convinced' can be variable. Some people are one hundred per cent sure that God exists, and one hundred per cent sure about everything that a particular religion says about God. Some people are convinced that God exists, but have lots of questions about what that means. Who is he? What he is like? Is God a "he" at all? How does God want us to live? For myself, I am actually one hundred per cent sure that there is a God, and I always have a hard time understanding how other people do not understand that. Intellectually I know, but it just seems odd to me since all my life I have firmly believed that. Once you say God exists, the real question is more about what God is like. I hope that is making sense," he added.

"Sure, that makes sense," I told him. "But I am not, and may never be, at the one hundred per cent place. This is the first time in a long while I've had the thought that I might even *want* to believe in God. He may or may not exist, I don't know, but either way I wasn't interested in believing … and either way, I don't have a clue which rendition of God it would be. I don't think I could ever be Christian, because it's too counter to my instincts of being born Jewish. 'God' I can kind of wrap my head around. 'Jesus' … no."

"Well, perhaps the most important question for you is actually whether or not you want to—or can—believe in God," he replied. "The other questions will follow. But that basic question, does God exist or not, is the most important. As for why you might want to believe, some do simply out of intellectual curiosity, but most people believe because it makes a difference in their lives."

"I don't know that it would make a difference in my life," I said, "but when I think about how it might, it might help me feel more content to know that everything will turn out OK in the end. Maybe I would worry less if I believed life was in someone else's hands ... but that just goes counter to what I feel the truth really is! I do believe that either we end up where we are and who we are through random luck, or that we propel ourselves through life by our own motivation."

Then I added, "But I guess the point is, I *want* to believe there's more. It's driving me crazy trying to understand how I can be so fortunate in life to have everything I do—people who love me, health, good fortune—while other people have nothing. I want to believe that someone brought us together, as well as bringing me and Heather together. It's hard and confusing for me to believe that I just won some sort of cosmic lottery to end up where I have and with who I have."

"Well, belief in God will not answer that basic question," Joseph admitted. "Theologians have tried to answer that one forever. But belief in God can bring a lot of meaning into life, whether what is happening in life is good or bad. The irony is that usually the people who have the least, who are suffering the most, believe in God the most."

"I don't find that ironic at all," I told him. "I find that logical. People who are in those situations need comfort, and I'm sure believing in God allows them that. They can believe that even though life is rough now, they'll get their rewards later. But I get it. OK, so no amount of believing in God will tell me why I have ended up where I am in life."

"No, it won't," he said. "But believing in God can add a lot of meaning to where you have ended up in life. And going back to your initial question, one can choose to believe even if they are not one hundred per cent convinced, just like one can believe in the theory of global warming even if they are not entirely convinced. Belief does not always mean 'I know everything I can'; rather it should always be a starting point for us to examine and learn more."

I admitted that was a good analogy, but I still felt like adding, "So, I don't know. I just feel, and have felt for a while, as though someone is watching out for me in a way that could not be attributed to random chance. Is that a good enough reason to believe in God?"

"It certainly is a good enough reason to be open to the possibility and continue to explore it," Joseph pointed out.

"Well, I don't exactly know what the point of this has been," I said, "but I have been feeling abnormally grateful to God or whomever lately."

"I don't know if there has been a point to our conversation either," he told me, "other than just to reassure you that belief in God is not a bad thing, and is possible even for skeptical people. And I am always happy to talk with you about religion, God, and all that any time, Sir."

Part IV: Deeper Down the Rabbit Hole

LETTER FROM AN APPRECIATIVE OWNER

Joseph and I had been together more than six months and each day of our relationship, I grew more and more certain that I had found someone I wanted to keep forever.

My experiences with relationships have trended towards instantaneous, intense, chemistry but time and time again that attraction has fizzled out within weeks or at most a few months. Having made it this far, with things only building, gave me both great pleasure and satisfaction and terrible angst. The truth of the situation was never far from my mind. Joseph was mine, sure. But he had promised himself to me only for a set period of time and in order to change that, he'd have to go beyond anything he'd ever done before and make a decision that would drastically alter his life. For Joseph, who I knew had always followed the path of least resistance and rarely (if ever) made a difficult decision for himself that would not be met with approval by his family or religious community, I wasn't convinced he was even capable of *making* the decision even if he wanted to; even if he felt it was the best one for him.

This decision, *his* decision, his future, our future…it all became my obsession and my preoccupation. We were seven months away from when he would have to return to Nebraska for his new assignment there, and I felt as though he had grown into an extension of my self and my will. To lose him would be as unthinkable as chopping off my own arm.

Being separated for two weeks while he was away for the holidays was hard enough. With reminders of him everywhere, I wrote a letter on the eve of his arrival home.

Wednesday, January 12, 2011

Dear pup,

As I lay here in bed, drifting off to sleep, I felt compelled to write to you. I feel the soft, clean sheets under me and I think of you, and it's because of you that they are here and I'm enjoying them. I was down in the kitchen and opened up the cabinet to get a drink, and all of the glasses were neatly put away because of you. Reminders of you are everywhere I look. It makes me feel constantly loved and cared for because I know that your energy has gone into making my life better, more comfortable, more enjoyable. So thank you. And know that your service is never overlooked or unappreciated. Home is filled with reminders of my beautiful and loving boy.

See you tomorrow,
Melissa

NEEDLES

Joseph arrived back in town and started his final semester of classes. Just a few days later, I had to leave for a family gathering down South, so we were once again apart, albeit briefly. While I was away, I sent Joseph on a shopping trip to Mid-Atlantic Leather, a large Leather event that takes place in Washington, D.C. each January. A young friend of mine accompanied my boy and helped him navigate the relatively large vendor area. A pup could get overwhelmed and lost on his own there, after all.

To my delight, Joseph purchased a leather chest harness at the conference and as soon as I was back in town, I wasted no time breaking it in on him.

Scene Report: Thursday, January 20, 2011

I was excited to show you my harness. I was excited when I bought it, too. Not only was it my first harness, which is a major step for me to purchase, but of course I also really like the way it looks on me, so I was hoping that you would like it just as much. Fortunately, it led to a wonderful play session. The way you played with me hurt, obviously, but I accepted it all gladly as signs of your love, as your right to use your property, and feeling thankful that you have such control over me. This was harder to do when you had your arm inside my harness holding me down—I was completely unprepared to be whipped in that position. As a result, it was hard to stay in any "good state of mind", and I just fell into doing my best to bear up under the pain for as long as I could. In the end, though, I was surprised that you had drawn blood with your whip, as I just didn't think your play was hard enough to draw blood, and it made me feel very proud that you were able to play with me that hard. As you already know, being fucked by you feels so good. Not only is the sensation great, but knowing I am being used by you in such a way and feeling a special connection to you in that activity are even more wonderful. I felt most honored and proud that you were able to come while fucking me. I know it had nothing really to do with what I did (so that, for example, if you don't come while fucking me it isn't a failure on my part), but it just makes me very happy that you can have that experience and pleasure.

Knowing that you had needle play in mind next did not make me nervous, at least in the moment. I think that outside of the immediate situation, I tend to focus only on how hot the idea is to me, and ignore the fear and pain that it causes. I also tend to focus on the moment and leave what might happen, or what is going to happen, for when it actually does happen. That is part of my personality in general, and being with you only enhances that - I tend to let you worry about the future, not think too much about things, and just do what I am supposed to do in the moment. So even as I was getting the table ready and kneeling on the floor waiting for you to come I was not nervous. I had no real desire to look at what you had brought in, in part because I didn't want to know, but also because I enjoy not knowing what you are going to do to me next.

Once I got on the table everything seemed to change. I got immediately nervous and couldn't keep myself from shaking. As you started preparing my cock and balls with antiseptic, I couldn't help but think about needles being put into them. I tried to calm myself, but I couldn't, even after your comment about not doing anything we hadn't done before. It was then that I told you how nervous I was. I didn't know what you would do, and I was very glad that you took the time to calm me down. I was amazed at how quickly I could feel calm again once you told me to breathe and relax.

The needle play started off fine—the first needle did not hurt that bad, and my nerves remained pretty calm. But with each following needle, while the pain did not really increase that much, I got more and more nervous. By the fifth needle I was frightened and uncomfortable, getting closer to crying with each new needle you inserted. It was a great relief then to be done and have them removed. After you finished, I really did feel worn out—not tired physically so much as emotionally exhausted. After the strong emotions of the last scene, I felt spent. All I wanted to do at that moment was curl up in your arms and enjoy the feeling of being cared for.

I was unsure when you said that you weren't finished with me and hoped that I would be up for it, but I was pleasantly surprised when you said you wanted to use your cock. It felt very good, but I did my best to remember that it was not just about me, but also about your enjoyment of the activity. I held out as long as I could so that you and I could enjoy it for as long as possible. It was a great release to be allowed to come, and I felt even more worn out afterward. As I lay back in your arms I only wanted to be put to bed by you. As I said, it would be the perfect end to a great day to be used in so many ways by you, to be worn out from all your use, and then to be put to bed when the day is done.

EXPANDING HIS COMFORT ZONE

Despite everything that Joseph and I had experienced and explored, he was still new—very new—to the realm of relationships and sexual interaction. I often had to remind myself that in the body of a thirty-four-year-old man, I was easily dealing with the sexuality of a sixteen-year-old boy. I don't say this to demean him, and in fact he has been, from the first moment, an amazing lover and partner to me sexually. But his comfort with his own genitals was minimal, and he was even less so with mine.

People in the BDSM community throw around the word "training" quite a lot. There is anal training, chastity training, house-boy training, and so on. These words are used as if they have some sort of standard meaning, but that's not the case. Anyone who tries to tell you otherwise is only trying to sell you something. But Joseph and I had been doing our own type of training since the day we established our relationship. It was the only kind of training a Sir and boy really can do: training him to be *mine*.

Scene Report: Tuesday, January 25, 2011

Dear Sir,

There was one point about last night that I wanted to bring to your attention. When you told me to touch you and get you in the mood to fuck me, I was quite nervous. I really did not know what I was supposed to do. Ideas of what you might want me to do were very few, as I obviously do not have much experience in getting someone "in the mood." In fact, the nervousness I felt was tinged with a bit of fear thinking about the disappointment you might feel if I didn't figure something out and get you in the mood, even despite the "hints" you were giving me.

So, I started with what I knew, and knew that at the very least massaging your legs would make you feel good even if it didn't get you hard. The idea of kissing you had crossed my mind earlier, but I just wasn't sure if and where to do so. But in the course of massaging you the moment just seemed right, and so I started. It felt very natural to the situation, but most important I was relieved to get your words of affirmation and so I continued, first on the one leg and then on the other.

It made me feel very happy and proud that I could get you in the mood, not so much for the pleasure it would give me to get fucked by you, but because you wanted it and I was able to do it for you. Given that the task seemed so foreign to me and I was almost lost at the beginning, it made me more proud to be able to give you what you wanted. The feeling of being thrown onto my stomach by you was itself the greatest confirmation I could get about how well I did, and I rejoiced in that feeling (and what followed as well). Time to get to class. I hope you have a good afternoon.

Love you.
Joseph

◆◆◆◆◆

Joseph and I had been playing for eight months at that point, and only one or two times had he felt what he imagined "subspace" would be like. And even then, not more than a hint of it, really. All the websites, forums, blogs, and classes talked about it, but despite my best intentions, the most he ever reported was some light-headedness while playing that we attributed to endorphins.

As a sadist, it's not that my ultimate goal is to have a slave that's ecstatic or mentally orgasmic in every scene. I actually do enjoy real suffering of the type that happens when subspace doesn't set in. The kind of suffering where pain is just pain, and every stroke of the whip feels not like a miniature orgasm or burst of cosmic energy, but just like what it is: a beating. So it may come as no surprise that I've never had a problem playing with Joseph, and never cared much that he didn't go to "subspace." It's never ruined my enjoyment. Still, my biggest kink, even more than inflicting pain, is control, and the idea that I couldn't put him in that kind of state even if I wanted to had always irked me a little.

But it had begun to get worse. Instead of simply enduring, he started experiencing something quite the opposite of the peace and bliss many submissives describe during play. When I played with him even moderately hard, he began to erupt into fits of anger—banging his fists, screaming, and writhing against whatever bondage I had him in. He would curse, and after that he would become a brick wall, determined to withhold any reaction from me. We had been battling this anger for a month or so since it started really taking over; before then it was just occasional. When it became a regular occurrence, I told him explicitly to inform me if he started getting angry. I don't like surprises and as a control freak—er—dominant, I certainly don't like not knowing what's going through his head while I play with him. When this happened, I would stop what I was doing and redirect him to a place where he was mentally capable of suffering more for me happily—or if not happily, at least without fighting it. Or I might stop the scene entirely. At least that was what had happened up to that point.

Then, one Saturday, we had a pretty bad scene. A party was going on at my house, and I had told him the day before to prepare himself for a hard whipping. He has always appreciated knowing in advance if we're playing hard so he can prepare himself. I don't always tell him, as I like to keep him guessing as to what he'll endure any time we play, but I thought I was being nice by giving him the heads-up.

Saturday night came and we started playing, but the dungeon was crowded, and people were watching and having their own loud scenes just feet away. Something seemed off as I warmed him up with some flogging, and when I asked, he told me that he was already having a hard time not getting angry. Aware that his anger was already brewing, I continued flogging and soon moved on to my signal whip, one of my favorite toys. For safety, I use a removable cracker at the end of the whip so that it can be thrown away any time I play with a different person or break skin. (Joseph actually makes and attaches these for me.) The only problem is they keep falling off every time I play hard, so as I ramped up my whipping that night, the cracker flew off and I commented offhandedly that it had happened again. Since Joseph is the one who makes and attaches them, he took my comment as a personal criticism or judgment of him as a failed cracker maker, and started to become angry.

He didn't say anything at the time, so I assumed he was all right. That is, until the classic signs of his anger appeared and it was too late to stop it: he was majorly pissed. There were lots of things going on in that dungeon; it was distracting, and I just wasn't feeling it. It certainly wasn't conducive to me getting him into a better headspace, so I took him down from the cross and sat him in my lap to talk. We soon retreated to the privacy of one of my upstairs rooms to talk further about what had happened. It may not be the sexiest solution to read about, but this relationship involves a lot of talking through our problems.

We did end the night in a good place, after some conversation and other activities that put us both back in a good mood, but the whole thing had made me think about what Joseph is really capable of. Perhaps he just wasn't able to be a heavy bottom for me, even if he wanted to be. The relationship itself is so much more important than any act of play, but at the same time, both of us wanted me to be able to use him for anything I desired. *Well, that's fantasy and this is reality,* I had to remind myself. Our desire for me to be able to use him to the fullest extent didn't change what might be the truth of the matter.

After Joseph had left for his own place, I spent some time journaling and thinking about the best course of action to take. I came up with a few ideas of how to continue on in the face of this obstacle. I could hold back from playing with him so hard, and prevent the anger from developing. I could get him to that point and play through it, which was something we've never done. Or I could decide to slowly, deliberately reprogram him to let go of negative emotions and surrender to what I want to give him at all times. Of course I think I'm going to choose the crazy answer because I like a challenge.

I'm no expert at this; just a young person feeling my way through, but not doing a terrible job, and the boy is on board and fully aware and willing for me to restructure his feelings on many things to suit my preferences (assuming I can pull such a thing off). I'll take a few days to think about it and I'm going to consult a few more experienced dominants I know, but why not? I'm ambitious.

The first chance I got to put my new theory into practice was the following Friday. I don't remember us doing any heavy play in the six days between the party and the next time. We were at a large local BDSM event and had attended a few minutes of a class on cock and ball torture where I realized for the first time how much Joseph truly enjoyed having "my" cock in bondage. He had told me before how great it was to have his cock and balls tied tightly, but it's not an area of great interest on my part, so I'd never done much of it. Now I know not only can it be saved as a reward for him, but used to my advantage.

Later that afternoon, I took him up to my hotel room for our final hour together, got him naked, and tied up his (my) cock and balls the way I had learned in the class. I put him in a chest harness with his arms behind his back, and connected the cock bondage to it, then I had him lay face up on my bed and I did a bit of teasing to his cock before getting out some canes. He really hates the thin rubber cane in particular, so I got that one.

Before I started doing anything I explained that I wanted him to tell me how he interpreted the intensity of my strokes. We decided that on a 1-10 scale, 0 would be entirely pleasurable, and 1-3 would be a mixture but more on the pleasure side with a twinge of pain. A four would be the border between pleasurable and painful. Five would be definitely "pain", but the annoying type he could endure for a while. 6-7 would be increasingly painful, and 8-9 would be very strong pain. I told him 10 should be the worst he could imagine and I'd hope not to get up to that point. So with these instructions, I started caning him very lightly and slowly. I increased my pace but not my force, and then decreased speed and increased force. I asked him questions about where each level fell in the number scale till I had discerned the type of strokes he actually liked from the ones he could tolerate, and the ones that he hated. We had actually only made it up to about a 6 on the scale when I told him that I wanted him to take more for me. Just one to start with, and I wanted to know what number it ranked. I did a few light taps for aim and then, wham, came down at a decently hard intensity.

Joseph drew in a breath sharply and moaned, or whimpered, I'm not sure which. His whole body shook as the sensation washed over him and a red, nearly bloody welt rose instantly to the surface of the pale skin of his upper thigh. I looked him in the eyes and saw the suffering that feeds my desires. I felt my dick grow hard instantly, and stroked his face, telling him, "Good boy." He thanked me, and when he had recovered I asked him if he thought he could take another. When he said yes, I repeated the process on his other thigh, aiming to create a matching stroke. Again, I could feel his pain quite powerfully, but unlike the time when I could feel him struggling against it, this time it was is if he just allowed the sensation to go through him and then out—neither fighting nor holding onto it, just feeling the pain and allowing it to dissipate.

"You're so beautiful when you suffer for me." I told him, looking into his blue eyes that nearly melt me every time.

"Thank you, Sir," he whispered back.

I asked him if he could take another hard stroke, and he told me that he could take several more, he was sure of it. I decided to underestimate and end on a good note by telling him I was going to do two more equally hard ones in succession without recovery time. And I did ... and it was wonderful. After that, he told me he could have taken several more but of course I know he was relieved I didn't want that of him.

I rolled him onto his side and untied his arms and cock and balls from all of their bondage. He had four beautiful marks on his thighs to prove just how hard I had hit him, and the only emotions I could sense were peace, love, and happiness at being used the way he is meant to be and wants to be.

We parted ways that evening happier than I can remember being after a pain scene in a long while. I was hopefully optimistic of more to come. Little did I know my next opportunity would be just two nights later.

◆◆◆◆◆

Joseph was not supposed to be able to come back to the conference after Friday because there are only so many hours in the day and he's got to focus on schoolwork and thesis writing and all of that important stuff. But on Sunday evening he admitted he was tempted, even though he had to be up early Monday for class, and I am the queen of rationalization. *The event doesn't happen every weekend, it'll be OK to come out. Just for a little while.* I knew he wouldn't have even mentioned the idea if his schoolwork were not already completed. Joseph agreed that he could spare an hour and a half and since I hadn't expected him to be free at all, I was thrilled. Even more so because I had bought a long awaited new whip that afternoon in the vendor area.

I have become very good at using my signal whip and decided a while back to move up to a snake whip, a bit longer, a bit more difficult. So I was anxious to try it out on him. But after we spoke a little I knew he was tired and not up for anything intense so I decided to do something he always loves: rope bondage. We went into the dungeon and there was one piece of equipment free: a suspension frame, just our luck! I tied him up nicely and suspended him face down a few feet off the ground. It was relaxing and nice and he loved it except there was this woman being beaten bloody a few feet away and the sounds of her screams ranged from distracting to annoying to laughable. I guess we tuned it out for the most part though. I put him up, I let him dangle, I kissed him a bit, and then I took him down.

With 30 minutes left until I had to release him back into the wild and the space plenty large, I decided to test out my new whip. It's only a 4-foot (same as my old one) but the difference in style between signal and snake whips gives this one about 12 extra inches. It doesn't sound like a lot but it feels like a massive difference when you throw it. I'm sure I'll get used to it.

I positioned Joseph under the frame, facing the wall, but not bound or holding onto anything. I reminded him of the 1-10 scale we'd come up with the other day and told him to raise his hand if anything felt above a 5. This seemed like a good idea since it was so loud in the dungeon and I felt so far away with the extra foot between us. My goal was to start practicing throwing the new whip but very lightly, just like I did with my first one when I was learning. No point in using force if you aren't sure where it's going to land or how it's going to act. So I threw the whip from a far distance and inched my way closer to where it was barely touching his back. Then a little more and a little more. Once in a while I would get a good, harder, hit and he would raise his hand but for the most part he stood still and reacted mildly to the sensations.

I went up to talk with him and ask how he liked my new whip. He said it "felt good" but when I asked for further comparison between the new and old one he wasn't able to provide it. So I said I would bring out my old whip for a minute so he could compare side by side. Note that Joseph does *not* like my whip. He has told me as much. He doesn't like it, it scares him, and it just plain hurts. So when I said I was going to use it on him I saw a definite change in his face.

It seemed as thought he might protest but only for a slight moment, then just acceptance. "Yes Sir," he said, as always. I knew something was different so I prompted him to tell me what it was. I asked if the idea of me using the other whip made him angry, as that has been the main emotion on my radar with him recently. He said it did not and I believed him, but still something was off. I reassured him that I really wasn't bringing it out to hurt him, but just to give a side by side comparison to the new whip so that he could give good feedback.

After a couple of minutes of using my old whip I approached him again to ask what he thought. He told me that the new one, though it could hurt at times, tended to feel better, less intense, and less stingy than the old one. He said the range of intensity was more in the 1-4 range whereas the old one just plain hurt all the time and stung significantly even on the lighter strokes. All good information to know, and I thanked him for it. I also told him that I appreciated his ability to accept what was going to happen without getting emotional or upset or especially, angry.

After this we sat together for a few more minutes but that was all the time we had. I'd committed to let the boy go at 11:00 so he could get back to his place and sleep enough for his early morning. After two good scenes in a row, I was feeling very positive and couldn't wait for more. Luckily, Monday is our normal day together, so I wouldn't have to wait long.

◆◆◆◆◆

Joseph always came over to serve on Monday evenings and I would cook dinner for him and Heather, we'd watch some TV, and then I would play with him. He had to be leaving at ten, so we made the most of our time. That Monday I was off work for President's day and we were coming home from (and coming down from) the large event, so it gave us more time together than usual. I could never complain about that! I grilled salmon for dinner, and Heather, who was suffering from the "con crud" (a term for any kind of communicable disease, normally a cough or cold, that gets passed around at conventions) ended up falling asleep early.

After a great massage and dinner, I took my pup downstairs to our own dungeon. It was not as fancy as what you'd find at an event, but pretty amazing for something in a house. I'm not one to do much planning of scenes in advance; with a few exceptions, everything I do in play is just because it feels right to do in the moment. This night, I decided to try a few new things that I thought my boy would like. Given our recent struggles with his anger and our even more recent progress on that front, it was my intention and desire to give him an enjoyable experience. To do that, I could always stick with the standard activities that I knew he loved but something pushed me to try something different and take a chance on the result.

I told Joseph to stand under the bondage frame while I clipped up two suspension cuffs to the eyebolts on either side of the top beam. He obediently held his arms behind his back, in their proper place, until I removed them one at a time to buckle into the wrist cuffs. It is such a small detail that he kept his left hand behind his back while I buckled in his right, but such things don't go unnoticed either. I grabbed my new blindfold, one I had been eyeing for ages and finally purchased at the conference that weekend, and adjusted the Velcro straps around his head. The new blindfold is super-heavy-duty and Joseph looked like an alien or insect, but he certainly couldn't see anything.

Next I utilized the cock and ball ties that I had learned on Friday, but this time with the twist of adding some weight. I don't actually own any ball weights, so I improvised with my large steel butt plug that conveniently has a handle on the end. I tied the excess rope from his cock and balls around the handle of the plug. It might have weighed about eight ounces: much less than I knew he was used to from his own self-experimentation with ball stretching. Then I added a metal carabineer and some metal chain for a bit more weight. All of this I did slowly and gradually, listening to my slave moan in pleasure as I worked. When the genitals were the way I wanted, I moved on to the nipples.

His right nipple had been pierced six months prior, so I'd mostly left it alone since then. This was the first time I dared use nipple clamps, but from his reaction, he was more than ready for them. As he stood and I added one accessory after another, I felt the boy slip away from the here and now that he always seems so present in when we play, and could only imagine he was having a good time. He deserves a good time, but then again so do I!

I went for a thick wooden cane (on the thuddy side of things as canes go) and started tapping his ass lightly and rhythmically. He only moaned more and breathed heavier; there was not the slightest indication of pain coming from him. To my surprise he stuck his ass out towards me as if to invite each stroke of the cane, and I continued hitting him with increasing force, but didn't go above what I would have imagined a 5 would be on our newly created scale.

My dick was starting to get hard, though, and my mind was wondering if I could get more out of him by mixing the caning with some fucking. I have tried things like this before, but he reports back that the pain overrides anything pleasurable from other sensations. But something felt different this time, so I put on a glove, lubed up my hand, whacked him hard with the cane, and immediately shoved my finger into his ass before he could release a response to the cane stroke.

With one finger I probed his ass, teasing him because he knows as well as I do that it could easily accommodate my entire fist, but somehow one finger still feels like a treat. That's my boy: both willing to take as much as I give, and grateful for however little.

I gave him a few moments of fingering that made him squirm, moan, and sigh, before abruptly pulling out and starting with the cane again, this time harder. With each stroke, I saw something I've never seen from him before. He seemed to push into me, into the cane, into everything. His body was dropping forward, ass pushed back towards me and arms dangling in their suspension cuffs from the frame above him. It was as if he went limp, but not in a bad way. Limp like putty, like clay to be made into whatever I wanted.

The energy coming off him in waves cried "Please, Sir, more, Sir, please Sir, give me more!" even though he was silent other than the increasingly heavy breathing. He sounded like he was nearing orgasm, and his body danced in its restraints, its nipple clamps, its ball weights. He moved like a lover begging for more, not a slave begging for mercy, even though I was hitting him harder than I had in a long time. It was simply incredible.

My dick was getting harder by the minute, and I decided that if I was going to really fuck him he'd have to take some even harder strokes first. I slipped on my harness, put a rubber on my cock, and added more lube to my still gloved left hand. With the cane in my right hand I methodically beat him with increasing pressure and force and observed his reactions, which were still positive. Any other day these strokes would be earning a 7 or 8 on his pain scale, but in this moment I could only imagine they felt dulled compared to the overwhelming pleasure he was feeling. I was happy—so extremely happy—to finally have been able to make my slave feel this way.

I hit him a few final hard times on the ass with my cane and then plunged into him with my silicone cock. His pleasure only heightened as I fucked him silly—grabbing onto his collar, pulling his head back towards me so I could bite his neck, then letting him fall forward again to the position he'd established for himself as a limp body. He barely stood on shaking legs, arms clinging to the suspension cuffs and ass pushed in my direction as though he were offering it to me. Because he was. Even though no words were spoken, I could hear it in every breath and moan, him telling me he is mine.

When I was so aroused that I couldn't stand it anymore, I discarded the nipple clamps and untied his cock and balls. I freed his hands from the cuffs, but left the blindfold on. Quickly tossing my cock and harness aside, I spun him around, told him to kneel, then pulled him onto the floor on top of me and pressed his face into my own real dick. I knew I would eventually come, but not right then. Instead, I flipped him over, pounced on top, pinned him down between my legs, and tore off the blindfold to look into his peaceful eyes. Like so many times before (yet so rarely from a session such as this) I looked straight into his penetrating deep blue eyes and saw nothing but pure happiness and contentment.

Later on, Joseph told me he thinks he may have experienced "subspace" for the first time. He said he finally understood why people talk about it like it's a good thing; why people would enjoy all of this stuff. I had figured as much and I was thrilled. It's not that I wanted to let him escape to happy-land all the time and never truly hurt him again, but I loved the idea of being in control of that too. For the next few months, all of our play went back to being hard on him in one way or another except for those scenes that he inherently likes, consisting of bondage only or light spanking. But it was a great thought to know that when I wanted, I had the ability to make him suffer so badly he couldn't stand it and then send him to a place of ecstasy, all at my whim.

IN HIS OWN WORDS

Somewhere around the nine-month-mark in our relationship, Joseph and I realized that his scene reports were becoming more and more repetitive. There wasn't much new information, and by now I basically knew what he was thinking and feeling to my own satisfaction. He had also become increasingly good about communicating with me during and after scenes, so there was less of a need for him to write about it. Instead, we focused on occasional journal entries, which covered a variety of important topics, the most significant of which are included below.

Journal Entry: Wednesday, February 23, 2011

In The Cage

Experiences with my counselor and spiritual director each of the last two days had left me in a vulnerable and confused place. I always have productive sessions with them, but talking about deep-seated and emotional issues is not easy for me. Most especially, it was frighteningly clear that I needed to make a decision about my future.

As I recovered from the emotional shock of meeting with my director, I felt that perhaps the best solution was to stay at my place and enjoy a quiet evening, so that I would be well-rested and well-prepared for time with Sir later. This was my intention until I began chatting with Sir later in the afternoon. As I told her about how I was feeling, and gave voice in my mind about my need to feel secure amidst the turmoil I was feeling, the thought suddenly popped into my head about having some time in Sir's cage. It has been a while since I spent time there, and it occurred to me that being in her cage would really help me feel safe and secure and calm. We made arrangements for this, and I found myself excited to think of how wonderful it would be for both of us to know that I was locked in there, waiting for her to come home.

I arrived home a little ahead of schedule, wanting to make sure everything was ready so that I could spend as much time as possible locked up. Unfortunately, as soon as I arrived home I had to attend to Shadow, who had been home alone all day, had gotten himself trapped inside one of the bedrooms, and had an accident. As much as I just wanted to run down to the dungeon and throw myself into the cage, I knew there were other things needing to be done, and I could not help but want to be helpful to Sir.

Once Shadow came back and the cage was set up, another pang of guilt hit me. I knew he had made a mess in the bedroom, and I felt bad not doing anything about it and leaving it for Sir, but I also knew that cleaning was not why I was there, and that Sir would want me to care for myself in her cage. I texted her to try and get some direction, and while I waited for her response I continued doing little things around the house. Finally it dawned on me that she was at an appointment and would not get my texts for a while anyway, so a decision needed to be made. Since I was even more stressed now, I happily crawled into her cage, hoping that Sir would understand that I was not just blowing off service.

Laying on my back in the cage, my first response was to check and make sure everything was secure. It was; I would not get out until Sir came and let me out. I felt the bars with my hands and feet, and let the feeling of being locked in wash over me. As it did, I felt a sudden wave of emotion come back from my morning appointment. After a few tears flowed, I felt a sense of peace and calm. I didn't have to worry about anything. I was locked in Sir's cage, and that was now my world; nothing outside of it really mattered. I listened to some relaxing music on Sir's iPod and let myself doze off while the minutes ticked away. Part of me never wanted to leave. I was content to let the cage be my world - safe, secure, understandable - with Sir there to watch over me and protect me.

I was enjoying this experience when I heard the sound of footsteps above, so I turned off my music and waited patiently for her to come. I didn't know if she would come right away, or how long she would let me stay there, and it didn't matter to me. I was hers, and I was right where she wanted me to be until she let me leave. When she came into the dungeon at last, knelt on the floor by the cage, and grabbed my nipple through the bars, all I could do was smile - and feel completely happy.

◆◆◆◆◆

Journal Entry: Wednesday, March 2, 2011
A Day In The Life

The more that I have thought about the differences between what I thought slavery would be like when I first started versus how I view it now after months of real service to Sir, the more I realize that I had no clear concept of what a normal day as a slave would be like when I first began. I guess that shouldn't surprise me, as I was not intending to be a slave when I started—I was just looking to play with someone, and never really considered my life going beyond that. So in the beginning all I had were general ideas of how slaves were treated by their owners.

For example, I would have expected the slave's day to be strictly regimented (7:00 a.m. - wake up; 7:00-7:30 showering and getting dressed; 7:30-8:00 breakfast; 8:00 leave for work, etc.). I would have expected the slave to be denied any real comforts (sleeping on a mat rather than a bed, no snacks between meals). I would have expected the slave's activities to be always directed to the comfort, pleasure, good of the owner with very little time devoted to himself or his own wants. I would have expected the owner to treat the slave harshly, or at least coldly with little or no real affection or intimacy. In short, I had a very crude and unrealistic idea of what it was like to be a slave, and did not realize that the idealized fantasy view of slavery would be hard to actually accomplish in real life.

These days, my idea of a normal day as a slave with Sir would be similar in some ways, but with a completely different tone. My life would be controlled in many, if not all ways, but that control would not always be so strict or rigid. I would have a list of chores for the day—things to do around the house, work, things to do to care for myself such as exercise—and a certain period of time in which to accomplish these tasks, but it would not necessarily be regimented. I could determine the order or exact time of doing any one thing. I would be denied many of the comforts of life, but not to that extreme - for example sitting on furniture except for what was specifically allowed by Sir. Food and clothing, would be controlled in a general kind of way (Sir has provided what she likes and I can choose from among them unless told specifically what to eat or wear). My relationship with Sir would be a relationship of power exchange, and that could be expressed differently on any given day, but underneath it is always a relationship of love and care for one another. My focus would always be primarily upon serving my owner, but she would know that effective management of her property demands a certain amount of time and care for myself, and so "down time" would be allotted by her in order to keep me in good condition.

In short, the current idea I have of slavery is one that is much more realistic, and much more fulfilling. It is not some idealized notion of being a "worthless slave"—which would be almost impossible to actually live for any period of time—but a real relationship where I belong to my Sir completely, serve her as best as I can in every way, and in return she does her best for her property as well.

◆◆◆◆◆

Journal Entry: Wednesday, March 9, 2011

Stress
A recent post on the Internet posed the following question: "Whatever your

starting point before your enslavement, how do slaves process stress now? Better? Worse? About the same? Has it changed differently in different areas?" The question immediately resonated with me. I have always been fairly good at dealing with stress, both in the past and now, and it has not caused me to react in negative or destructive ways. In the past, I would have found ways to relieve stress on my own such as exercise, going out for a walk, or listening to music. Only on occasion, and only to a small extent, would I confide in other people as a way to relieve stress.

However, what really helps relieve my stress now is spending time with Sir. As that realization dawned on me, it struck me as one way in which I have become dependent upon her. When we are together, whatever stress or anxiety or anger I have been feeling goes away. Whether that is due to the stress being relieved, or simply forgetting about it for a while, the fact remains that I look to Sir a great deal to help me relieve my stress. While this is a wonderful thing, it does perhaps mean that I am less able to relieve stress on my own, which makes me more dependent upon Sir.

I am not sure if this is better or worse, but it certainly is different. In many ways it is surprising that I had not thought of this before, although I know that subconsciously I was aware of it. I think back to last week when I wanted time in the cage to help me recover from a bad day, and it is clear that my time with Sir helps me overcome stress in ways that I cannot do for myself. I do enjoy the feeling of dependence it gives me upon Sir, as well as knowing that she has that kind of power over me. In a small way, however, it raises a caution in my mind about my loss of independence. Is it a good thing to lose any of my ability to deal with stress on my own? To what extent would that be a good idea? What happens if I am feeling stressed and Sir is unable to relieve it (for example, if she is away, or is dealing with her own issues and cannot meet mine at the moment)? This is a real concern, but a small one. The overwhelming feeling this gives me is one of security knowing that Sir is there to help me in so many ways.

LOSING IT

The following piece is the last of Joseph's journal entries before the practice fell by the wayside. I felt it was important enough to separate out from the others because of the weight of this topic in our lives.

Joseph came to me as the ultimate virgin. He had not even had as much as a casual girlfriend growing up. In fact his relationships with others—male, female, platonic, friends—had been limited, to say the least. Early in our relationship even ejaculating was a limit he was not willing to sacrifice, and so we avoided all sexual contact other than me using his ass.

After a short while, ejaculation became something he was comfortable with, as long as it was only hands or toys inducing an orgasm. Other forms of sexual contact were still off the table. After a little while longer, he became comfortable with the idea of both giving and receiving oral sex, touching my "dick", and making me come. By that point, as I have mentioned before, everything except penile-vaginal penetration was free for my taking, if I desired it.

With my physical attraction to Joseph being as intense as it was, I certainly desired to use him in every way possible; but I can honestly say that I could have continued with all of that indefinitely and been completely satisfied without ever having "sex" of the (apparently) biblical variety, because my sexual gratification doesn't rely on having a cock inside of me. I also want to reiterate that I never pushed Joseph to drop any of these sexual limits. Each and every time he decided to do so, it was because he felt compelled to offer those things up to me. I am very happy we did it this way, because I do know that each and every part of himself he gave to me (not just sexually but as a whole) was given because he *wanted* to give it. Each time a former limit was revoked, it was because the thought of limiting my use of him felt unappealing and wrong.

So around the ten-month mark of being together, Joseph thought more and more about giving up the final barrier to my use of his body—his "virginity". I hate using the term because it's such a heteronormative paradigm. I mean, really? We're talking about a boy who had been regularly fucked in the ass, received hand jobs, blow jobs, had performed oral sex on me, and gotten me off in various other ways. We fucked like bunnies and more than that, we *made love* on a regular basis. So to claim he was still a virgin because his peepee had never entered my weewee? It seemed ludicrous to me … but according to everything Joseph grew up being taught, that was what really mattered, so I wasn't going to take it from him until he was certain it was something he wanted to give.

Joseph had already come to the decision that he wanted to offer it to me, but it took several months and lots of thought on my part before I concluded that it would be the right thing to do. Assigning Joseph this journal topic was just one exercise in my consideration of his offer.

Journal Entry: Friday, April 1, 2011

What would it mean to me to lose my virginity?

Other than actually getting publicly involved in the BDSM scene, this is probably the biggest step that I could take in my relationship to Sir. For me, losing my virginity is almost like taking on a different identity. I will no longer be "a virgin". This does not mean I will be a better or worse person for having done so, but it does mean that I will forevermore never again be a virgin. Although I just wrote that this is not necessarily better or worse, I cannot help but feel in some ways that it will be a bad thing. It does not mean that I don't want to go through with this, but given my upbringing in the Catholic faith and my life as a priest, being a virgin has always been seen as a very good thing, and so losing that will somehow be less than the ideal. However, if seen from a different perspective, having that experience can also be a good thing for my work, in terms of relating to other people and the experiences they have in life. So with that as the background, for me personally, losing my virginity would be a big step.

However, the most powerful and important aspect is what it would mean in terms of my relationship to Sir. I have served Sir in many different capacities, and all of them are fulfilling for me as a slave. Losing my virginity would mean one last boundary removed in my service to her. This is not to say that she would use me in that way very often, but knowing that she has, and could again in the future, would mean that there would be virtually no way in which she could not use me if she wanted. Being that open and available for her use is an amazing feeling for me as a slave.

Losing my virginity would also create a unique and special bond between Sir and me. No matter what would happen in the future, we would always have the knowledge that she was the one who took my virginity. Not to overly romanticize it, but having said how important virginity is to me personally, having that memory would be very special. My hope would be that sharing something that powerful would strengthen and deepen the special and unique relationship we already share.

OUT OF BODY EXPERIENCE

On the rare occasion that we played in a new and different way and I felt there was something worth reporting, Joseph still composed scene reports. As someone who doesn't experience "subspace" or any altered state on a regular basis, Joseph's description of a very detached feeling while we played one night intrigued me, and I requested a more detailed account of it from him. He wrote:

Once the blindfold went on my world began to shrink. I knew where I was, and from the sounds I heard I could imagine what was going on around me, but I soon began to have a strange experience that my world was reduced to a very few sensations. I could feel only a few things (where my hands, feet, etc. were secured in place). I could hear only a few sounds (mostly you typing and the sound of silverware on the plate). That was my world.

Being fed was like a strange invasion—suddenly something was put into my mouth. It was different, yet somehow fun, to experience the taste when you don't know what exactly you are eating. I began to have the experience not so much of being fed or being cared for, but only of doing what you wanted. I was eating because you wanted me to eat; it was my way of serving you at the time. I was chewing because you wanted me to chew. As that reality sank in, my other thoughts and emotions seemed to flee. I was no longer "Joseph" or "your pup", but only a slave, there to do whatever you wanted. I felt at that moment that whatever you had asked I would have immediately done with no second thoughts. If you had asked me to walk back to my apartment dressed like that, I would have started walking.

This feeling of "detachment" continued as long as I wore the blindfold. You told me to finish the plate, so I did, as quickly as I could. You had me bend over to be used as your footstool and I did. There were no thoughts about why, or wishing I could be used in another way, or wondering what was next. You said it and I did it. Anything else connected to my "personality" was in a different place in my brain, still aware of what was happening to me but no longer in control of it.

When you had me lay down and were hitting me, I could feel the blows and sometimes a bit of pain, but it was as if I couldn't really react unless you told me to. Only the stronger blows brought about any kind of response. It was much the same when you put the vibrator inside of my ass. It felt pleasurable, but there was no feeling of "enjoying it." The part of me that would enjoy it wasn't there. I only felt a very nice sensation. Soon it almost felt that I was being overloaded with sensation: the vibrator inside of me, the pain of the clothespins on my nipples, the condom you put on your cock, the other ways you were touching me. At one point the sensation was just so intense I couldn't stop myself from squirming around. You were completely manipulating my body, controlling it. The same was true when I finally came. It was not so much that "I came", but it really was you who made my body orgasm.

Only once you removed the blindfold did I start to come back to myself. The experience of last night was positive, definitely. I cannot say it was "enjoyable", at least in any subjective way, since the part of me that would enjoy something like that wasn't there to experience it. Honestly, though, I think I am still coming to terms with what exactly happened - not in any negative sense, mind you. I think I can look back and say that it was a great experience to have been used as your object, to have been so detached and such a complete slave.

ANOTHER PERMANENT MARK

From the point when Joseph and I first began to refer to him as my property, we both had agreed that permanent marks on his body were my jurisdiction. Not that he ever would have had the desire to pierce or tattoo himself, but the rules we established officially prohibited that, as well as permitted me to make any changes to his appearance I liked. We started with the nipple piercing, which turned out to be quite an asset to his appearance (and our play). As we got closer to the year mark, the opportunity arose to get Joseph marked with his first tattoo.

Back in August of 2010 I had discovered a tattoo shop that celebrated each Friday the 13th with a special set of thirteen-dollar tattoos. Each tattoo was a small image containing the number thirteen, and to get the $13 special you had to choose from one of the images offered on that day. No other choices are given, and no other tattoos were performed.

When I first learned of this arrangement, I went out to get a tattoo for myself. Since I already had several, the idea of a small "meaningless" one didn't bother me. Joseph was back in Nebraska at the time, and I had no other friends who wanted one, so I went alone as an adventure. As it turned out, Friday the 13th tattoos were more popular than I had expected. I took a number and got in line for my turn, but hours went by before they even got close to calling my number. Luckily, the event was being held at a restaurant instead of a regular tattoo shop, so there was food, entertainment, and (most importantly) free Wi-Fi. I used my iPod to pick up Internet and was happy to find Joseph online as the night dragged on.

Finally, around 10 p.m. my number was called, and I was allowed upstairs to the tattooing area. I finally got to see the artwork choices, as they had not been displayed in the main waiting area beforehand. At the time, our relationship was just getting started, but as I looked over the tattoo options, I noticed one in particular that I felt could have meaning to me amongst all of the other silly symbols. There, between a butterfly and a flower, stood a sacred heart: one of the most recognizable symbols of Catholicism. I debated getting it, unsure if I should, being that I can't call the religion my own. The shop assistant came to take my ID and money, telling me I only had a couple of minutes left to decide on my design. I quickly typed up a message to Joseph.

"Getting tattooed, finally! Which one do I get? Flower or Sacred Heart?"

"Sacred Heart." The response came back instantaneously. So only two months after meeting him, and before I marked his body with any reminders of me, I marked my own with a beautiful reminder of him.

Fast forward to April 13th, 2011. Once again, it was a Friday. This time, Joseph was in town. I had planned in advance to skip work and take him back to the shop so that he could get his first tattoo: a replica of the same sacred heart I had gotten.

Though Joseph really didn't want a tattoo for his own sake and was not looking forward to the pain of it, he was definitely excited to experience the profound sense of ownership as his body was permanently altered at my command. We had every reason to believe that the shop would once again offer the sacred heart in their collection of Friday the 13th flash, but we were disappointed to learn that it was not one of the several dozens of designs being offered this time around.

Regardless, we were not going to change our plans and after looking through all of the choices, I decided on a small flower that I would get on my left upper thigh and Joseph would get on his right hip. I chose a spot on him that would show when wearing a jock strap (my favorite form of underwear for obvious, ass-accessible reasons). The details of the day were tedious and do not warrant recounting, but the important part is that by the end of it, Joseph was no longer a tattoo virgin. We had our first matching marks, which made us both exceedingly happy.

24/7 TEST DRIVE

From as early on in the relationship as we knew things were "serious", Joseph and I had been trying to plan for some real "24/7" time together. We both realized that if he were going to make the decision to leave the priesthood and be my slave "for real", it wouldn't be the same as spending a day or two with me. Up to this point, the only uninterrupted time we had managed was what we could steal between school breaks. Each time Joseph managed to come home for a few days or more at a time, we found the whole arrangement feeling more and more natural.

Our opportunity for a true test-drive of the dynamic came in the month of May, a break between the spring and summer semesters of class. Joseph told his family in Nebraska he would be staying close to the library to work on his thesis. This wasn't a complete lie, since his main responsibility while at home during this time was to continue writing it. And he told Father Patrick that he was "going home" (assumedly to Nebraska), even though that statement wasn't technically false either. My boy was indeed coming home.

Our time together was originally supposed to be the entire month of May, but life always seems to find a way to mess up the best laid of plans, and some outside family obligations popped up at the last minute. I was upset, but still grateful for the time we would get. So from May 6th through 15th, Joseph and I had the longest period of uninterrupted service and ownership we had yet experienced. I'm sure that we did all kinds of delicious things that I could write about, but the real important part is that we lived our everyday lives. We shared the same roof and sometimes the same bed, saw each other each morning and night between my job, and Joseph learned that my everyday routine was one he could easily see himself fitting into long-term. In fact, after returning to his place to deal with the last minute out-of-town family-visit-fiasco, he told me that the time had gone better than he would have expected (since we'd never spent so long together before), and that it only made him feel more comfortable with the idea of living at home in the future.

As soon as he was gone, I was already missing him. But we were luckily only "apart" (of course, still seeing each other every couple of days and not truly apart) for a short time before getting to experience another relatively long stint of time together- a trip I had been looking forward to for months that turned out to be better than I imagined it could be.

♦♦♦♦♦

Every Memorial Day, a group of close friends (better known as "family") get together in Pittsburgh for a four day house-party that consists of a lot of eating, socializing, and of course playing and sex. I had been hoping to take

Joseph along with me to this or another "family" event for quite some time, but given his discomfort with large groups and new people, I wasn't sure how he would fit in, or if he would enjoy himself. With Memorial Day available, I decided to just go for it, and we drove the five hours out to Pittsburgh to spend five days and nights together. Despite his recent longer stay with me, the opportunity to spend so much uninterrupted time together was still truly rare and special.

Earlier in our relationship we had assumed Joseph would need to make a decision whether or not to leave the priesthood before he graduated school, but I determined that it was too much pressure too soon. I suggested that he go back to Nebraska as planned at the end of July and spend the next five months in his new life, figuring out if he wanted to remain there or return. That way, if he decided he did want to request a release from his duties as priest, giving the diocese notice in January would allow them to assign someone new to his position for the following July rather than interrupting the cycle.

So with two months left, which felt unbearably short, we were fortunate enough to get some more time living in our own world where only the fact that he was my slave and I was his owner mattered. The weekend turned out to be such an experience that as exhausted as I was upon our return from Pittsburgh, I couldn't contain the excitement and wrote about it.

Sunday, May 29, 2010:

We left home at 2pm, on schedule and had an easy drive out to Pittsburgh. We split the driving and I fell asleep for the last hour or so. When we arrived, we had some great dinner at one of the host's houses, and then went off to where we were staying, nearby, with a couple of pit stops at some sketchy liquor stores for beer and wine requested for the next night's dinner.

Thursday we woke up and had no formal plans until 7:30 p.m., so I started trying to figure out what we should do. I explored local options via the Internet on my phone and finally discovered Kennywood, a nearby amusement park. They even sold discounted tickets at the supermarket, and since pup and I both claim to enjoy amusement parks, we ventured off. I have never been to a park with him before, so I wasn't sure what to expect, especially as the pup is not much of a thrill-seeker when it comes to social activities. But boy, was he a pro at roller coasters! He rocked that amusement park and navigated us around, making sure we got to ride everything we wanted. He kept me entertained while we stood in line, and laughed with me when we were screaming at the few actual scary drops, or when I goofily made noises on some of the sillier rides. We split some traditional amusement park food and got soaked in the afternoon's ten-minute-long rainstorm. We had a really wonderful time.

We did have to stop at the electronic store to see about getting a new power cord for my GPS, because my car charger died. They didn't have the right kind, so for the rest of the weekend my "GPS" was "a boy and a map" ... which turns out is really all you need.

The dinner went very well; Pup retreated upstairs for a bit to get away from all the noise, but later he joined me to drive over to the other host's house. I whipped him outside - which I haven't done in a while and it was great - and then we got into the hot tub and made googly eyes at each other until we were so tired we had to drag ourselves out to sleep. Regrettably, there were no marks from the whip even though I used it pretty hard. Saturday morning was a trip to the Milkshake Factory where we split a red velvet milkshake for breakfast, then we made our way over to The Strip District of Pittsburgh and literally ate our way from one end to the other, picking up a mung bean pancake, calamari, baklava, and buckeyes.

That night was a Mediterranean-themed dinner, but more importantly, I told the pup that I wanted to remedy the "no marks" situation from the night before. I told him I was going to cane him until it left some good marks, no matter how much it took. My boy was really worn out after this, physically and emotionally, so we went inside and just sat for a bit before I decided it was time to leave. Once we were home and in bed, I decided I wanted to be inside of him so I stuck some fingers into his ass and began thrusting.
Normally, he is more than ready to be fucked at any time, and this night was no exception on a physical level, but mentally he was already three-quarters of the way to sleep, and really wasn't into the idea of being penetrated. That only made it more exciting for me, and I continued adding fingers and gripped his cock with my other hand, stroking until he was hard. He admitted he felt used and that he would prefer I stop. These things only made me keep going more enthusiastically.

Finally, I found myself tired as well and pulled out—also leaving his cock hard. We cuddled, and I allowed him the rare chance of sleeping next to me in the bed, because I just couldn't let go of him.

Sunday morning we woke up in time for breakfast at a third person's house— brunch, actually. It was oh-my-fucking-god-amazing. Waffles, bacon, quiche, cakes of all types, amazing coffee, I can't even name everything. We sat around eating and having great conversation which lasted hours, moved to another house and visited some more, and finally it was time to go. Once home, we ate dinner and watched a little TV, and then I broke the news to him.

Well, he'd sort of guessed it already. This weekend I had single-tailed and caned him already—two things I really enjoy and he dislikes. I decided we needed to go for a trifecta of evil by doing needles, his absolute worst activity on a scale of hate to abhor, which only makes me want to do them more. The needle scene was amazing. I only got nine in; the tenth was too much, but to his credit it was a larger gauge than any of the previous nine, and the poor boy seems to be immune to the normal endorphin rush most people would have after nine needles. So I stopped before the tenth one was in.

It doesn't matter to me; he'd long since been sobbing by that point, which gets my dick hard so I'd gotten what I'd wanted. I removed all the needles and he even bled a little. I put Band-Aids on him, took him over to the couch, and proceeded to attack his body with my mouth. I made him come on command as a finale to this amazing five-day weekend.

A YEAR AND A NEW CONTRACT

It had been one year since Joseph and I first played, and even though he wasn't actually owned at that point, I still count the first night we played as the true start of our relationship. Even then we both felt that incredible connection, which even the passage of time has not diminished.

Joseph's departure date had been set for August 2nd. He would spend his last day at home with me before driving back to Nebraska and we would come up with an interim contract to sign at that point, which would outline how the relationship would be maintained while he was away. For now, with about two months left to fully enjoy each other and our previous contract expired, we created a new version to reflect the current status of our arrangement. The most notable difference was that one year later, all of Joseph's limits had fallen away.

On paper, he could no longer lay claim to "his" body, "his" sexuality, "his" time, "his" money, "his" free will - or anything else that might have once been his. In reality, not much changed because over the course of our relationship we had hammered out so clearly what I actually wanted to control, and to what extent. I certainly don't have the time or energy to fully micromanage every facet of his life! However, just knowing that he had officially given up all self-imposed limits on my use of him, and any choices on how to do so or not do so would rest on me, made us feel the ownership more profoundly.

I guess the obvious question at this point became whether there was still a doubt about him remaining a priest, or whether he would return to being my property for the long-term future. If I own him as I say I do (and as he will also say I do), then why can't I just demand he give up everything? The answer is basically one of my mottos: "Just because you can, doesn't mean you should."

Maybe I can make that choice for him. Maybe I am entitled to by the nature of our agreement. But I don't believe that I should … and so I won't. There were all sorts of options going through my mind about how I was capable of forcing him to stay, and in some ways he might even prefer it if I did just that. But just as every part of him I own was given freely to me by him, so too I believe this ultimate decision should be given freely as well.

◆◆◆◆◆

It's not unusual for me to write about things that have happened between myself and my boy, both in journal entries and online discussions, in a way that might give strangers the impression that our relationship is one-sided. This couldn't be further from the truth, but of course I tend to write about the things that turn me on the most, which are inherently the things he likes the least or are the most difficult for him. I don't write about the other times when things are just pleasant and lovely for him.

However, I should show a bit of balance, because it doesn't do justice to the relationship as a whole to only write about the scenes and time together that feel like a porn novel in my mind. In reality, he is a very well-cared-for and spoiled slave.

For example: The pup arrived home early today, but since I wouldn't be able to get home from work until after 7, I had him run an errand and pack up my toy bag for camp. I should say that he did an excellent job and I only had to substitute out a couple of items that were different from what he packed. For not being a mind reader, he came awfully close.

When I got home, I greeted Heather and Joseph and started pulling all sorts of leftovers out of the fridge for dinner. We're leaving for camp tomorrow, so my goal was to empty out anything that would go bad. We ended up with one pork chop, one piece of barbecued chicken, two polish sausages, five ears of corn, some green beans, some cornbread, and some fresh cupcakes I had brought home from work. Joseph, Heather, and I all sat on the sofa and watched episodes of *The Soup* while we ate. They were very funny, and when Joseph and Heather were done eating, I lounged back into Heather's lap and put my legs on Joseph so that he could massage my calves. I am always up for a massage, as those who know me are well aware; and I've been running every day for a month now with only a couple of days off, so my muscles are getting overly tight. Joseph had worked out some knots in my calves on Saturday, and they needed some more of that.

Heather eventually left, and I decided to tie Joseph up because we both enjoy it and I was feeling kind of low-energy. Bondage is one of the few things I can always count on him enjoying. Ass play is another, but even then there is that once in a blue moon where it doesn't quite feel right to him. I don't think he's never not enjoyed bondage, though.

After tying him into a chest harness with his arms behind his back and the extra rope going between his legs just for fun, I positioned Joseph on the couch and started up the DVD. (We'd been making our way slowly through Buffy the Vampire Slayer from the start because he'd never seen it.) I lay back on the opposite end of the couch, rested my foot in his crotch ... and then fed him cupcakes.

Since I wouldn't be seeing him for a week due to our camping trip, I decided to let him come. It would probably be the only time during the week he could get an orgasm, unless I felt compelled to instruct him to again while I'm away. You never know. Being as I love cock, and I especially love cock that I own, I went down on him (still tied and lying on the couch) and gave him permission to come. After that and some nipple and neck nibbling, I got him up, untied him, and sent him to get dressed and go back to his place. I reminded him how lucky and spoiled he is. It's not always about pain or suffering; not even most of the time, really. I enjoy being in control and doing whatever I want, and lucky for my boy, I'm actually a very nice person.

Part V: End In Sight

PLAY RAMPS UP AS TIME WINDS DOWN

Journal Entry: Monday, July 11, 2011

I don't like to think about the reality of it much (though of course it's never far from my mind), but tonight marks only twenty-one days left with my boy before he leaves. Neither of us wanted this, but it's life and prior commitments and we knew it when we met, and all of that crap. So maybe I was just making the best of the time we have left, or maybe I would be craving this intensity regardless, but I was definitely itching for something good tonight.

I wouldn't say we've been playing harder on a regular basis. I think it comes and goes with my energy level, and having had a mostly restful weekend helped tonight. Many evenings, especially weeknights, we just eat dinner, watch TV, cuddle, and all that icky stuff. (OK, normally there is at least some fucking, ass-fucking or fisting thrown in at a bare minimum, but that all still counts as a pretty mellow evening.)

I told him that actually I wanted to hurt him quite a lot tonight, and then asked if he had figured that might have been brewing on my mind. Sitting in my lap, the way he gulps in air, swallows, and seems to shrink into me even more when I say things like this makes my dick instantly hard. He answered yes, that it had occurred to him he was going to be in for some suffering. He's not a masochist by any stretch, but I love that he's never attempted to sway me away from using him however I want and to whatever degree. We walked down to the dungeon and I had him shed his jock and stand with his back against the St. Andrew's cross.

I put his arms up in cuffs attached to the top of the cross, and then had the idea to vet-wrap each of his legs to the legs of the cross so he was standing spread fairly wide apart and unable to move. I added a rope chest harness that bound his torso to the cross as well. By the time I was finished, he could wiggle a few inches in any direction, but that was the extent of it. Lastly, I tied a lark's head around the head of his cock and attached this rope to the chest harness, so his cock was pulled taut in an upward direction.

He was fully erect at this point, and I vaguely considered abandoning the rest of my plans to hurt him in favor of using him as a human dildo for myself. I was already quite turned on. But I am infamous for losing interest in sadism after coming, which is one reason I allow him to come before me on many occasions (Isn't it great that something so seemingly "nice" can actually result in more pain for him?)

So there he was, tied pretty firmly, turned on as all hell, blindfolded, and ready to be tortured. Of course I used the opportunity to remind him how much he belongs here with me, and how good it makes him feel to be owned and used by me, always. Not that he needs reminding, but it never hurts to get those thoughts in his head before inflicting the type of pain that might make his body or mind unwittingly rebel against me in the heat of it.

He certainly seems to have moved beyond the anger he had trouble with earlier. I'm trying to recall what all I did to him, and things are mostly a blur up until the caning. Eventually I decided to get down to serious business and make him suffer the way I was craving. I can't explain why I want this or how intoxicating the feeling is. I hit him hard on the top of his thigh and instructed him to begin counting, but only when he had recovered enough after each one that he was ready for the next. Each time I hit him and he released screams, moans, grunts, cries, and whimpers, my dick grew harder with lust and the desire to just throw him onto the floor and fuck him. Yet at the same time I had to keep going to reach the climax of our play, because his pain is addictive, and I am a junkie. Each time the wooden cane connected with his flesh and he reacted, I felt higher and higher on the rush of using him. I don't feel this way with everyone. Play with others can be enjoyable, but euphoric and emotionally orgasmic? No, not even close. I wonder if I will feel it with someone again in the future ... and for the moment I wonder if I even want to.

I continued caning him and it took a couple of minutes, but we got to ten. I asked him, "How many more do you think you can handle?" I was half expecting him to say "As many as you want to give me, Sir," which might have pushed me over the edge and made me forfeit everything else to pound into him right then and there. Instead, he replied that he could at least make it to twenty—and he did, at which point I asked him again how many more he thought he could handle. Note the use of the word "think". I am not asking him how many he can take, but how many he thinks he can. The reality is always more than he would think. He said five, so I decided five more per thigh was a good idea. But I also knew that if we kept going in the same fashion, with me only applying a new stroke when he had recovered enough from the previous one to count and thank me, the reality was he would need to go a lot more than 10 before I got the kind of suffering I wanted out of him. So I told him that for the next five, I would choose the pace and he was not to count. If he didn't already, he now knows that this is bad news.

I started with the left thigh, and he sounded like he was crying by the fourth. I applied the fifth and he thrashed so violently in his restraints that some of the rope began to unravel. His body doubled over forward, and though the cross is heavy and I had no fear of it moving or falling, I instinctively caught him and held his torso up against mine for a few moments while he heaved and gasped.

His cock was so soft it was disappearing into the rope, but my own dick was harder than ever. I love holding him and soaking up all of his suffering as he lets it flow out of his body. I feel so close and connected to him, and the love I have for him runs through me like blood in my veins. I'm sure he hadn't let it leave his mind that we weren't finished, but I reminded him anyway, telling him "Good job," and "You're halfway done."

I secured the rope that had come undone and went over to his right side for the second set of five. I intended them to be just as hard, but it seemed as though the first four didn't move him as much. The fifth was good, though, and he was back in the same position against my chest by the end. I know I could have done more, I could have moved to another toy, I could have done anything, but our time this evening was getting short and I couldn't stave off my lust any longer. Even though he would have gladly endured more if I'd wanted it, his suffering up to this point was not minimal, so I felt no slight in putting an end to it.

I untied my boy and rubbed out his arms a little before leading him over to the couch. He lay with his head up against my chest, still naked, and small as ever. I always find him so beautiful, but never as much so as when he has been put through whatever I want to inflict on him, and then looks up at me with blue eyes deep as oceans—expressing gratitude for being mine without saying a word. That look only makes me crave him more, and since his body is mine for the taking in every way, I put our last thirty minutes together tonight to good use.

EVERY. LAST. SECOND.

On Sunday, Joseph gave his final Mass at the Parish he had been living at for two years, packed up the last of his things, and said goodbye to everyone. He would leave for Nebraska early Monday morning, or so they all thought. In fact, he was on his way home to spend his final twenty-four hours with me. This was a day I had been looking forward to for weeks, and simultaneously dreading since nearly the first day we met. The entire fourteen months of our relationship seemed to be building towards this one inevitable day. At the same time, we'd managed to deny it enough that we had still thoroughly enjoyed the time we had together.

A side note on this for a moment: I realized during our last day together that one thing that had made our entire affair so amazing was that we literally didn't take a single minute for granted. Knowing from the start that this could only last until a given time made us value each other immensely. I know I have never had such a successful relationship as this, and if I am blessed with the gift of it continuing, I hope we will never lose that sense of urgency to love each other as much as we possibly can every second of the day. We had a few little hiccups over the course of the year, but compared to what I have encountered in other relationships, I can sincerely say that we both acted as though our time together was too precious to waste on anything but building our relationship and engaging in our love.

But now Monday, August 1st, had arrived. I took off work and made special plans for how we would spend our final day together. We had planned to go out to a nice dinner, but we were pretty tired from the day so we got Mexican food instead. (I love making Joseph order for us in Spanish. Goofy as it sounds, it gets me hot every time!) And we ended up watching a movie, having some sex, and lots and lots of cuddling. I had thought we might have some sort of last hoorah in terms of play, but when it came down to it, we did a lot of talking and a fair amount of crying, and I didn't have the desire to hurt him at all. The kind of pain we were both starting to experience—which I knew would hit us much harder as the hours drew closer to saying goodbye—was more than enough to make any other type of pain unappealing to me.

To be completely honest, I also had the vague notion that if I started hurting him, I would go too far out of sheer anguish at the experience of losing him. Ultimately, I have to believe that this wouldn't be our last time together as Owner and property, so I didn't want to go making a big deal out of our "last scene".

Upon arriving home, we took a shower together, and I bathed him the way it has become common for me to do. I have never bathed anyone before, but I learned very early on in our relationship that I liked it. A lot—and he feels the same way. Usually being bathed by me involves fingers in his ass, lubed up with soap or body wash, getting him clean all the way inside. Sometimes it turns from that into more blatant fucking with him bent over in the shower, arms braced against the wall of the tub, and me fucking his ass with one hand and stroking his cock with the other while the hot water pounds down all around us. Just the thought of it right now is making my dick hard, and it saddens me that I have months to go before I'll get to experience this again.

After our shower we got on the bed and I put in a DVD. *Hedwig and the Angry Inch* is one of those movies I've loved since college and made every friend watch with me since then. I couldn't believe I hadn't made him watch it sooner, so we had to remedy that. Pup enjoyed it, though he said he'd need to watch it again to really understand all of it.

By this time we were still thinking we'd go down in to the city for dinner, but it had started raining and we were tired. I think it hit us both about the same time that we had only eighteen hours left together, eight of them probably spent sleeping, and we didn't want to waste time driving in and out of the city. We ended up going to bed relatively early, but not before I had jumped on top of him and used his cock to get myself off. He was not allowed to get off that time, and he went to sleep hard.

We both tossed and turned all night. I wish we hadn't; I wanted him to have a good night's sleep before his long drive. We finally gave in to waking up around seven so that we had a few hours to spend together before he departed. There was still so much to do.

First, I put on my harness and cock and fucked his ass for what would have to be the last time till we met again. I was very turned on, but I didn't want to get off that way, and I had been thinking about something for a while. In all the times we've had sex since I took his virginity, he's never been on top. As kinky as I am, it's funny to me that I still enjoy good old fashioned missionary style sex once in a while. But hey, it feels good, so what? I told him I was going to use him in a new way this morning and directed him into the proper position. I have to admit it felt so very good to have that cock I own inside me as I lay back and relaxed.

Afterwards, we started the process of getting dressed and getting down to our final business. This was the part I was not looking forward to in the least. It makes me sick to my stomach just to recount it in detail again, and I pray that I will never have to experience this again. In fact, I have already started thinking that I may tell him not to even return home in December if he's not going to be delivering me good news, because I can't stand the thought of going through another "last day" together. Hell, that last hour was one of the most painful and heartbreaking experiences I can ever remember.

9:00 Tuesday morning. There was no more putting it off. It was time to remove his metal ankle cuff and sign our (possibly) last contract. The metal cuff had been locked on his right ankle for over eleven months at this point. It went on August 26th, 2010 and was coming off August 2nd, 2011. It still amazes me that it was on him for that long without a break, and at the same time I look forward to putting something on him in the future that will stay on much longer. I had thought about allowing him to keep wearing the cuff while he was gone—after all, we agreed that he's still mine—but he has other more permanent reminders like his nipple piercing and tattoo, so there's no way he can forget that his body still belongs to me. I decided ultimately that the ankle cuff should be worn only when he's under my direct ownership.

Joseph and I had spent a lot of time over the past few months talking about how our relationship would be once he left. We wavered back and forth between cutting off contact entirely to keeping contact minimal; releasing him from ownership entirely; keeping it full-fledged, and everything in between. The agreement we finally decided made most sense was to draw up a new contract that would be in effect for the next five months.

As you can see below, as opposed to prior versions, this one consists of me taking a more hands-off approach to my ownership. It may be just semantics, but we feel better saying he is still owned even if I'm suspending the exercise of the details that ownership entails.

It's funny, I'm trying to write about the scene that came next and I am having a hard time. As difficult as it was to go through in the moment, it is equally difficult to recount. I told him to kneel down in front of me, and I sat on the bed where we had slept (not so well) the night before. I handed him the copy of our contract, which was now only one page as opposed to the three or four it would normally be. I instructed him to read the contract aloud just as he had the first time we'd ever signed one, more than a year earlier.

The first time, July 14th, 2010, he had been on the verge of tears due to overwhelming happiness that this long-held dream to belong to someone was finally coming true. On August 2nd, 2011 I heard his voice crack as he began to read aloud.

AGREEMENT OF OWNERSHIP: INTERIM CONTRACT

Contract Version 3.1
Effective August 2nd, 2011 - December 31st, 2011

Statement of Purpose

Ownership, as understood in this contract, is an act of power exchange in which the property surrenders authority of his life to the Owner within mutually agreed parameters. Becoming Owner and property is a conscious and fully informed relationship into which both parties freely enter. It is not an admission of inferiority or statement of superiority, but a mature relationship between equals in which one, the property, voluntarily and without coercion agrees to cede control of his life to another, the Owner, according to the subsequent stipulations as a means of providing personal fulfillment and enrichment of life for both parties.

Special Terms & Conditions

All rights and duties of the owner and the property as detailed in contract version 2.3 are still valid, however, for the interim time period between August 1st and December 31st, 2011 the owner is suspending her option to exercise these rights in order to allow the property the time needed for the discernment of his future, free of most obligations associated with being owned. During this time, the only requirements of the owner and the owned will be as follows.

Owner and property agree to keep in contact with a minimum of one weekly phone call at a regularly scheduled time (to be determined based on schedule.) Above and beyond a weekly 1 hour phone conversation (which can be substituted with an online conversation if necessary) any contact will be strictly optional on both parts and should not interfere with the daily life of the owner or property. The owner will keep her ankle cuff in her possession until the point in time the property returns fully to her service, whether temporarily or permanently.

The property will retain the owner's leather collar and dog tag but will only be permitted to wear it as instructed by the owner (i.e. during normally scheduled phone calls or if granted special permission.) The property is not permitted to engage in sexual, service, or S/M activities or conversations, in real life or online, with any person whatsoever. The property agrees that this area of his life is still maintained by his owner and is not his to freely explore in any capacity while this contract is in effect. The property agrees to make a trip home that will last no less than two days in order to present the results of his discernment process to his owner. This trip will take place no later than December 31st, 2011. For the duration of this trip, the property will return to his former state of full service and the terms of contract version 2.3 will apply.

Depending on the results of the property's discernment period, a new contract will be written and signed OR the current contract will be allowed to expire with no intention of continuation.

Terms of Contract

Duration of the Contract: The obligations of this contract, freely assumed by both parties, shall be binding for the duration of 5 months, ending on December 31st, 2011 unless terminated prior to that date. The only acceptable way for the contract to be terminated prior to December 31st is the establishment of a new contract or the agreement of a complete dissolution of the relationship.

I have read, understood, and agreed to the above contract and hereby vow to uphold my obligations as outlined therein to the best of my abilities.

Though he had started off shakily, Joseph quickly regained his composure, and his voice grew stronger and calmer as the reading went on. I do fully realize how hard it was for him to do this, but I needed to make sure that he was feeling the sting of what we were doing, and grasping the full impact of the pain of our separation. Of course, my instinct as the protective owner is to gloss over everything; to make it as easy and painless for him as possible ... but that would not benefit the situation in the end. If the decision is on him, then he needs to truly feel the consequences of that decision. I want him to feel the loneliness and sadness of a life without me, and the torture of his ankle being naked of the symbol of my possession. I want each word of the new contract to penetrate him like a needle, so that when he weighs all of that against the difficulty of returning to me (and thus leaving other obligations behind), he will in fact be weighing the true ramifications of both and not some lesser, more pleasant, version of what leaving me behind was like. Damn, do I sound like a bastard? I hope not.

Having read and signed the new contract, there was nothing left to do but say goodbye. We carried everything he'd come with out to his car. I hugged and kissed him, and asked if he'd wait outside to close the garage door behind me as I pulled out of the driveway. (My electric opener has been broken for a while.) So I pulled out, watched him close the garage door, saw him walk over to his car ... and then my heart broke into a million pieces and I just couldn't drive away. I stopped, jumped out, and grabbed him. "I just can't..." I said through tears. What I wish I could have done was throw him back inside the house and lock him in the cage, but I had to be satisfied with just holding onto him as tightly as I could and sobbing into his shirt for the hundredth time that morning. I tried to make a mental imprint of his body next to mine so that I could remember the feeling of holding him, but I knew already that it wouldn't last, and I think that knowledge upset me even more. I just couldn't wrap my head around the simple concept of him being with me in the moment and so close to not being with me for so long ... or ever. I think that instant when you have to switch from saying goodbye to having said goodbye is one of the most difficult things to do. Once a person is gone, you can start moving forward, but for a few minutes it feels like time is standing still and you wish nothing more than being able to suspend the world and never leave that moment. I feel it so deeply right now, just retelling the story.

Finally, after a few minutes that I wished could have been years, I separated myself from him. I kissed him deeply, told him I loved him and to be a good boy (how silly, he always has been and always will be). I said goodbye. I got back into my car. I drove to work where for the rest of the day I somehow pretended that I was fine, just tired. I don't know how I made it through that day, but I did. I keep making it through each subsequent one, too.

If it's any comfort, I know one hundred per cent for certain that we loved each other for every last second we could, and if that's all the seconds we ever get, then no one has been luckier than us.

~ ~ ~

Gifts are very important to me in terms of showing someone that I love them and being shown love. It doesn't matter how big or small the gift is; it's about being thought of, being remembered, being considered. When someone walks down an aisle at the grocery and remembers to pick me up something they know I like, I feel loved. I also really like giving people gifts, and so it should have been no surprise to my boy that he would receive a few before he left. I didn't expect anything in return, but I had assigned him to organize the photos from a recent shoot into an album for me. I was hoping he might do something along the lines of what he did, and I was pleased to find out that he had.

The gift he gave me on our last Saturday night together was a beautiful purple photo album (my favorite color) filled with the best photos from our shoot, decorated with quotes from our contract or other captions that were appropriate. The album is gorgeous, and was evidence of his care and love in preparing the gift for me.

My gifts for him were a few handmade "art" projects (I use the term loosely), and a couple of picture frames for some of the best photos of us from the same shoot. All of that he expected, because I'd been working on them for a while and he was aware of my plans … but then there was the surprise gift that he never would have seen coming. Oh, I love it when I can do that!

I had an older model iPod shuffle that held about a gigabyte of music. Twelve and a half hours, I would come to find out. I had been thinking for quite some time about making a mix tape of all the songs that reminded me of him, or of us, or our relationship … but it was only as I started to compile the songs that I realized I could arrange them in a way that told our story. I don't know how clearly the narrative played out in his mind, but it was certainly there in mine.

I made the playlist—forty-six songs long—and then added several albums that I thought he would like onto the iPod as room allowed. I filled that thing to the brim, and then I wrote him a long letter on an (overly sentimental) card and sealed the iPod, charger, and card into a giftwrapped box with the message "Do not open until your first rest stop. Text after opening!" written on the wrapping paper.

This was to be my final gift to him. He would be able to open it in the privacy of his own car where his emotions could come full force and uncensored. I wanted that for him. I imagined him crying as hard as I had when I put together that playlist, because every song spoke to me on a visceral level as if it had been written just about us. I saw in my mind's eye a level of misery and suffering he never had shown to me in our year together, and I doubted he would allow himself to, had I given him the gift myself in person.

Around noon I got a text: "Stopped for lunch and opened your gift. Thank you so much, Sir! It is truly special and will be a great reminder of us. I love you, Sir."

And for the twentieth time that day, the tears welled up again.

IT'S OVER

Wednesday, August 3, 2011

He's hasn't even been gone one day and my email box is already piling up with letters started but never sent.

Dear Joseph...
Dear boy...
Dear Pup...
Dear my love...

I know we agreed only to speak once a week so that our communication did not intrude on your discernment process, or keep you from your obligations with the Parish ... but I keep asking myself, "What's so wrong with making sure we at least say hello every day?"

No, I will not intrude. I will not burden you with all of the crap in my head, as you undoubtedly struggle and suffer as much as me. I will write letters, but leave them unsent and post them here where the world can read them, but you don't have to. Because I love you and want what's best for you more than I care about relieving my own pain. You always did make me feel better just by talking, but it's time to do it on my own and leave you to your own needs. Here is a letter I started today. I didn't finish it. I saved the draft and went back to work, hoping to distract myself long enough to make it home and cry in Heather's arms. Poor Heather, who has had to watch me go through this entire doomed affair from start to finish, and never stopped supporting me or told me I was going to regret it when it ended.

Finally, I wrote a letter that I actually felt could be sent.

Dear Pup,

My moods have been oscillating today between relief that your leaving is over and I don't have to go through it again, depression that you're gone, joy at counting down the days till I see you again, fear about the future, and more. I don't tell you this to burden you with my feelings, I just don't know what else to do right now than to write you. I don't know if talking would make things better or worse (for either of us).

The last thing I want is to make this harder on you than it should be. Memories of this morning keep replaying in my head. I can't believe that I had you in my arms and now I don't know when the next time that will be is. This sucks so much and I'm angry at myself for not thinking in advance about driving with

you and flying back. 2 more days together now seems like it would have been a miracle but I know it only would have prolonged the painful goodbye, not made it better.

Saying goodbye is one of the hardest things in life and though I'm good at a lot of things, this is not one of them.

With love,
Melissa

◆◆◆◆◆

"How are you doing?" I asked him over my instant messenger program because he didn't want to talk on the phone tonight. I knew the reason without having to ask. We'd both just lose it.

"Well, I haven't cried for almost two hours now, so I guess that's good," he replied. His admission nearly made me break down again because in all of our goodbyes, I had been the emotional one and I knew that he was holding it in.

"The drive was very surreal. Listening to your playlist. Trying to take in what was happening."

"Did you cry when you opened my gift?"

"Yes, and nearly the entire rest of the drive as I listened to the songs."

I feel bad for admitting it, but knowing his reaction was so strong did make me happy in a strange way. I guess it's in part because I anticipated it, and I like knowing that I'm correct. But it's not just that. I feel cruel even saying this, but I want him to hurt as much as I do. I can't handle the thought of it being one sided, un-reciprocated. It comforts me to know that he feels the loss as acutely as I do, and it gives me hope that his decision might end up in my favor, even though I know the decision will be based on much more than emotions.

This whole day has been one I would never wish anyone to go through, yet I can't stop reminding myself that we chose to be in this position. *It sucks! It sucks! It sucks! I feel like a six-year-old. Life isn't fair.*

All day I've been on the verge of tears. They threaten to well up constantly and then spill over for no particular reason. Thoughts float in and out of my head, like "It's over," and "I can't believe it's over," and "Was this past year just a dream?" Impulses to buy a plane ticket or just take off driving keep passing through my brain. I feel as though I've lost a part of myself, a part I never knew I had until I found it just last year.

My mom used to tell me that maybe I was just "one of those people who would never be happy", and I accepted that for the longest time. I figured I was just born neurotic and anxious and I'd never be able to let go and just be happy. Well, she couldn't have been more wrong. For the past fourteen months I have been happy, content, satisfied, peaceful, and blissful. It's not just being in love

- I've been there before. With Heather, the first couple of years were magical as they always are in a new relationship but even then we had our share of arguments and conflict—misunderstanding, hurt feelings, and the like. Not with Joseph. The relationship was so amazing that at times I wonder if I didn't just make it all up.

So am I prepared that someday the shiny newness of blissful love will wear off? Yes, it might. But there are elderly couples that are still just as much in love as they were fifty years ago, and I am also equally prepared to be one of them. In fact, more so. It feels so powerless, as an Owner, or even as a lover, to not be able to tell him to just get back here or to go to him myself, but I've said over and over again that this has to be his choice. I don't have the right to change the course of his life in this way … yet. I will fully accept responsibility for everything about him once the choice to be mine forever is made, but I can't make that choice for him. For now, I can only pray that he'll make the right decision—the one that will return him to me.

THE AGNOSTIC'S PRAYER

Friday, August 5, 2011

Journal Entry:

Dear God. Are you there? Are you even real? I'm going to assume that you are for now. I don't know if I'm even doing this right but here goes. Please, please, please, please, please, bring Joseph back to me. Please help him realize that being mine is what will make him happy. Please give me the strength to accept whatever happens even if it's not what I really want. Please let him be happy, whatever that means. And thank you for bringing him into my life. But please don't take him away from me.

I haven't spoken too much about religion, and yet it seems this story should have contained a lot more of it, since it's at the crux of this whole saga.

I was raised Jewish, but I never felt very connected to the religion. Sometimes the traditions and culture still feel meaningful, but for the most part I don't have any connection. I really don't even know if I believe in God - or maybe "didn't know" is more accurate now. My time with Joseph has changed me. I guess it's only logical that spending this much time, so intimately, with someone that knowledgeable on religion and spiritual matters would do that to me. I have found myself thinking about God more in this year than I ever remember doing in the past, and as Joseph's departure became imminent, I realized how very little control over the situation I had and the only thing I might really do to make a difference was pray.

My old self would have laughed and said that praying would be silly, but today's self, even though she doesn't know anything for sure, believes that praying might just make a difference. I've been saying this prayer twice a day— first thing in the morning when I wake, and last thing at night before I fall asleep with his old leather collar in my hands and held against my heart. I beg like I have never begged for anything, hoping that even a fraction of my prayer is heard.

OH, RIGHT, I REMEMBER NOW

It's been a long time since I was actively looking for anything in regards to a relationship, a submissive, or service. Before Joseph, I was served for seven months by a very competent, capable, and sincere boy who really opened my eyes to what D/s could be with someone who took it as seriously as I did, but due to him already being partnered, I didn't feel I could own him the way I craved. As both of our lives got busy, we drifted more into the friend zone.

So in reality it's been over two years since I was actually *looking*. I met Joseph while in a "keeping my eyes and mind open" stage, but wouldn't have been disappointed if our first coffee meeting lead to nothing more. I certainly didn't expect it to.

About a month ago, in anticipation of Joseph leaving and me finding myself with a giant hole in my life, I put up a new profile on the same website I had met Joseph on. I made a new handle and started from scratch to try to separate myself from the same profile I've had on there for five years. I wanted to start fresh and be very clear about what exactly I needed and didn't need. Specifically, I am on the hunt for someone to serve me in all the useful ways I will miss so much now that Joseph is gone, and I'm willing to play with someone as part of their incentive for serving, but I'm not looking to own anyone. So far, I have been contacted by hundreds of people, most of whom obviously never even read my profile, but a few who seem sincere and with whom I continue the conversation.

One such—we'll call him M—contacted me last week, and despite a few initial gut feelings on my part that he was a little too good to be true based on what he was saying, I decided we could meet. We first made plans to meet for dinner last Thursday, but before we could finalize the location he logged off. Three days later he instant messaged me again and apologized, saying his computer had a major meltdown and he just got it back from the repair shop. Fair enough, so I asked if we were still on for dinner Thursday, as we had agreed. He said no—he had to work Thursday night, but he was free this weekend. I thought it was kind of odd, but shrugged it off, and we made plans to meet Sunday 11am for brunch at a mutually convenient location.

Even with firm plans in place, I still had some inherent doubts about his sincerity. To get one last confirmation before showing up, I emailed him Friday evening asking him to confirm, but never heard back. Saturday afternoon I tried messaging him, but again got no response. He was shown as "online" Saturday night, but never responded to my email or message, so I gave up. I am not going to show up on Sunday because it would prove pointless. He won't be there.

It doesn't bother me on a personal level. Nothing was lost but a few hours of chat time over the past week and a half, but it's frustrating. How does a person think this is the way to treat someone under any circumstances, much less under circumstances where he's professed to be a submissive who is highly interested in meeting a dominant and "being given a chance to prove he's serious"? Yes, those are actually his words. He had told me numerous times over the past week that he looks forward to meeting me and showing me his sincerity, and how happy he would be just to have someone to serve even in the most mundane sense like house cleaning. Oh well, like I initially thought: too good to be true.

But yes, I remember now why I hated this so much. It's enough to make you crawl back in your hole and give up on finding someone who means what he says. I know my boy is still out there, and I know that he wishes more than anything he could be the one serving me, meeting all my needs, making sure I'm happy and well taken care of so that I never have to look for anyone else again. And someday he will, I am confident. But until then, I guess my choices are to put up with the game players and weed them out best I can or to stop looking at all and just live without this in my life for a while.

With Joseph gone and Heather out of town for the weekend, I tried to fill my time with friends to keep my mind off any potential loneliness. Saturday I had planned a sleepover with a former submissive-turned-friend I'll call L, whose partner was also away at a conference this weekend. We met at my house at 5:30 and went to dinner and a movie, and then went back home where we stayed up chatting till almost two a.m. Everything was going fine and he let me ramble on and on and on (and on!) about Joseph. L had met my boy a few times and seen us together, and he knows me pretty well after serving me before I met Joseph. So he knows how much this relationship has meant and how hard it's been to lose. Having his company was invaluable and I even got a nice leg rub while we talked.

When it was time for bed, I invited him into the master bedroom not only because it was the only bed in the house large enough to sleep two people without any squishing, but because it was the only bedroom with a ceiling fan and we were in the middle of a heat wave. Earlier that night we had briefly discussed what kind of physical contact was acceptable, which was an odd topic for me to bring up because he had spent seven months serving me, during which he had no right to dictate what I did to his body. Fortunately, he told me that anything we'd previously done was still allowed. This left a pretty broad range of possibilities on the table; I knew I was nowhere near interested in pursuing most of them, but touching someone would feel good: or so I thought.

We lay in bed next to each other, him naked, and I ran my hands over his body, particularly interested in his five-month-healed nipple piercings. I stroked the side of his face and pinched his inner thighs, which were still tender from a huge scene he had done about a month ago. I asked him if my touch felt familiar, and he said it did ... and I could just feel the unspoken "Sir" following his reply. He had told me it's still sometimes a struggle to not say it. I hadn't ever told him to refrain from calling me Sir, but I also didn't know how I was going to feel being called by that title now by anyone else.

As I listened to his reactions—soft moans as I touched his hyper-sensitive nipples—I felt a sudden wave of sadness. My eyes teared up and I dared not speak because my voice would surely break. In my mind I could only think one thing: *You're not him.*

CELL PHONE SERVICE

Tuesday, September 6, 2011

"I am ready."

The text message arrives just after 10pm. This means he is lying in bed naked and waiting for me, even if he is a thousand miles away. I dial his number, and he answers in a way that is quite different from his usual "Hello," or "Good evening."

"What can I do for you tonight, Sir?"

The immediate recognition that I require his service, that this is not just a chat between friends, makes my dick hard.

My dick has not been all that hard since Joseph left. Instead of playing and fucking several times a week at minimum, it has been two weeks now since I've even been turned on enough to think about my needs. But I just spent the whole weekend at the annual "Master/slave Conference". This event happens every Labor Day Weekend, and it's an environment celebrating these relationships. The conference is oddly non-sexual, considering the relationships it focuses on are usually intensely so. I spent my time listening to brilliant speakers talk about relationship struggles and spiritual work on the mastery and slavery paths, but underneath everything I felt a gaping hole that my own boy was not by my side.

In years past I have looked at other people's relationships and thought, "I want that." and imagined how amazing it would be to have that. But this year it was a whole different kind of pain and longing. I would look at respected masters and slaves of this community and see between them the same thing I see within myself and Joseph. I had the joy of knowing "I finally found it," but the fear and sadness of also knowing that I might lose it.

The emotions ran high for me all weekend, but I managed to keep them under the surface. I didn't get down or feel truly sad for the entire conference, but when I got home I was hit with an intense urge and longing for my boy. Not to mention an intense sexual desire.

"What can I do for you tonight, Sir?"

I quiver, and I am still in awe of how something so simple as this phrase can make me feel. "I want you to reach down and touch the piercing that I gave you."

"Yes, Sir." I hear him moan as he tugs on the nipple ring.

"Now I want you to run your hand over the tattoo I gave you."

"Yes, Sir." I imagine him running his fingers so lightly over the permanent reminder on his skin, and I know his cock is already as hard literally as mine is figuratively.

"Now put your hand on my cock."

"It's so hard, Sir."

"I know, but you're very good at keeping it that way without going any further." It's true. More than a year of being conditioned by my constant stimulation and rare allowance of release has given my boy all the stamina I could ask for.

"Yes, Sir. Thank you, Sir."

We continued to talk, not sure what about, while I got closer and closer to coming. I asked him if he enjoyed hearing me come (I already know he does, but hearing his throaty "Yes, Sir" was just for my own enjoyment.)

There was no reason to hold out longer, I came. It was hard, intense, but somehow the actual orgasm itself was not as pleasurable as it normally was. It didn't matter, because the buildup to it had been so nice, but it does make me wonder if coming so infrequently has influenced my orgasmic patterns.

As for the boy, I could have easily told him to remove his hand from "my" cock and go to sleep, and of course he would have. He probably even would have enjoyed the denial for its own sake, as he finds a way to revel in every aspect of my control over him, even if it is not directly pleasant. But I wanted to hear him come as well, so I instructed him to do so. One thing that struck me was how outwardly vocal he was. I don't remember him being that way in the past. Maybe because it had been a while since he last came; maybe because we were on the phone and he knew I wanted to hear him. But I appreciated it, whatever the reason.

Almost immediately after he came, I began to cry, for no real reason other than an overwhelming wave of emotions. He told me it made sense; I'd been keeping a lot of emotion under control for several days without any type of release. My tears soon turned into laughter as we kept talking about other things and I shared with him some of the highlights of the weekend. Just another thing I love about my boy: his ability to guide me through my own emotional bumps with his empathy and understanding.

It was later than I had wanted when we finally said good night, but it was well worth the loss of sleep. Not quite midnight yet, I was feeling in such good spirits - feeling so much love both *from* and *for* my boy, that I couldn't help but get myself off a second time thinking of him and how fortunate I am to have him. I was reminded that though we are apart, he is not lost. The thought is comforting.

In some ways it feels like it was only a moment ago that we parted, and in others it feels like lifetimes ago. Over the past months, I do have to admit it's gotten easier to go about everyday life. I don't think about him constantly like I did the first few days, but he's never actually far from my mind. The littlest things remind me of him—something as simple as cleaning the kitchen and putting away dishes, and then seeing the system of stacking the plastic-ware that he established, makes me feel love, joy, and sadness all at the same time. I've been making a point to keep things the way he left them - not only because it feels more familiar that way, but because it reminds me that he is the one who did it. Somehow, in continuing to place things back where he would and take care of the house the way he would, it feels like he is still serving me.

After being apart for two months, Joseph and I were reunited for five short days when I flew to Nebraska for a visit. Even though we hadn't planned on any visits between August and late December, we both were missing each other enough to warrant one. After the long weekend was over, we exchanged letters to one another, which tells a better story than anything I could recount.

◆◆◆◆◆

Monday, October 24, 2011
Dear Pup,

As hard as it was to believe I was actually there with you Tuesday night, it is now just as hard for me to believe I'm back home without you. Coming up, I was nervous and not as giddy with excitement as I would have thought I'd be at the prospect of seeing you. I knew that this was because I was afraid. My biggest fear and insecurity (in relationships in general) has been that what I experience is not "real" - not just with you and really not because of you in any way. You've heard me say this before. And despite you never, ever giving me a reason to think this about us, it still creeps in once in a while. Most significantly because what we "are" is so extraordinary that it often feels hard for me to believe I'm not just making it up.

I know you are not pretending or lying or doing anything other than being your absolute true self with me, but still it just feels impossible sometimes that I could have found someone this compatible who wants what I want. But particularly when we are not together, it starts to creep into my mind that there is no way I actually felt what I did or that you felt what you did or, who knows, maybe we won't even like each other the next time. This time apart has been the first and only real test of our relationship we've had in that sense. Though we'd spent a few weeks apart before, we never doubted how we'd feel upon reuniting. I never actually doubted it this time either, I want you to know, but it was that fear and insecurity wondering if you really needed or wanted me anymore. Now I can say with confidence that you do. I felt very wanted and needed, and I also know now that if you don't choose to come home, it won't be because you "don't need or want" me, but because it's just not the right decision for you. This brings me a lot of peace and comfort and the ability to know I can accept the future. After all, what choice do I have?

But yes, I now know that life will go on and I will live and be OK. Of course, on the other hand, seeing you again only acted to cement my feelings of what's right, and certainly us being together is what I know in my heart to be right, for whatever that's worth. Knowing that I will be OK doesn't make me feel any less sure that I don't want it. I want the kind of passion and love and joy I feel when we are together and when I know you are mine.

All of that to say, upon arrival, things did seem kind of weird. I told you as much at the time. Luckily, through our time together Tuesday night, I was soon back to normal and everything just felt right. The rest of the week went by effortlessly, as our time together tends to for me.

In bed Tuesday night, I clearly remember lying in bed with you and deciding to tell you what's been on my mind recently since my very helpful conversations with Larry (the guy I met at the Master/slave Conference this year). We both work at computers, and have been able to chat a good bit in the past couple of months, and it's been really nice to have another owner to talk to who shares a lot of my beliefs about these relationships. We both admitted that our properties were the only people we felt we could relax around, because we trusted them as much as we trust ourselves. It was great to hear someone else say to me exactly what I feel and had been thinking.

So, we've been chatting a good bit and occasionally I'd mention my upcoming trip to see you, but not often. Until one day I asked him some advice and he provided me with something that hadn't occurred to me before. That trusting you to make the right decision is about all I can do here, and in fact what I "should" do, according to him. This is in opposition with everything I have been thinking and feeling in terms of how to get you to make the right decision, how to convince you to do it. He says if I trust you that much, all I can do is trust you to make the right decision.

Hearing this and really letting it sink in changed my perspective a bit, and I had been trying to think of when and how to tell you this. I didn't plan to do it that soon into our visit, but the timing seemed right. And judging by your reaction, I am so happy I did. I remember after telling you that, you starting to kiss and nibble on me and there was no stopping it then. Whatever happened in those moments, I felt suddenly as though we'd never separated, and I knew exactly what to do and how to be, without any awkwardness from there on. I can't say if that was your intention, but still, thank you for taking the first steps to initiate the physical contact that lead to such good things. Waking up next to you is one of the most pleasurable feelings of complete love and comfort I know. "Good morning, my beautiful pup." or something similar, seemed to be the only fitting way to acknowledge how lucky I felt to be waking with my property right beside me where he should be. I enjoy cooking breakfast for us and I'm happy I got to do so much cooking or at least food-prep if not actual "cooking." It makes me feel very much in control and

Owner-like to always feed you. It felt a bit odd at first, or just different, to be cooking at your place and not in my familiar environment but I learned my way around the kitchen quickly and as you know, I really liked your pan!

Sadly, that is as far as I made it with my own email before yours arrived. I am off to read it now!

With love,
Melissa

♦♦♦♦♦

Monday, October 24, 2011
Dear Sir,

After thinking about it, I decided to make this more of a free-flowing recollection and discussion rather than try to do the "scene report" style. I just thought that there was too much to try and go over in that format, and that the overall impressions are probably most important anyway. Of course, if there were individual events that you thought were important that I don't talk about I will be happy to do so.

Your visit was wonderful. In some ways it didn't seem that we had been apart for as long as we had. Perhaps that was due in large part to how often we have been able to stay in touch over the weeks since I left home, but your stay here certainly reminded me of how much I value your love and support, and of the love that I have for you.

Your visit was also rather surreal. I guess it was one thing for me to be engaging in this other lifestyle while back east, but to do so (to whatever extent) here in my "home" was very different. It brought a different sense of reality to the decision I have to make. It also brought a certain level of stress to the week knowing that this is not a big place and that the chances of being "discovered" were much greater. Fortunately that went fine and nothing of the sort happened, but there was always the threat of that looming in the background more so than when I was at home with you.

By the end of the visit I could also feel myself getting worn down a bit just from lack of having personal time. This was in part because of your visit, in part because of everything I had been doing to help my friend Greg recently, and in part due to work. I'm not saying this in any accusatory sense, only mentioning it in case you noticed anything toward the end. I could feel that happening on Saturday and especially Sunday, but given the amount of time you were here, I didn't want to take away from that so I just gutted my way through, knowing that I would have plenty of personal space after your visit. I was very happy about how naturally I was able to go back into "full submission." I haven't had any desires to not be fully obedient or anything of the sort, but given the time we had been apart and some of the difficulties that had happened in that time, I wasn't sure how much of an adjustment there would be getting back into the swing of things. Also, given that you were coming here to "my place" in "my home", I didn't know how much that would affect things, but I was able to be your pup right away without much effort. I think there were a few times I needed some reminders—which I think was natural and to be expected—but other than that it was pretty seamless. It helped to be able to wear your collar while you were here—and just having the experience of kneeling while you placed it on me reminded me of my place and your control.

Something that I have always enjoyed about our relationship, and that I enjoyed while you were here, was simply being able to enjoy time together. I have mentioned before that often being with other people is a lot of work, but it is rarely (if ever) that way with you. Being able to go out to eat, to show you around town, and to go shopping was wonderful. It helped that the weather cooperated enough so that you could enjoy the beauty of the river and the bluffs and the trees. I was also not surprised that by the end you were pretty much "done" with the city, as that is how it goes with smaller towns. But I was glad I was able to share that with you. The city, and my college located here, has been a major part of my life, as I have spent more years here than anywhere else except for the town where I grew up.

I have always very much appreciated, and been more than a little surprised by, your openness to my faith. It goes without saying that I have not been, and will not, try to force you to believe certain things or cram religion down your throat or anything of the sort, but given your background I have been surprised at how open you are to going to Mass or talking about religion. I was very happy to be able to have you experience my parish here. Even more so, I was very happy to share night prayer at the monastery with you - not so much for the prayers being said but for the beauty of the experience. And I was glad that you enjoyed it.

I was very pleased by the play time that we were able to have. Given everything that was going on, I was not in a frame of mind to want harder play, but I obviously enjoyed the play that we had. Not only was it fun and enjoyable, but I found many of the experiences meaningful. I was very pleased by my control from the very beginning - that you were able to use your cock the way you wanted and I would not come until you wanted. That made me very proud not only that you could use me the way you wanted, get the pleasure from me you wanted, but also that I was still able to have such control. Along those lines, I was not so much proud but more just intrigued by my experience of "coming" without coming. I don't know why exactly it happened or what exactly it was that happened, but to me it seemed like I "came" because you told me to and I wanted to obey you and come, even though my body did not ejaculate.

Overall, it was a wonderful time together and another great reminder of what it feels like to be so owned and loved by you.

Your Pup,
Joseph

ANOTHER BIRTHDAY

Saturday, December 3, 2011

I just got off the phone with Joseph. Today is his birthday. A year ago we were in the middle of one of the most intense nights of both of our lives, and it's hard to believe it's really been a year. This year, we're not together and it's been about six weeks since we last saw each other, but the good news is that it's only three weeks until we will see each other again. The thought makes me happier than I can express. Though the original plan was for him to fly back home for a few days, it turned out I had more time off around the holidays than I had expected, and it made more sense for me to drive to Nebraska, spend Christmas and New Years there, and for Joseph to ride back home with me for a few more days after that.

For his birthday this year, I ordered a gift that I was hoping would arrive to him in time, and thankfully it did. As instructed, he called me before opening it last night, and I got to hear the excitement in his voice as he unwrapped the package and found a shiny new shower-enema-nozzle set. Since using his ass is one of my favorite activities, I have always been happy that my pup was into enemas, and knew how to give them to himself so that he's always clean and ready for my use. Over the past year, I have learned to give them to him and I do enjoy it sometimes, but the last experience we had with it when I visited him wasn't the most pleasant for either of us, and I decided I'd like to have a different mechanism for administering them other than the traditional hanging water bottle. It was no task at all to find a set online and have it sent to him for his birthday. I teased him that the kidnapping was coming later.

So last night as we spoke on the phone, Joseph quickly installed the device into his shower, and by the end of the phone call he was eager to give it a try. I got a text before bed that read simply, "It works!" with a little winking face. I wrote back this morning that he was going to have to do better than that in terms of details, and he told me he'd be available to speak tonight. So we did— and I wasn't disappointed. After hearing all about it, there didn't seem to be much left to talk about, but I wasn't ready to say goodnight yet.

I asked my boy if he would like to come for me tonight and he obediently replied, "If you want me to, Sir." I did want him to, and I wanted me to as well, since that hasn't happened in a couple of weeks. I went downstairs and found a toy I wanted to use on myself, sprawled out on the couch, and began instructing him to touch his body in places as I normally would. I told him to play with his nipple piercing, to touch "my" cock, imagining me nibbling on him all the way from his collarbone down to his thighs. I knew it wouldn't take more than this to make him hot, and I was already close, myself. We spoke briefly about how he used to enjoy being denied and now enjoys being made to come at my command but ultimately what he finds most fulfilling is just being used whichever way I decide.

I told him that I wanted him to come for me and that he was allowed to, as long as he described what he was thinking about to me aloud while he did so. Joseph told me that he imagined me using "my" cock to get myself off, and then leaving him hard and desperate but denying him release until I was good and ready or possibly not at all. It was a lovely image, but I wanted him to come tonight, so I instructed him to do so.

After he came, we both mused over it being only three weeks until we see each other again, and how pleasant of a thought that is. It was time for him to go to bed though so I wished him a happy birthday, told him I loved him, and we said goodbye.

Now, I'm about to drift off to sleep with fantasies of his birthday gift and how I will use it when I make it out west.

YOU AND I

Friday, December 23, 2011

For nineteen months now, I have thought about little else than how this story will end. It became clear very early in my relationship with Joseph that we belonged together and that we needed to do whatever we had to, overcome whatever barriers we must, to be together in the end. It is impossible for me to believe that two people so well suited for each other and so thoroughly in love would be dropped together by random chance—or by the will of God, even—and not allowed to be together more than this brief time. I know I may be suffering from an extreme sense of entitlement, but nonetheless, I refuse to believe that Joseph was given to me only to be taken away again. He has also said before that my love and this relationship were the answers to many years of prayers he had voiced. If God answered those prayers and brought us together, then how can we not be meant to make it work?

But still, I've had to give him the freedom to make this decision for himself. Yes, I've tried my best to enslave, master, and own him to the point that the decision would be a no-brainer, and there are certainly ways I could force the decision I want. However, my own ethics will not allow me to do so.

Whatever the result may be, I can honestly say that I own him as much as I possibly could, given the limited time I had to work with. I can hardly believe that I have done this with no road map, no real guide or mentor of any type; just my own intuition leading the way and the empathy and advice of countless friends who have witnessed this whole saga from start to finish. People have listened to me go on endlessly about the trials and tribulations of the whole situation, but at the end of the day, it's just me and it's just Joseph, and whatever ownership exists in our minds is there because we created it together.

For five months now we've been apart. We saw each other briefly in mid-October and the visit washed away any doubts on my part that crept in during his absence. Now I am on my way to Nebraska to see him again, and he will come back home with me after New Year's Day and stay for five days before flying back. During this time, he will give me the answer to the looming question. The decision.

I am driving west and taking Shadow with me. It's a long drive, and the dog isn't even doing his fair share of it, but it's nice to have the company for this leg. My other pup will provide a much better travel companion for the trip home.

Tomorrow is Christmas Eve and I'll be arriving in the early afternoon. For a while now, I've had this strange compulsion to see Joseph celebrate Christmas Mass. I can't really figure out why, but there is something so special about it, for some inexplicable reason. I just want to be there and see him do what may be his last Christmas mass, if I am so lucky.

My stomach is filled with butterflies. I am nearly shaking with nerves. It keeps running through my head on repeat. "This is it. Decision time. He's going to be mine or he's not. This is the moment that past two years have been building toward." It's a lot of pressure, yet I cannot be worried. I cannot believe anything other than he's going to fall into my arms and tell me that he's mine forever and that he'll be coming home as soon as he gets permission to leave his station. This may not be true; I know all too well that Joseph is likely to make the choice that's really not a choice at all—to stay where he's at, doing what he's supposed to be doing. But my optimism runs eternally deep when it comes to matters of love. In fact, I think this moment is one of the happiest for me because I'm suspended in my own reality, between the bliss of having him and harsh truth of being without him forever.

Looking out towards the endless horizon, I feel my entire life spread open in front of me. A life that includes Joseph. A life of happiness I never knew possible until meeting him. Like the endless miles of empty highway between where I am now and where I will find him, my life is a blank slate awaiting whatever future we choose to etch it with. A sense of freedom like none I can ever recall feeling before envelopes me. I am flying. Free of the burden of the future, feeling only the here and now. Knowing that it will all work out.

And Lady Gaga plays on the radio: "...Something, something about my cool Nebraska guy. Something about, baby, you and I..."

I smile and sing along to the last refrain as the sun sets and I enter Ohio.

"Been a long time since I came around. Been a long time but I'm back in town. This time I'm not leaving without you."

ABOUT THE AUTHORS

Melissa Cohen is a native of the Bible Belt who quickly escaped to New York City and found her kinky roots at a young age. Since 2004 she has been exploring BDSM and consensual power dynamic relationships. Though she has written prolifically online in forums and blogs, this is her first book.

Pup Joseph is from the Midwestern United States and has been a sick puppy (in his head) for as long as he can remember. Because of his ordination as a Catholic priest, Joseph never explored his desires until mid-2010 at which point he met Melissa and magic happened.

As of 2016, Melissa and Joseph live together in Wisconsin and are proud to say that their relationship is happier and stronger than ever. The authors can be reached for feedback, comments, and questions by email (MelissaOnTop@gmail.com) and on Fetlife.com (screen name MelissaOnTop and FatherJoseph).